MW00464126

THE
REPUBLICAN
REVERSAL

THE
REPUBLICAN
REVERSAL

Conservatives and the Environment
from Nixon to Trump

JAMES MORTON TURNER
ANDREW C. ISENBERG

Harvard University Press

Cambridge, Massachusetts   London, England   2018

Library of Congress Cataloging-in-Publication Data
Names: Turner, James Morton, 1973– author. | Isenberg, Andrew C.
(Andrew Christian), author.
Title: The Republican reversal : conservatives and the environment from
Nixon to Trump / James Morton Turner and Andrew C. Isenberg.
Description: Cambridge, Massachusetts : Harvard University Press, 2018. |
Includes bibliographical references and index.
Identifiers: LCCN 2018009744 | ISBN 9780674979970 (alk. paper)
Subjects: LCSH: Republican Party (U.S. : 1854–)—History—20th century. |
Anti-environmentalism—United States—History—20th century. |
Conservatism—United States—History—20th century. |
United States—Politics and government—History—20th century.
Classification: LCC GE197 .T87 2018 | DDC 333.70973—dc23
LC record available at https://lccn.loc.gov/2018009744

For my parents—JMT
For Amy—AI

Contents

Introduction   1

1   Conservatives before and after Earth Day   19

2   Visions of Abundance   54

3   The Cost of Clean Air and Water   98

4   American Exceptionalism in a Warming World   145

Conclusion   196

Notes   219

Acknowledgments   259

Index   261

THE
REPUBLICAN
REVERSAL

Introduction

ON OCTOBER 18, 2015, during an interview on *Fox News Sunday* with the journalist Chris Wallace, Donald J. Trump suggested that, if elected to the White House, he would eliminate the Environmental Protection Agency. "What they do is a disgrace," he told Wallace. "Every week they come out with new regulations." "Who's going to protect the environment?" Wallace asked. "We'll be fine with the environment," Trump answered. "We can leave a little bit, but you can't destroy businesses."[1] Over the next year, culminating with his victory in the November 2016 presidential election, Trump regularly reiterated his belief that environmental regulations harmed the American economy. At a Republican presidential primary debate in February 2016, Trump repeated his pledge to eliminate the Environmental Protection Agency (EPA), arguing that environmental regulations were a waste of money that weakened the nation's ability to compete globally.[2] Elsewhere on the campaign trail, Trump promised to restore jobs to the coal industry by rescinding environmental protections and opening public lands for energy development. In late 2015, he described climate change as a "hoax" at a campaign rally, and promised to pull the United States out of the Paris climate accord aimed at reducing greenhouse gas emissions from fossil fuels.[3]

Trump's environmental agenda put him in lockstep with many of his Republican contemporaries. By the time he announced his candidacy, his most extreme statements, such as his pledge to eliminate the EPA and his dismissal of climate science, had become familiar conservative talking points. In 2003, Senator James Inhofe (R-Oklahoma) described the threat of catastrophic global warming as the "greatest hoax ever perpetrated on the American people." Inhofe was one of hundreds of elected officials to sign a pledge orchestrated by conservative lobbyists promising opposition to a carbon tax.[4] By 2013, many Tea Party Republicans echoed such language. Representative Dana Rohrabacher (R-California) claimed that "global warming is a total fraud" concocted in order to erode individual freedoms. "Liberals" at the local level, he argued, had ceded decision making to liberals at the state level, who in turn had ceded it to liberals in the federal government, who "want to create global government to control all of our lives. That's what the game plan is." The end result, Rohrabacher predicted, would be a "government official" in some developing country taking away "our freedom to make our choices."[5] Rohrabacher's views were the product of decades of rightward movement in the Republican Party, which increasingly dismissed scientific expertise and saw in environmental policy an insidious political agenda that put global interests, not American interests, first.

Thus, when Trump assumed office in January 2017, he could count on the support of a large number of elected Republicans who had long nurtured an opposition to environmental protections and were ready and eager to advance his environmental agenda. Within weeks of Trump's inauguration, Matt Gaetz, a newly elected Republican representative from Florida, introduced a one-sentence resolution into the House of Representatives to eliminate the EPA. Three House Republicans quickly joined Gaetz as co-sponsors of the resolution.[6] As eliminating the agency seemed unlikely, Trump settled for drawing from the ranks of the Republican Party a new EPA administrator, Scott Pruitt, hostile to the agency's mission. Pruitt had made a name for himself as Oklahoma's attorney general, an office he won in 2010 not on a promise to fight crime, but to fight President Barack Obama's "radical" regulatory agenda. In following through on that promise, Pruitt sued the EPA fourteen times as Oklahoma's attorney general to block administration rules addressing issues such as mercury pollution, smog, and greenhouse gas emissions. In every case but one, regulated industries were also party to the suits.[7] That agenda made Pruitt a leader among both conservative Republicans and industry supporters. The Republican Attorneys General Association, which Pruitt chaired twice, drew millions of dollars in support from the likes of Koch Industries, Murray Energy Corporation, and Continental Resources. When the Obama administration ramped up its climate agenda at the start of Obama's second term in 2013, one lobbyist described Pruitt as "the lawyer-in-chief" for the opposition.[8]

To head the Department of the Interior, which oversaw energy development, endangered species protection, and national parks and wildlife refuges on the nation's public lands, Trump tapped a Montanan, Ryan Zinke. During his one term in the House from 2015 to 2017, Zinke earned a rating of 4 percent from the League of Conservation Voters, an environmental group that evaluates congressional voting records.[9] As a member of the House, Zinke had opposed the protection of endangered species, the development of clean energy, and the regulation of toxins in the air and water. Despite that record, on April 25, 2017, Zinke described himself as "a Teddy Roosevelt guy," when he appeared before reporters to explain Trump's signing of an executive order authorizing him, as secretary of the Interior, to review all national monuments that the three previous presidents—Bill Clinton, George W. Bush, and Obama—had created since January 1, 1996 under the Antiquities Act. Ironically, it was Theodore Roosevelt himself who signed the Antiquities Act into law in 1906 and immediately used it to protect the unique Devil's Tower geological formation in Wyoming. In 1908, because Congress was hesitating to make the Grand Canyon a national park, Roosevelt used the Antiquities Act to protect it as a national monument.[10]

With Pruitt and Zinke at the helm, the Trump administration vigorously pursued its anti-environmental agenda during Trump's first year in office. One of Trump's first acts was to sign into law a congressional resolution that overturned protections the Obama administration had put in place to protect streams and downstream communities from mountaintop removal coal mining. Representative Bill Johnson (R-Ohio) promised the law would keep electricity prices low and "thousands of hardworking

Ohioans" out of the "unemployment line."[11] In February, Trump directed the EPA to take action to narrow the scope of the Clean Water Act, describing it as a "destructive and horrible rule," that unfairly burdened farmers, ranchers, and agricultural workers across the nation. In March, flanked by coal miners, Trump directed the EPA to review the Clean Power Plan, a centerpiece of the Obama administration's effort to reduce carbon dioxide emissions by, in part, reducing America's reliance on coal. Upon signing the order, Trump said to the miners: "You're going back to work."[12] In June, Trump announced the United States was initiating steps to withdraw from the Paris climate accord. He described the commitment to greenhouse gas reductions and financial support for developing countries as a "bad deal." "The Paris Accord is very unfair at the highest level to the United States."[13] In December 2017, the president acted on Zinke's recommendations, and issued executive orders drastically reducing the size of two national monuments in Utah, arguing they far exceeded the law's requirement that monuments be "confined to the smallest area compatible with proper care and management of the objects to be protected." Such sweeping actions were only the administration's most publicized initiatives. It also adopted orders that called on agencies to eliminate two regulations for every new regulation developed, arbitrarily capped the length of environmental impact statements at 150 pages, and took steps to accelerate the opening of federal lands for oil and gas development.

The scope, speed, and precision with which the Trump administration attacked the nation's environmental protections was, in some respects, surprising. In its first year, the Trump administration struggled to find its bearings and Trump's presidency seemed to hinge on impulsive decisions and poorly planned initiatives, sending mixed signals on issues including immigration, healthcare reform, and international trade. But no such confusion and few such missteps characterized the administration's approach to environmental policy. With determined leaders in place at the EPA and the Department of the Interior and Republican majorities in the House and Senate, the Trump administration moved swiftly and decisively to advance its anti-environmental agenda.

What Is the Republican Reversal?

To many observers, it appeared that the Trump administration aimed to dismantle nearly every aspect of the Obama administration's environmental legacy—much as Trump had promised on the campaign trail. But the significance of the Trump administration's environmental agenda was greater than just that. The Trump administration represented a complete break with an older and equally important tradition of Republican environmentalism that dated back to the nineteenth century. It was under Republican presidents—Ulysses S. Grant and Benjamin Harrison—that the United States created its first national parks and national forests. At the beginning of the twentieth century, it was a Republican president—Theodore Roosevelt—who made the conservation of natural resources a federal policy priority. Republican support for environmental protection was also important when the modern environmental movement gained momentum in the 1960s and 1970s. It was a Republican president—Richard Nixon—who signed the National Environmental Policy Act (NEPA) on January 1, 1970, and declared it the start of an environmental decade. That same year, Nixon created the EPA by executive order and signed the Clean Air Act—one of a dozen environmental protection laws passed with overwhelming bipartisan support that Nixon signed into law. Ronald Reagan's administration starting in 1981 marked the beginning of Republican backpedaling on environmental protections, but nonetheless some Republicans continued to support such protections. In 1986, Reagan, who most often opposed environmental regulations, signed a pathbreaking global environmental treaty, committing the United States to aggressive efforts to address the stratospheric ozone hole. Moderate Republicans played a key role in building on the environmental gains of the 1970s and 1980s. In the early 1990s, George H. W. Bush described himself as the "environmental president" and pushed through an amended Clean Air Act that tackled acid rain and supported the international agreement that established a framework for addressing climate change.

Indeed, Republicans once took great pride in the party's long history of environmental leadership. But that was not the case with the Trump administration or the 115th Congress. Not since Reagan's first term in office had a president so forcefully marshaled his administration in opposition to existing environmental laws and regulations. This turnabout on environmental protection, which was nearly four decades in the making, starting with the Reagan administration and reaching its fullest expression at the start of the Trump administration, is what we describe as the Republican reversal. Certainly, the Republican Party has reversed itself—or at least wavered—on other issues in the last four decades. In the 1980s, Republicans backed away from their support for women's rights, refusing to endorse the Equal Rights Amendment in its party platform.[14] Most Republicans supported civil rights legislation such as the Voting Rights Act in the 1960s; by the time of Trump's election victory, Republicans in numerous state legislatures sought to disenfranchise nonwhite voters by raising the chimera of voter fraud. Yet the Republican reversal on the environment stands out: elected Republicans were almost unanimously in support of the landmark environmental laws of the early 1970s; by the time of Trump's election, rolling back environmental regulations had become a Republican rallying cry. It is one of the most profound and far-reaching transformations in modern American political history, on par with the transformation of twentieth-century Democrats from the party of states' rights and segregation to the party of the New Deal and civil rights.

Three characteristics distinguish the Republican reversal on the environment. Through the 1970s, the Republican Party (1) viewed environmental issues with a sense of urgency that demanded action, (2) put faith in scientific research and professional expertise, and (3) embraced an essential role for government in regulating business and industry to safeguard the environment and public health. Indeed, in this context, the Republican Party championed its role as an environmental leader. In the 1972 election, the party's platform trumpeted President Nixon's leadership on environmental issues at home and abroad and chided the Democrats who controlled Congress for failing to enact more of his environmental agenda.[15] But such a strategy stands in sharp contrast to the party's 2016 agenda. Since the 1980s, the Republican Party has increasingly (1) viewed environmental concerns as alarmist and exaggerated, (2) cast doubt on scientific research and dismissed professional expertise, and (3) viewed many environmental regulations as unnecessary burdens on the economy and as threats to individual freedom and the free enterprise system. As the party explained in its 2016 platform, "We firmly believe environmental problems are best solved by giving incentives for human ingenuity and the development of new technologies, not through top-down, command-and-control regulations that stifle economic growth and cost thousands of jobs."[16]

In approaching the history of environmental politics and the Republican Party together, this book aims to place the histories of conservatism and environmental politics into conversation with each other. Although both are rich fields of study, and while at least one political scientist, Judith Layzer, has studied conservatives' anti-environmentalism, no work of history provides an overarching analysis of the ways in which environmental issues have contributed to and been affected by the rise of modern conservatism.[17] Most histories of environmental politics, many of them excellent, focus foremost on environmentalists, the issues they sought to address, and their successes. Such histories often start with a few scientists or citizen activists who first became alert to a problem before raising the alarm that resulted in the enactment of new regulations.[18] The political scientist Roger Pielke Jr. has characterized such science-driven activism as "tornado politics"—a subject to which we will return in this book's conclusion.[19] Much of this book addresses how conservatives responded to the environmental laws that tornado politics produced in the 1970s. In many histories of the environmental movement, opponents of environmental reform are often cast as foils for environmentalists. But Republicans who came to oppose environmentalists and the policies they advanced saw themselves as commonsense realists unwilling to defer to elite scientists, ready to set aside their emotions, and committed to keeping the nation's core priorities—for individual freedom, economic growth, and international competitiveness—at the forefront of their agenda. Thus, what this book advances is not a history of environmentalism, but a history of environmental politics, focused on the contentious and evolving debates over the urgency of environmental issues, how best to address them, and how those issues and strategies should be weighed against other public priorities.

We contend that those debates have played an understudied, but central role in shaping the rise of modern conservatism and the evolution of the Republican Party. Most studies of the conservative transformation of the modern Republican Party since the mid-1970s emphasize the importance of social issues, such as right-to-life, race politics, or gun rights, in forging a coalition of the white working class, evangelical Christians, and suburbanites, especially in the South and Sunbelt. But many scholars have noted that the conservative turn in the Republican Party hinged on the ability of party leaders and politicians to fuse together social activists and business interests in common cause against big government. Although few studies consider how the Republican Party repositioned itself on environmental issues, joining cultural concerns and business interests has been especially important for Republican strategy on public lands protection, energy policy, and climate change. In this book, we contend that we cannot fully understand the success of the modern conservative Republican Party since the 1980s, especially in rural areas, such as the American West or Appalachia, and deindustrialized areas such as the Rust Belt, without accounting for the effectiveness with which it mobilized conservative interest groups, citizens, and legislators in opposition to environmental reform and in favor of policies that favored energy development, extractive industries, and manufacturing. Indeed, an unwavering faith in the market, skepticism of scientific and technocratic elites, and a belief in American exceptionalism have become distinguishing characteristics of modern conservatism and the Republican Party.

What Explains the Republican Reversal?

The Republican reversal began in the early 1980s when Ronald Reagan broke with the bipartisan consensus on the importance of environmental protection. But conservative opposition to environmental reform was not fully formed at the time of Reagan's election. Although many factors contributed to the evolution and consolidation of the Republican reversal, in the pages that follow we focus our analysis on three interrelated factors which have proven instrumental in this political transformation.

First, conservative ideology played an important role in reorienting the Republican Party. If Republicans were going to roll back the expanding regulatory state, they needed a message to counter environmentalists' narrative of the need for state regulation to manage resources, curb pollution, and protect public health. Beginning with the ascendancy of Reagan, Republicans drew on conservative ideology to create a vision of an American economy that, if left unfettered by regulation, could be the engine not only of a higher standard of living but of technological solutions to environmental problems. Conservatives suggested that the environment was neither as limited in its resources nor as polluted as environmentalists believed; those environmentalists, they argued, were alarmists.[20] Reagan called them "doom-cryers." The United States, conservatives argued, was an exceptional nation: extraordinarily productive, blessed with abundant natural resources, and populated by optimists who refused to bow to limitations of any kind. Reagan called the United States "a shining golden hope for all mankind."[21] Persuading Republicans of this gospel of exceptionalism happened by degrees. Reagan's sweeping electoral success in 1980 hinged on his ability to bring together a new Republican majority that included business interests, social conservatives, Christian evangelicals, and rural Americans.[22] Despite Reagan's electoral success, many Americans remained deeply concerned about the environment. In Congress, there remained a bloc of moderate Republicans, many of whom hailed from New England, who saw an important role for government regulations, especially in protecting the environment. Yet, as the political center of the Republican Party continued to shift to the rural West and the South, the party's moderate wing weakened in the 1990s and 2000s, which helped a conservative Republican Party consolidate its power and its opposition to environmental reform.

One of the emerging tenets of conservative ideology was a growing suspicion of scientific research and technocratic expertise, especially when it pointed toward the need for restraints on a free market economy and exploitation of resources. Naomi Oreskes and Erik Conway have described how a network of conservative and libertarian think tanks, supported by conservative business interests, cultivated academics and other experts to question mainstream science. It was a tactic that conservative interests had pioneered in debates over regulating smoking, leaded gasoline, and the pesticide DDT.[23] But as the strength and sophistication of conservative interests grew in the 1990s and 2000s, they pursued this tactic aggressively. Such misinformation campaigns, spearheaded by conservative think tanks such as the George C. Marshall Institute and Heartland Institute, are most often associated with debates over global warming. But since the 1980s the strategy has been important to conservative efforts to derail policies meant to address acid rain and protect endangered species, among other issues. In the view of conservatives, environmentalism was a house of cards that rested on a foundation of faulty science. If they could cast doubt on the science that informed environmentalists' arguments for addressing issues such as the ozone hole, acid rain, endangered species, or climate change—which they argued was often theoretical and model based—then the entire house of cards would collapse. Such misinformation campaigns found a ready audience among conservative legislators, media pundits, and citizen activists in the 1990s and 2000s.

The hardening of the Republican Party's anti-environmental agenda rests, in large part, on the growing importance of conservative interest groups in shaping the party's agenda. This is the second factor we focus on in this book. Although there has been much attention to the role of money in politics since the Supreme Court lifted limitations on corporate campaign contributions in the 2010 *Citizens United* decision, that is only the most recent chapter in a longer history of corporate political mobilization. As the historians Julian Zelizer and Kim Phillips-Fein have argued, in response to the wave of new regulations in the 1970s, including new environmental, occupational safety, and health rules, conservative interests have been "seeking to establish new ways of lobbying, developing new political identities, devising regulatory approaches, building broad popular campaigns . . . and creating new ways of thinking about the economy and politics."[24] New organizations, such as public interest law firms, including the Mountain States Legal Foundation and Pacific Law Foundation, and think tanks, such as the Heritage Foundation, Marshall Institute, and the Cato Institute, were all organized by business interests in the 1970s and 1980s, with the goal of marshaling the research of conservative intellectuals and academics in a concerted campaign to shape the reach and power of the regulatory state in the name of protecting free markets and American competitiveness.[25] These new organizations were matched by the reorganization of existing lobbies, such as the U.S. Chamber of Commerce, which positioned itself as the "voice of business," rallying entrepreneurs and business people, to a conservative social and economic agenda.[26]

The importance of these think tanks, lobbies, and trade groups, which together we refer to as the "public interest right," in shaping environmental politics grew in the 1990s and early 2000s, as conservative interests gained influence in the Republican Party, caught up to their counterparts on the left, and invested more resources in mobilizing conservative activists.[27] Grassroots opposition had played a limited role in early environmental debates. Starting in the 1980s, however, conservative citizens, often supported by and in coordination with the public interest right, began to organize more effectively. Groups such as People for the West! and Americans for Prosperity contributed to an uptick in grassroots activism in response to issues such as endangered species protection and energy taxes. Such campaigns, led by citizens and often supported by business interests, countered the efforts of environmentalists, leading to protests, letter-writing campaigns, and citizen testimony at hearings. These efforts made it clear that it was not only corporations, but workers, farmers, and ranchers, who were concerned about the implications of environmental policies that might curb resource extraction, farming practices, or consumer choices.[28] During these years, evangelical Christians, who largely stood on the sidelines during environmental debates before the 1990s, also became more involved. While some evangelicals adopted an ethos of "creation care," which emphasized environmental stewardship, other evangelicals subscribed to "dominion theology," which found in Scripture a biblical mandate to exploit natural resources and harbored a deep suspicion of secular environmentalists. Each of these strands of evangelical thought has been important to modern environmental politics in ways that belie easy generalization, but it was dominion theology that has more often aligned with conservative approaches to energy policy, resource extraction, and climate policy. It is what the historian Darren Dochuk has described as a "providential view" of resource extraction that "fused Christianity and capitalism" together, with powerful consequences for the Republican Party.[29]

The ferocity with which conservatives organized in response to environmental issues in the 1990s was not simply a product of changes from within the Republican Party and the growing power of conservative interest groups and ideas, however. This brings us to the third factor that helped drive the Republican reversal: the ways in which the nature of environmental problems and the scope of environmental governance changed after 1970s. When the bulk of the nation's environmental laws were passed with overwhelming bipartisan support in the early 1970s, those laws were forged in a moment of environmental crisis. Scientists warned of a "population bomb" and impending famine in developing countries, rivers polluted with petrochemicals caught fire, pesticides had brought species such as bald eagles an brown pelicans to the brink of extinction, children bore the consequences of lead pollution, and growing cities regularly suffered through days of smoggy skylines. Thus, when Democrats and Republicans came together to pass laws such as the National Environmental Policy Act, Clean Air Act, and Endangered Species Act, those laws were enacted in response to a clear and present danger.[30] By the 1990s, however, the urgency of environmental issues was no longer so pressing, at least in the view of conservative critics. Debates over endangered species increasingly hinged on little-known animals such as the delta smelt or gnatcatchers. Debates over water pollution revolved around protecting seasonal wetlands or limiting pollutants measured in parts per billion. Debates over forestry policy shifted away from setting aside specific wilderness areas to ending below-cost logging. And, by the early 2000s, the most pressing environmental challenge, climate change, was seemingly abstract, global, and on a distant time horizon. A clear example of how the evolution of environmental problems has affected environmental politics is the Clean Air Act, which Congress approved in 1970 by votes of 73–0 in the Senate and 375–1 in the House. Republicans were united behind the legislation, which regulated pollutants that were obvious threats to human health, such as carbon monoxide, particulates, and sulfur dioxide. In 2009, however, when the Obama administration determined that greenhouse gas emissions endangered public health and the environment and, therefore, required regulation under the Clean Air Act, Republicans uniformly denounced the plan—even among the small proportion of Republicans who acknowledged the reality of global warming, few considered it an urgent or pressing problem demanding government action.

At the same time that conservative Republicans dismissed the urgency of environmental issues, they recoiled at the unanticipated scope and effectiveness of the environmental regulatory state. In the 1960s and 1970s, few people had anticipated the reach of the new environmental laws or the power of new agencies, such as the Environmental Protection Agency. By the 1990s, however, environmental regulations played a central role in regulating public and private enterprise. Government funded or permitted projects—whether building a bridge or approving a new pesticide—required the completion of environmental impact statements that could be thousands of pages long and take years to complete. Endangered species listings could place constraints on the development of public and private property. Laws such as the Clean Air Act and Clean Water Act required billions of dollars of public and private investment in pollution-control technologies. In short, the laws created legal "trumps" that prioritized clean air, water, or the recovery of an endangered species over economic interests; and it empowered citizens to sue the government to enforce the laws. The upshot of these regulations were significant gains in environmental quality for most Americans. Indeed, the Clean Air Act and Clean Water Act have been among the most important environmental and public health laws enacted in American history.[31] But conservative critics saw in the growth of the environmental regulatory state clear signs of regulatory overreach, not in the name of addressing basic environmental problems, but for less pressing, more abstract, and often trivial issues—such as the protection of a species like the Delhi Sands flower-loving fly from extinction. As the conservative commentator Peter Huber warned in 2000, "For people who like big government and are a part of it, this is political ambrosia."[32]

The Republican reversal did not hinge on any one of these factors alone. Republican legislators were not simply bought off by corporate interests; misinformation campaigns about climate science do not fully explain Republican opposition to energy reform; nor do the teachings of free market thinkers or dominion theologians alone inspire the sustained conservative opposition to environmental reform. At moments, each of these factors was pivotal, as we will show in the chapters to follow. But the Republican reversal is a profound reorientation of the Republican Party's political agenda, extending beyond any one moment, single environmental issue, or constituency. It has depended upon the mobilization of think tanks in Washington, D.C., the ideas of environmental economists, and the engagement of rural citizens in places such as South Dakota or California. To understand how this Republican reversal has accelerated over the past forty years, we argue that each of these factors—the rise of conservative ideology, the mobilization of interest groups and activists, and the changes in the environment and regulatory state—together best explain how and why Republicans came to embrace an anti-environmental agenda with vigor.

This book advances this argument in four chapters. The first chapter is a concise history of the origins of the Republican reversal before and after Earth Day. It follows the role of moderate Republicans, including President Richard Nixon, in enacting the nation's core environmental laws and how that bipartisan environmental consensus began to fracture in the 1970s, as the Republican Party began its conservative turn, exemplified by the election of Ronald Reagan and the elevation of his anti-environmental agenda. Although Reagan's election was pivotal, Republican anti-environmentalism was not fully formed in the 1980s. The Reagan administration introduced the beginnings of positions and strategies that an increasingly conservative Republican Party would pursue with greater, although uneven, success in the decades that followed. In this way, the first chapter sets up the next three chapters of the book, each of which takes the Reagan administration as a starting point in explaining how the conservative right came to reshape American environmental politics in ways that culminate with the Trump administration. Chapter 2 focuses on the public lands, where debates over energy development and endangered species highlight the role the rural American West played in the consolidation of the modern Republican Party's anti-environmentalism. Chapter 3 focuses on the Clean Air Act and the Clean Water Act, highlighting the continuing role of moderate Republicans in safeguarding the most successful public health laws. Chapter 4 examines the debates over climate change and how, in the aftermath of the Cold War, the United States retreated from its historical role as a global leader on environmental issues, not because of economic concerns or scientific misinformation alone, but because of the threats addressing climate change posed to core conservative interests and values. The conclusion considers how these trends culminate with the Trump administration, which harnessed conservative anti-environmentalism to an "America First" agenda.

The Consequences of the Republican Reversal

Although much of this book concerns the origins of the Republican reversal, it is equally concerned with its consequences—how effective have conservative Republicans been at rolling back environmental laws and weakening public health protections? For those concerned about the future of the environment and public health, this history offers both cause for despair and a measure of hope. Although this is not a book about the environmental movement, one cannot understand the consequences of the Republican reversal without considering the ways in which environmentalists and their allies have mobilized to defend the nation's environmental laws and policies. Indeed, advocacy groups such as the Sierra Club, policy think tanks such as the Environmental Defense Fund, and public interest law firms such as the Natural Resources Defense Council, Earth Justice, and the Center for Biological Diversity have anchored the mainstream environmental movement and played a key role in establishing and defending the nation's environmental regulations. Thus, an important part of this story is the ways in which such groups have responded to the Republican reversal, mobilizing citizens, pursuing legal action in the courts, and lobbying legislators and administrators.

To understand the consequences of the Republican reversal, and the moments when environmentalists have succeeded in deflecting it, requires reconsidering an important assumption about how environmental policy gets made and unmade. Many people's idea of what happens in Washington, D.C. dates back to Schoolhouse Rock, a 1970s educational video series that told the story of a lonely bill that had dreams of becoming a law: it was an arduous journey, but in time Congress passed good bills and they became the law of the land. And, in the 1970s, there was some truth to this: a bipartisan Congress responded to environmental crises by passing major laws, like the Clean Air Act, Endangered Species

Act, and Toxic Substances Control Act, to create new regulations and programs to protect the environment and public health. But since the mid-1990s, few major environmental laws have been enacted or reformed. In part, this is due to the divergence of the Republicans' and Democrats' environmental agendas. The League of Conservation Voters has assessed politicians' voting records on environmental issues since the 1970s. Their research shows that the gap between Democrats and Republicans has steadily increased each decade, with most of the divide occurring in the 1990s (see Figure 0-1). This party divergence has contributed to an unyielding state of legislative gridlock: few legislative initiatives, either to address new problems, such as global warming, or to reform (or eliminate) earlier laws, such as the Endangered Species Act, have become law since the 1990s.[33]

But congressional gridlock has not brought environmental policy-making to a halt. Instead, it has made other avenues to policy reform more important. As the political scientists Christopher Klyza and David Sousa have argued, as congressional gridlock has deepened since the 1990s, both proponents and opponents of environmental reform have pursued initiatives to both advance and roll back environmental policies through what Klyza and Sousa describe as "alternative policymaking pathways."[34] The result is that most of the heavy lifting in recent environmental politics has been done through executive orders, administrative rulemaking, congressional appropriations, and the courts. Those have become the most dynamic and consequential arenas of modern environmental policymaking, ushering in (and out) efforts to address climate change, reduce smog, end mountaintop removal coal mining, and protect wild lands. What this history reveals is that the passage of a law is never the end of the story: just as important is how a law is implemented, litigated, and defended. And, despite conservative Republican efforts to roll back environmental laws since the 1980s, environmental advocates and their allies have been diligent in their efforts to not only defend these laws—in Congress, within administrations, and in the courts—but to ensure that they are implemented fully. Thus, environmentalists not only weathered many of the challenges posed by the Reagan administration, Newt Gingrich's Contract with America, or George W. Bush's administration, at times they used these pathways to their advan-

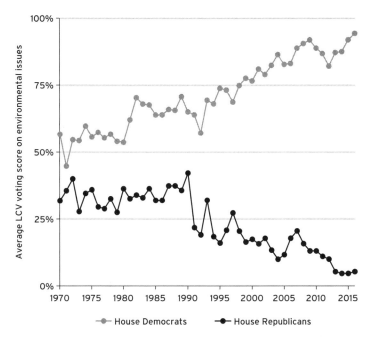

Figure O-1   The growing partisan divide on environmental issues. Each year, the League of Conservation Voters assesses the environmental voting record of each member of Congress. The gap between Democrats and Republicans widened rapidly in the mid-1990s and has continued to diverge. *Data source:* League of Conservation Voters.

tage, succeeding in expanding the protections for clean air, clean water, the public lands, and public health.

In sum, what we aim to do in this short book is tell a clear story about the surprising aftermath of the landmark environmental laws of the late 1960s and early 1970s. It is a story of great successes—the overarching arc has been to build on the legislative framework of the 1960s and 1970s to strengthen protections for the environment, usually through expanding the power of the federal government, in ways that have materially improved public health and environmental quality—and great failures, such as the United States' unwillingness to make a binding commitment to reduce greenhouse gas emissions, to fully address water pollution, or to prioritize issues of environmental justice. Ultimately, it is also a story about how environmental protection has become more perilous, as it has become both politically polarized and more volatile. The shift away from legislative action in Congress and toward alternative policymaking pathways has made the priorities of the president—who controls appointees, issues executive orders, and initiates rulemaking activities—increasingly important. Thus, never before have the potential consequences of the Republican reversal been so great as during the Trump administration.

1

Conservatives before and after
Earth Day

FROM THE MID-1960S through the early 1970s, environmental quality was both a subject of broad, overarching public interest and a matter-of-factly bipartisan issue. During this period, when the environmental movement was at its early height, its political appeal was so robust that most Democrats and Republicans eagerly endorsed its aims. Indeed, until the early 1970s, because environmentally minded voters helped to elect to office moderate Republicans willing to craft bipartisan compromises on environmental protection, environmentalism helped to blunt the rise of another, even more far-reaching, movement in twentieth-century American politics: conservative Republicanism. Conservatism had its roots in the 1930s, when business leaders began to support anti–New Deal and pro-free-enterprise think tanks and to court the support of evangelical Protestants. By the mid-1960s, the conservative movement had gained enough strength that one conservative, Barry Goldwater, had won the Republican nomination for president (though he was decisively defeated in the general election by the incumbent, Lyndon Johnson), and another, Ronald Reagan, had been elected governor of the most populous state, California. Yet in the 1960s and early 1970s, both Gold-water and Reagan struggled to reconcile their conservative ideals with the expanding role of government in protecting the environment; both supported bipartisan environmental initiatives, notably laws to improve air quality. Whether it was political conviction or political calculation on the environment that drove them, neither was willing to apply to environmental protections the same scorn that they heaped on other government regulations. By the late 1970s, however, oil crises and a slowing economy sapped environmentalism of some of its popular appeal: in a faltering economy, fewer Americans had much enthusiasm for environmental regulations that might impede growth. The economic anxieties of the 1970s presented conservatives with an opportunity to accomplish what had long eluded them: win the White House. To do so, Republicans began to reverse many of their positions on environmental protection. Reagan, who by the time of his presidential run in 1980 had spent two decades honing his conservative pitch—largely focused on the toxicity of government regulation and the blessings of American free enterprise—added caustic dismissals of environmental regulation to his campaign speeches, inaugurating a new partisan era of environmental politics. With Reagan, the Republicans, once champions of environmental protection, began a campaign to assert new policies more favorable to business interests that put ascendant conservative values—the free market, economic growth, and individual freedom—before environmental protection. This marked the beginning of the Republican reversal on the environment.

The Origins of Conservatism and Environmentalism

Few movements in recent American political history have been as consequential as either conservatism or environmentalism, and few have such muddled origins. When environmentalists narrate the beginning of their movement, they variously point to moments dispersed from the early 1950s to the early 1970s. Some locate the origins of environmentalism in the Sierra Club and Wilderness Society's fight, waged between 1950 and 1955, to prevent the federal government from building a dam on the Green River within the boundaries of Dinosaur National Monument on the Colorado-Utah border.[1] Still more believe that the movement started in 1962, with the publication of *Silent Spring,* the biologist

Rachel Carson's blockbuster exposé of chemical pesticides.[2] To others, the movement did not begin in earnest until the first Earth Day in 1970, which drew 20 million participants to a "teach-in" at hundreds of locations across the United States.[3]

The first important legislative success for the environmental movement—and, as such, another foundational moment of environmentalism—was the Wilderness Act, which President Lyndon Johnson signed into law on September 3, 1964. The act was neither the first environmental law nor the most important. Yet the scope and ambitions of the Wilderness Act were strikingly new. The law immediately set aside 9.1 million acres of federal land as part of a new National Wilderness Preservation System. Defining wilderness as places "where the earth and its community of life are untrammeled by man, where man himself is a visitor who does not remain," the law largely barred industries such as mining and logging from the newly designated wilderness areas. Over the next decade, environmental policymakers would amplify this approach into what would become a defining quality of environmental laws: a "legal trump," that prioritized environmental quality over economic interests.[4] Congress would create wide-ranging legal trumps in environmental laws it enacted in the early 1970s, including the Clean Air Act, Clean Water Act, and Endangered Species Act. Moreover, the Wilderness Act mandated that the secretaries of Agriculture and the Interior review other roadless areas in the national forests, parks, and wildlife refuges to assess their suitability for inclusion in the wilderness system. Before the secretaries could submit such recommendations to Congress, the law, in what would become another defining quality of environmental regulations, required the agencies to provide public notice and hold hearings, setting an important precedent for citizen involvement in environmental decision making.[5]

The Wilderness Act, like most environmental laws in the 1960s and early 1970s, enjoyed broad bipartisan support. Representative John Saylor (R-Pennsylvania) introduced the bill in the House; Senator Hubert Humphrey (D-Minnesota) introduced the Senate version of the bill. Its staunchest foe was a Democrat, Representative Wayne Aspinall of Colorado, who worried about the law's consequences for economic development in the West, where much of the land proposed as wilderness was located. Saylor's support for wilderness protection was entirely in keeping with the traditions of the Republican Party. From the time of its founding in 1854, the Republican Party had favored industry, championing legislation liberalizing access to natural resources—largely in the West—in order to stimulate industrial development.[6] Yet the first Republican in the White House, Abraham Lincoln, deeded Yosemite Valley to the state of California for "public use, resort, and recreation." In 1872, Ulysses S. Grant created Yellowstone National Park. In 1891, Benjamin Harrison created the first national forest reserves—later renamed the National Forests. Theodore Roosevelt dwarfed his predecessors in protecting public lands: he created 150 national forests, fifty-one bird preserves, four game preserves, and five national parks. Altogether, he set aside roughly 230 million acres of land, more than any president, Republican or Democrat, before or since.[7] In short, in the century preceding the passage of the Wilderness Act, the Republican Party had a stronger claim to be the party of environmental protection than the Democrats. In 1964, both parties supported the Wilderness Act enthusiastically. The House of Representatives voted in favor of the law 373–1. In the Senate, the vote was 73–12.

One of the twelve senators to vote against the law was the Republican Party's leading conservative, Barry Goldwater of Arizona. He had risen rapidly from being an outspoken conservative critic of the New Deal in the 1930s, to a member of the Phoenix city council at the head of a nominally nonpartisan party of business leaders in the late 1940s, to the U.S Senate in the early 1950s.[8] Because the Wilderness Act empowered officials in the Interior and Agriculture departments to identify public lands for review, Goldwater feared that the law concentrated power in the executive branch. Perhaps more importantly, like the Democrat and fellow westerner Aspinall, he believed that the legal trumps embedded in the law would slow economic growth by withdrawing land—notably mineral resources and timberland in the western United States—from development. In the summer of 1964, Goldwater had a prominent public platform from which to articulate these conservative principles. Exactly seven weeks before Johnson signed the Wilderness Act into law, Goldwater accepted the nomination of the Republican Party for president of the United States, delivering an acceptance speech that has become infamous for its invocation of what would become a refrain of conservatism: "extremism in the defense of liberty is no vice." In that speech, Goldwater argued that the state was not the protector of American liberty but its enemy: "Those who seek to live your lives for you . . . who elevate the state and downgrade the citizen . . . who seek absolute power, even though they seek it to do what they regard as good . . . are the very ones who always create the most hellish tyrannies." Whether the state was Johnson's Great Society or Soviet Communism (and Goldwater viewed the former as merely a milder version of the latter), the only antidote to the expanding power of liberty- and soul-destroying statism was capitalism. "We see, in private property and in economy based upon and fostering private property, the one way to make government a durable ally of the whole man, rather than his determined enemy. We see in the sanctity of private property the only durable foundation for constitutional government in a free society."[9] Although Johnson trounced Goldwater in the 1964 election, winning 43 million votes to Goldwater's 27 million, conservatives looked to Goldwater's nomination in 1964, as many environmentalists looked to the Wilderness Act that same summer, as a foundational moment in their movement.[10]

Just as environmentalism did not spring into being with the signing of the Wilderness Act in 1964, conservatism did not simply begin with Goldwater's nomination that same summer. Republican conservatism first emerged in the 1930s alongside and in opposition to the liberal consensus of Franklin Delano Roosevelt's New Deal. Capitalism, according to the New Dealers, aggregated economic power to itself, and it thus fell to the federal state to protect the economic liberties of ordinary people from the power of capitalists. Roosevelt's liberalism aimed to position the federal government as, according to one of the early historians of the New Deal, a "broker state" that would insulate workers, farmers, and consumers from the vicissitudes of capitalism, and thus prevent not only another economic collapse like the one that began in 1929, but the attendant social chaos that had fueled the rise of fascism in Europe.[11] By contrast, the conservatives who emerged in the 1930s saw the state's aggregation of power as the real problem, and they looked to capitalism to protect ordinary people's economic and political liberties. Running for a U.S. Senate seat from Ohio in 1938, Robert Taft, the son of the progressive

Republican president William Howard Taft, used, for the first time in American politics, the term "conservative" to describe his opposition to Roosevelt. The planned economy of the New Deal, Taft argued, "violated every constitutional principle."[12] By imperiling property rights, Taft believed, the New Deal threatened fundamental American liberties.

By the time Taft declared himself to be a conservative, business leaders had been stirring up opposition to the New Deal for several years, providing funds to found organizations that, while nominally nonpartisan, promoted the interests of business against New Deal regulation. In 1934, the wealthy du Pont family helped to create one such group, the American Liberty League, an organization committed to protecting what it saw as constitutional guarantees of private property in the face of the New Deal state. In 1938, Lewis H. Brown, the president of the asbestos manufacturer Johns-Manville, founded the American Enterprise Association (renamed the American Enterprise Institute in 1962), a think tank devoted to limited government and free enterprise. General Motors, Ford, Chrysler, and the du Ponts contributed funds to the AEA in its early years; Phyllis Schlafly, who became a prominent anti-feminist in the 1970s, was a staffer; the Nobel Prize-winning conservative economist Milton Friedman eventually served on the advisory board. Older business organizations, notably the U.S. Chamber of Commerce, which initially supported Roosevelt's National Recovery Administration, became increasingly opposed to New Deal regulations. During his 1932 campaign, Roosevelt had inveighed against privately owned electrical utilities, which controlled 80 percent of the electricity market, for the high rates they charged consumers. In 1933, electric utilities joined together to form the Edison Electric Institute to combat regulation.[13] In 1943, Leonard Read, the head of the Western Division of the U.S. Chamber of Commerce, founded a journal, the *Economic Sentinel,* in which pro-capitalist critics of the New Deal could publish their work. Altogether, it was, according to the historian Kim Phillips-Fein, "the start of a new kind of ideological mobilization."[14]

Ironically, although conservative Republicans such as Taft and Goldwater saw themselves as exemplifying intrinsic American values, much of the new conservative ideology that business interests sought to mobilize was a European import.[15] The foundational text of American conservatism was *The Road to Serfdom,* by the Nobel Prize-winning Austrian economist Friedrich Hayek. Hayek argued that when a state undertakes central economic planning, however well meaning it may be at the outset, it inevitably erodes individual liberties. In the wake of the Nazis' election to power and the ascendance of other authoritarians in Europe in the 1930s, Hayek and his mentor, Ludwig von Mises, scorned the idea that democratic government could protect freedoms; Hayek dismissed faith in democracy as a "fashionable concentration." Choices one made in the marketplace, however, unlike those one made in the voting booth, were hard-earned, and thus reflected what one truly valued. For Hayek, a government, even a democratically elected one, imposed on the liberties that the market made possible when it meddled in the economy. The free market, Hayek therefore argued, was not merely a guarantor of economic freedom but more importantly political freedom. "The substitution of central planning for competition" not only constrains economic choices, Hayek argued, but "could not stop at what we regard as our economic activities," leading the state inevitably to totalitarianism.[16]

Hayek wrote the book in 1944 while teaching at the London School of Economics as an exile from Hitler's *Anschluss.* The book was popular in the United States; *Reader's Digest* published an abridged edition in April 1945. In 1950, Hayek moved to the faculty of the University of Chicago, where he taught until 1962. His salary, however, was paid not by the university but by the William Volker Fund, a Kansas City-based charity that promoted free market values. Hayek was by no means averse to courting the support of wealthy business elites. In 1947, he and a group of like-minded economists who believed that a competitive free market was the foundation of a free society founded the Mont Pèlerin Society in Switzerland. Jasper Crane, an executive vice-president at DuPont Chemical, convinced Hayek to invite American corporate leaders to join his society. By the mid-1950s, J. Howard Pew, the president of Sun Oil (later Sunoco), and George Koether of U.S. Steel, among others, had joined.[17] Hayek's teaching and writings influenced generations of conservative economists and policymakers, notably his fellow University of Chicago economist Milton Friedman, who served not only on the advisory board of the American Enterprise Institute but on Ronald Reagan's Economic Policy Advisory Board, and David Stockman, Reagan's Director of the Office of Management and Budget.

Conservative business leaders sought to build support not only among university intellectuals but among religious leaders as well. In 1935, James Fifield, the pastor of a wealthy Congregational church in Los Angeles (it was one of the first mega-churches in the United States, with five Sunday services and a daily radio show) helped found Spiritual Mobilization, an organization devoted to encouraging Protestant leaders to support capitalism from the pulpit. "The blessings of capitalism," Fifield wrote, "come from God." Fifield's wealthy congregants supported Spiritual Mobilization; so, too, beginning in the 1940s, did J. Howard Pew.[18] When the National Association of Manufacturers—a group that included Standard Oil, General Electric, and General Motors, met in 1940, Fifield was one of the keynote speakers. For Fifield, financial success was a sign of divine blessings. He cheerfully embraced detractors' characterization of him as "the Thirteenth Apostle of Big Business or the St. Paul of the Prosperous."[19]

Goldwater's 123-page book, *The Conscience of a Conservative,* published in 1960, pulled together the disparate elements of conservatism that had been percolating in American politics for over two decades. The book (ghostwritten by L. Brett Bozell, the brother-in-law of the *National Review* editor, William F. Buckley) combined a loathing of state regulation, a belief in the ability of an unfettered marketplace to make Americans both prosperous and free, and a conflation of conservatism with religious faith. To Goldwater, or Bozell, conservative principles derived "from the truths that God has revealed." The invocation of God was not merely rhetoric—it was an appeal to the evangelical Protestants in the South and West who strongly supported Goldwater.[20] Chief among the principles was these: "Throughout history, government has proved to be the chief instrument for thwarting man's liberty." As a result, 'The businessman is hampered by a maze of government regulations."[21]

Despite his loss in the 1964 election, Goldwater's brand of conservatism was on the rise within the Republican Party. It succeeded by exploiting weaknesses in the Democratic coalition. Although in retrospect—and with a tinge of nostalgic hindsight on the part of Democrats—Franklin

Roosevelt's New Deal coalition seems rock solid, it was in fact a tenuous pairing of urban laborers, many of whom were Catholic first- or second-generation immigrants, with rural white Protestants, both in the West and in the segregated South. Roosevelt kept the alliance intact by suppressing social issues, especially those involving race, while emphasizing class solidarities. The coalition began to break down in 1948, when Hubert Humphrey's convention speech denouncing segregation caused white southern Democrats to bolt the convention and nominate Democratic senator Strom Thurmond of South Carolina on a States' Rights ticket. Despite his loss in 1964, Goldwater intuited the weaknesses in the Democratic coalition, laying the foundation for the resurgence of the Republican Party. As the historian David Farber put it, Goldwater paved the way for "anticommunist militants, anti-secularists, pro-states' rightists, and dedicated segregationists" to unite as "Republican Party conservatives."[22] Four years after Goldwater's campaign for the White House, the Democratic coalition cracked apart for good. In 1964, Lyndon Johnson's support for civil rights legislation had already impelled white southern Democrats to vote for Goldwater; in 1968 they supported either Nixon or the Alabama Democrat running on a third-party ticket, George Wallace.[23]

Yet in the late 1960s and early 1970s, the conservatives' time had not yet arrived. Moderates, such as Senators Edward Brooke of Massachusetts, Clifford Case of New Jersey, Mark Hatfield of Oregon, Jacob Javits of New York, Thomas Kuchel of California, Charles Mathias of Maryland, Charles Percy of Illinois, Richard Schweiker of Pennsylvania, Margaret Chase Smith of Maine, Robert Stafford of Vermont, and Lowell Weicker of Connecticut, as well as Governors Nelson Rockefeller of New York and John Chafee of Rhode Island, were a significant force within the Republican Party. What defined them as moderates? In the first place, they were pro-business yet they did not share the social agenda of conservatives such as Goldwater, who voted against not only the Wilderness Act but the Civil Rights Act of 1964; to a man or woman, all moderate Republicans supported civil rights legislation. Such moderates dominated the Republican Party in the 1960s: 80 percent of House Republicans and 82 percent of Senate Republicans voted for the Civil Rights Act. By contrast, because of the large number of conservative southern whites in their contingent, only 63 percent of House Democrats and 69 percent of Senate Democrats voted for the bill. Moreover, moderate Republicans largely accepted the New Deal's reformulation of the role of the federal government as a broker state that, as the economist John Kenneth Galbraith put it, enhanced the "countervailing power" of groups such as consumers and labor unions against business interests.[24] In the late 1960s and early 1970s, moderates' willingness to use the power of the state to mitigate environmental problems resonated with voters keenly interested in environmental protection. Moderate Republicans thus performed a delicate balancing act, positioning themselves both as pro-business as well as advocates of one or more social issues such as civil rights, women's rights, anti-poverty programs, or environmentalism. Many of them regarded conservative Republicans such as Goldwater as destructive forces within the party, whose extremism on both social and economic issues would make Republicans unelectable—Goldwater's resounding defeat in 1964 seemed to confirm this view.

Although the moderate Republicans took little notice of it at the time, in Goldwater's defeat, another conservative star had emerged: Ronald Reagan. Like many conservatives of the 1960s, 1970s, and 1980s, Reagan was once a liberal: he was a New Deal Democrat who voted for Franklin Roosevelt four times. As a Hollywood actor, Reagan had a successful but unremarkable career from the late 1930s through the mid-1950s. In 1954, as his film roles dried up, he readily accepted a job as host of the CBS Sunday evening television program *General Electric Theater*. Until the show went off the air in 1962, General Electric (GE)—a steadfastly anti-union company—employed Reagan not only as a television host but as a kind of traveling goodwill ambassador to its seventy-five plants in thirty-eight states. Meeting with plant managers and workers—and often addressing local Rotary or Kiwanis clubs as well—Reagan developed a stump speech that was cheerfully pro-corporate and patriotic. During the course of these travels stumping for GE, Reagan's politics drifted to the right. In 1960, while still a Democrat, he supported Richard Nixon for president; he became a Republican in 1962; and in 1964, he co-chaired Goldwater's California campaign.[25]

In the waning days of the 1964 campaign, Reagan filled in for Goldwater at an appearance in Los Angeles. He delivered a version of his GE stump speech, lumping the New Deal together with fascism and communism: "there is no left or right, only an up or down. Up to the maximum of individual freedom consistent with law and order, or down to the ant heap of totalitarianism." Like Hayek, he warned of the dangers of letting the state provide for its citizens; those who embrace social programs, he argued, "sacrifice freedom for security." Already, Reagan warned, "the hour is late. Government has laid its hand on health, housing, farming, industry, commerce, education. . . ."[26] In addition to embracing Hayek's anti-statism, Reagan revived an old strain in American conservatism: anti-intellectualism. "Either we believe in our capacity for self-government," Reagan said, "or we confess that a little intellectual elite in a far-distant capitol can plan our lives for us better than we can plan them ourselves." While the content of much of the speech was gloomy, Reagan leavened it with patriotism. After likening the Republican cause to Jesus on Calvary, he concluded that "You and I have a rendezvous with destiny. We can preserve for our children this, the last best hope of man on earth, or we can sentence them to take the first step into a thousand years of darkness." The speech reflected skills he had honed in his eight years as GE's public relations man. Reagan's words were not much different from those of his conservative predecessors such as Hayek, Taft, and Goldwater—but he inflected them with an upbeat sense that Americans had the ability to rise to the challenge that statism posed.

Bipartisan Consensus on the Environment

Despite business leaders' opposition to regulation and conservative thinkers' belief that the state should respect property rights, many early conservatives made an exception for environmental issues. "Certain harmful effects of deforestation, or of some methods of farming, or of the smoke and noise of factories," Hayek acknowledged in 1944, cannot "be confined to the owner of the property in question." The best solution to such a problem, Hayek thought, was to put a price on what economists now refer to as externalities or social costs. Yet Hayek recognized that sometimes the market alone could not mitigate environmental problems, and the state was justified in imposing regulations. Sometimes, he wrote, "we have to resort to the substitution of direct regulation by authority where the conditions for the proper working of competition cannot be created. . . ."[27]

Like Hayek, conservative Republicans in the 1960s were not implacable enemies of environmental regulation. Representative John Saylor of Pennsylvania was a virulent anti-communist and supporter of the war in Vietnam. He advocated for gun rights and prayer in school; he opposed federal aid for education and the Supreme Court's 1966 decision in the *Miranda* case that decreed that suspects must be apprised of their rights when arrested. He was also a genuine advocate for wilderness and the national parks who introduced the bill in the House that became the Wilderness Act. How could a conservative Republican be such an advocate for the environment? When Saylor introduced the wilderness bill, conservative ideology had not become Republican orthodoxy, nor had conservatism yet coalesced around an orthodox set of policy ideals. Saylor embraced many conservative ideas, yet he rejected others, supporting not only environmentalism but civil rights and Lyndon Johnson's programs to fight poverty in Appalachia.

Moreover, in the 1960s, regional identities often outweighed party ideology. Most Republican moderates represented states and districts in the Northeast, Upper Midwest, or Pacific Coast, where the electorate was relatively urban, wealthy, and well-educated. In the 1960s and 1970s, most college graduates—who tended to be relatively progressive on issues such as race or the environment—voted Republican.[28] Whether they were Republicans or Democrats, only 8 percent of representatives and 5 percent of senators from states of the former Confederacy supported the Civil Rights Act, while 90 percent of House members and 92 percent of senators from Union states supported the law. Regionalism defined many politicians' approach to wilderness, as well. Wayne Aspinall, a Democratic member of the House from western Colorado, where timber and mining interests were significant, was a fierce opponent of the Wilderness Act and other restrictions on resource development. Yet, Aspinall voted for the Civil Rights Act and Voting Rights Act. For Saylor, pristine wilderness was to be found in the West, not in his district in western Pennsylvania coal country. At home, where Saylor lobbied for federal highway spending and supported the coal industry, he would not have been mistaken for an environmentalist.[29]

Regional interests bounded even the definitive 1960s conservative, Barry Goldwater. Although Goldwater opposed the Wilderness Act, he did so despite his deep love of the outdoors. He feared that the Wilderness Act would keep loggers, miners, and ranchers off federal lands, slowing economic development in a state such as Arizona where the federal government owned 42 percent of the land. Goldwater's insistence that the government stay out of the economy was selective, however. For example, he was an ardent proponent of federal projects, such as the Colorado River Storage Project, which built dams in the West. He also pushed for restraints on private development when it threatened environmental quality. In 1957, he proposed expanding the boundaries of Grand Canyon National Park to protect the park's beauty from private developers on its borders. After his loss to Johnson in the 1964 presidential race, Goldwater briefly immersed himself in local politics in Phoenix, spearheading a successful effort to protect Camelback Mountain from suburban sprawl.[30] In 1970, two years after being re-elected to the Senate after having dropped out in 1964 to pursue the presidency, he published a book of political essays that included staunch support of environmental regulation. "While I am a great believer in the free competitive enterprise system and all that it entails, I am an even stronger believer in the right of our people to live in a clean and pollution-free environment," he wrote. "[W]hen pollution is found, it should be halted at the source, even if this requires stringent government action against important segments of our national economy."[31] Goldwater's conflicted support for environmental protection extended to the Senate floor. He co-sponsored the Senate bill that became the Clean Air Act of 1970, but was absent from the chamber when the bill came up for a vote—the bill nonetheless passed without opposition. He was also absent for the votes on the Clean Water Act of 1972 and the Endangered Species Act of 1973.

The bipartisan support for environmental reforms reflected the seriousness and immediacy of environmental problems in the 1960s and 1970s, when smog choked major American cities and sewage and industrial pollution fouled many urban rivers. It was also a response to the surge of public concern about environmental quality, manifest on Earth

Day in 1970, when twenty million Americans took part in Earth Day activities. To casual observers, the spate of environmental legislation that emerged in the late 1960s and early 1970s seemed entirely unprecedented. In truth, those laws, notably the National Environmental Policy Act (NEPA) of 1970, which established the requirement of environmental impact statements for projects permitted or funded by the federal government; the Clean Air Act of 1970, which established strict emissions standards for air pollution; the Clean Water Act of 1972, which did much the same for water pollution; and the Endangered Species Act of 1973, which protected not only species threatened with extinction but their habitats, were erected upon the legal platform of the New Deal. As the legal historian Arthur McEvoy put it, the doctrines that informed environmental laws in the 1960s and 1970s "came off shelves originally stocked during Franklin Roosevelt's New Deal in the 1930s." The New Deal expanded the authority of the federal government to tax, spend, and regulate interstate commerce; it empowered interest groups and created government bureaucracies to be responsive to them; and perhaps most importantly it established the legal trumps that anointed particular interests such as farmers, workers, or consumers, with protections that outweighed business interests. These powers were essential parts of environmental laws in the 1960s and 1970s. NEPA's requirement of environmental impact statements "redistributed political power by forcing developers to subsidize the information costs of environmental and community organizations," according to McEvoy. The Clean Air, Clean Water, and Endangered Species Acts authorized "citizen suits" that permitted lawsuits against both private-sector polluters and federal agencies that failed to meet their regulatory responsibilities. Those laws also established "rights trumps" that gave environmental concerns new consequence: for instance, actions that threatened endangered species were barred; pollution standards for air and water were set without regard for economic cost.[32]

In the 1960s and early 1970s, both Republicans and Democrats could embrace environmentalism because, in its early years, its inspirations were eclectic, simultaneously representing anxieties about pollution and overpopulation and desires for a clean and aesthetically pleasing environment (see Table 1.1). A handful of scientists who had

Table 1-1   The major environmental laws from the 1960s and 1970s passed with strong bipartisan support in the House and Senate. The % GOP indicates what percentage of Republicans voted in favor of the law in each chamber (of those who cast votes). Other major laws from the 1960s and 1970s are included as points of comparison.

	U.S. House		U.S. Senate	
	Vote	% GOP	Vote	% GOP
Wilderness Act of 1964	374–1	100%	73–12	76%
National Environmental Policy Act of 1970	372–15	96%	77–6	85%
Clean Air Act of 1970	336–40	98%	73–0	100%
Clean Water Act of 1972	366–11	97%	74–0	100%
Endangered Species Act of 1973	390–12	95%	92–0	100%
Safe Drinking Water Act of 1974	296–83	70%	Voice Vote	
Surface Mining Control Reclamation Act of 1977	325–68	72%	85–8	80%
Toxic Substances Control Act of 1976	360–35	84%	60–13	56%
Civil Rights Act of 1964	290–130	80%	73–27	82%
Voting Rights Act of 1965	328–74	85%	77–19	94%
War Powers Resolution of 1973	284–135	46%	75–18	64%

the ability to write for a general audience, such as the biologists Rachel Carson and Paul Ehrlich, helped to define environmentalism in the 1960s by raising the alarm about chemical pollution and overpopulation. Yet they were part of a broad and diverse movement. That movement included decades-old outdoors and hunting organizations that had long sought to protect wilderness, scientists concerned about the limits of the world's resources, public health officials concerned about the health consequences of air and water pollution, urbanites worried about an epidemic of lead poisoning, working-class city dwellers seeking access to recreational fishing and public beaches, rural whites in Appalachia fighting off strip mines, and suburbanites who wished to protect their new neighborhoods.[33] The nascent environmental movement's tactics and goals were so multiform that both Republicans and Democrats could find space under the new movement's expansive political umbrella.

Although many observers have retroactively grouped the environmental movement together with civil rights and the anti-Vietnam War movements as an artifact of the political left, much of the early support for environmental reform also came from middle-class, white, and largely Republican suburbanites.[34] Indeed, Carson's *Silent Spring* was prompted, in part, by a 1957 suit by thirteen Long Island suburban residents over the indiscriminate spraying of the pesticide DDT in their communities.[35] Prominent environmentalists in the late 1960s and early 1970s courted the support of both Democrats and Republicans. One such environmentalist was the biologist Paul Ehrlich, whose 1968 book, *The Population Bomb,* which posited overpopulation as the planet's most pressing environmental crisis, outpaced the sales of even Carson's *Silent Spring.*[36] Toggling between the two major parties, Ehrlich and his wife and co-author, Anne, registered as Republicans in 1968 to vote in the primary for their congressional representative, the liberal Republican Pete McCloskey. Ehrlich supported the Democratic nominee Hubert Humphrey in the 1968 general election, but after Nixon's election he wrote to the new president offering his help and support.[37] David Brower, who expanded the Sierra Club into a national organization advocating for wilderness preservation, raised its membership from 7,000 in 1952 to 70,000 in 1969 as he honed the organization's reputation for effective activism. In so doing, he took on both parties. In 1969, Brower founded the League of Conservation voters; the organization endorsed candidates of both parties in twenty-one elections in fourteen states in its first year. The League's first victory was the defeat of Representative George Fallon, a thirteen-term Democrat from Maryland and chair of the House Public Works Committee.[38] In the 1970 election, Environmental Action, an environmental advocacy group founded by the Earth Day organizers, tagged twelve gubernatorial and congressional incumbents who opposed environmental reform—a group that included both Republicans and Democrats—as the "Dirty Dozen." That campaign contributed to the defeat of seven of the twelve that November.[39]

Politics makes seemingly unlikely alignments possible: however improbably, Richard Nixon found himself at the center of the late 1960s and early 1970s bipartisan consensus on environmental politics. Environmental problems commanded his administration's attention from the outset. On January 28, 1969, eight days after Nixon's inauguration, an oil rig off the coast of Santa Barbara, California blew out. For eleven days, the rig spewed oil. Between 80,000 to 100,000 barrels escaped altogether, creating an 800-square-mile oil slick that affected thirty miles of California coastline.[40] The Santa Barbara spill occurred just days after the Senate had confirmed the former governor of Alaska, Walter Hickel, to be Nixon's Interior secretary. Hickel had not aligned himself with environmentalists before his nomination—indeed, the man who prepared Hickel for his confirmation hearings was a young lawyer from Wyoming and ardent proponent of mining and logging on federal lands, James Watt, who would gain notoriety as Reagan's first Interior secretary in 1981. Yet Hickel was shocked by the spill, and swiftly issued a moratorium on offshore drilling until new safety guidelines could be implemented. By 1970, Hickel's embrace of environmental reform impelled him to urge Nixon to declare Earth Day a national holiday. Nixon did not go so far—indeed, he fired Hickel in November 1970— yet in his first term, with public support for environmental reform at its peak, Nixon made environmental protection a centerpiece of his domestic agenda, issuing annual environmental addresses and championing expanded legislation to protect air and water quality. He signed NEPA into law on January 1, 1970. Seven months after Earth Day he created the Environmental Protection Agency (EPA) by executive order, justifying the new agency as part of his commitment to "the rescue of our natural environment, and the preservation of the Earth as a place both habitable and hospitable to man."[41] On New Year's Eve, 1970, he signed the Clean Air Act into law.

Nixon's endorsement of environmental reforms in his first term was partially to prevent Democrats from making environmental issues their own. Senator Edmund Muskie of Maine, whom many political observers believed would be the Democratic nominee for president in 1972, was one of the Senate sponsors of the Clean Air Act and one of the most outspoken advocates of environmentalism in the federal government. Muskie's keynote address at the Earth Day gathering in Philadelphia drew him national attention. He called for a whole society that "will not tolerate slums for some and decent houses for others, rats for some and playgrounds for others, clean air for some and filth for others."[42] Yet Nixon was ideologically pliable enough to embrace environmental reform. He had spent his political career tacking between the conservative and moderate wings of the Republican Party: as a Representative from California in the 1950s, he was an outspoken anti-communist on the House Un-American Activities Committee, but by the 1970s he had embarked on a policy of détente with the Soviets and Chinese; in his 1960 run for the presidency, Nixon was an advocate for civil rights and won 32 percent of the black vote, but by 1972 he had fully embraced a "Southern strategy" of wooing disaffected white Democrats angered by desegregation. Though it seems, in hindsight, contradictory for Nixon to have courted the support of both segregationists and environmentalists, it was a savvy maneuver. After a narrow loss to John F. Kennedy in 1960 and a narrow victory over Hubert Humphrey in 1968, Nixon's larger strategy to win reelection in 1972 was to peel away constituencies from the Democratic Party, whether they were environmentalists or conservative southern whites. Yet Nixon's embrace of environmental reform was not only political positioning. His executive actions in support of environmental causes reflected the strong support within the Republican Party for addressing environmental problems.

The Republican Party's 1972 platform is striking for its embrace of environmental reform and its celebration of the Republican Party's environmental leadership. The Republicans called for the passage of legislation to protect endangered species. They proposed expanding the existing wilderness system by over 30 percent, by withdrawing 3.6 million acres of federal land from the path of economic development and designating it for protection. They called for a clean energy program (although, in the short term, for increased exploitation of domestic fossil fuel supplies to wean the United States from dependency on foreign oil supplies), and a new Department of Natural Resources to administer integrated energy and environmental policies. The Republican platform in 1972 touted Nixon's environmental accomplishments during his first term. The platform emphasized the central role of the government in environmental protection, boasting that under Nixon, federal spending on "environmental improvements" had risen by a factor of three to $2.4 billion. The Republicans even claimed Nixon could have accomplished more, if it were not for a Democratic Congress that had let his proposals to improve water quality, mitigate toxic and solid waste, and ban ocean dumping languish.[43]

Yet over the summer and fall of 1972, while Republicans were renominating Nixon for the White House and appealing to environmentally minded voters, Nixon was quietly backing away from environmental reform. In the last year of Nixon's first term, a bill to ameliorate water pollution, known officially as the Federal Water Pollution Control Act Amendments but popularly as the Clean Water Act, worked its way through Congress. Much of the law was concerned with industrial pollution, which by the end of World War II surpassed municipal sewage as the primary cause of water pollution in the United States. By 1970, largely owing to the expansion of the American chemical industry, 80 percent of water pollution was industrial in origin, and industries released 22 million gallons of pollutants into American waterways every day, 70 percent of which received no treatment whatsoever to reduce their toxicity before they were dumped. The law targeted "point source" discharge of pollution from factories, mills, and other facilities—in other words, the industries that dumped pollutants into waterways. Like other environmental laws that were built on the New Deal's legal platform, the Clean Water Act made public health an interest that trumped the property rights of industry, imposed a strict command-and-control regulatory regime, and made possible citizen suits through which private citizens could force both industries and the federal government to abide by the law.[44]

Like the Wilderness Act and the Clean Air Act, the Clean Water Act enjoyed extensive bipartisan support. The Senate approved its version of the bill in November 1971 by an 86–0 vote; in March 1972, the House approved its version 380–14. Quixotically, perhaps, considering the bill's overwhelming support, Nixon sought to dissuade Congress from passing it. Publicly, Nixon's objection to the bill was that it was too expensive. The proposed law called for the federal government to fund 75 percent of the new municipal treatment plants that would be required under the law. The cost of this provision mounted steadily as Congress debated and modified the bill, rising eventually to $24 billion. Yet the Nixon administration also objected to the cost that complying with the law would impose on industries. The Nixon administration attempted to ease the law's strictures on industry, trying—and failing—to weaken the law by changing the wording that required industries to use the "best technology available" to mitigate pollution to the best "practical" technology.[45] Nixon's objections did not dampen congressional enthusiasm for the bill, however. In October, after the different House and Senate versions of the bill had been reconciled in committee, the Senate passed the bill 74–0; the vote in the House was 366–11.

Nixon had ten days to sign the bill into law or veto it. His hope was that Congress would adjourn before those ten days had elapsed, and thus allow him to kill the bill quietly by taking no action on it while Congress was not in session—the so-called "pocket veto." Congress, however, intentionally stayed in session in order to force Nixon's hand. He vetoed the bill on October 17, characterizing it as one "whose laudable intent is outweighed by its unconscionable $24 billion price tag."[46] With considerable Republican support, Congress overrode Nixon's veto within hours. Senator Charles Percy of Illinois spoke for the moderate Republicans—Peter Dominick, Margaret Smith, John Beall, Charles Mathias, Edward Brooke, Clifford Case, Jacob Javits, George Aiken, and Robert Stafford—who voted to override the veto. "There can be no doubt as to the critical need for cleaning up the Nation's waterways by establishing strict pollution standards for industries and municipal plants," Percy said. He was joined in his support of the bill by Senator Howard Baker—who in 1966 had become the first Republican elected to the Senate from Tennessee since Reconstruction and who in 1987 became Reagan's chief of staff. Baker said that "I have spent more time . . . on environmental legislation than on any other field of endeavor since coming to Congress" and that the Clean Water Act "is far and away the most significant and promising piece of environmental legislation ever enacted by Congress."[47] The Senate overrode the veto by a vote of 52–11; in the House, the vote was 247–23.

The debate over the Clean Water Act revealed growing fissures in the Republican Party. The override was a victory for Republican moderates from the Northeast and Upper Midwest. At the same time, Nixon's opposition reflected deepening reservations about the scope and cost of the new environmental regulatory state. Nixon's failed veto demonstrated to Republican Party conservatives that one could succeed without courting the votes of environmentalists—indeed, one could win reelection while risking alienating them. The 20 million Americans who had attended

Earth Day in 1970, as well as the successes of Environmental Action and the League of Conservation Voters in targeting opponents of environmental regulation, had caught Nixon's attention in his first term. Yet even as early as 1971, Nixon had concluded privately to his chief of staff, H. R. Haldeman, that "you can't out-Muskie Muskie," and that he should be more concerned with shoring up his support among conservative Republicans than trying to win over environmentalists. Gallup polls from the time that he was nominated until the election in November showed Nixon with the consistent support of between 59 and 64 percent of voters, far outpolling his Democratic opponent, Senator George McGovern of South Dakota. Over the course of the 1972 election year, Nixon calculated that for many environmentally minded voters, the environment was nonetheless a secondary issue, not the primary one on which they would cast their ballot. At the same time, by vetoing the Clean Water Act, Nixon bolstered his support among pro-business Republicans. According to William Ruckelshaus, who directed the EPA until 1973, and Russell Train, who started at the Council of Environmental Quality and then succeeded Ruckelshaus at the EPA, in his first term Nixon had little interest in the environmental agency he had created. By the end of 1972, comfortably ahead in the polls, that indifference bordered on disdain.[48]

The most prominent Republican conservative in the late 1960s and early 1970s—Ronald Reagan—initially accommodated himself to the political appeal of environmentalism as governor of California, much as Nixon did. In 1966, a group of southern California business leaders, impressed by Reagan's speech in late 1964 endorsing Goldwater, had persuaded Reagan to seek the Republican nomination for governor of California. Reagan was not the first conservative Republican nominee for the California governor's office. Senator William Knowland had lost badly to the Democratic nominee Pat Brown in 1958. Reagan knew from Knowland's defeat as well as from Goldwater's loss to Lyndon Johnson in the 1964 presidential election that conservative Republicans needed the support of moderates if they were going to win at the polls. That support was particularly crucial in California, where moderates dominated the state Republican Party. Reagan thus modulated his critiques of the state and his support for business interests, even lending support to environmental issues. Reagan tried to court the support of Senator Thomas Kuchel, the leader of the moderate Republicans in California, by expressing his interest in protecting the environment, saying that "I am an outdoorsman and bleed a little whenever a highway cuts through any of our scenery."[49]

Reagan served as governor of California from 1967 to 1975, just as the environmental movement became a popular concern. During these years, Reagan, like Nixon, tacked between appeasing environmental advocates and resisting them. He often steered toward compromise with environmentalists, in part because of the influence of his secretary of resources, Norman Livermore, a dedicated conservationist and member of the Sierra Club board of directors. An outdoors enthusiast, Reagan was most comfortable advocating for parks and scenic nature. In May 1971, he created an "Ecology Corps," modeled on Franklin Roosevelt's Civilian Conservation Corps, made up of conscientious objectors to the military draft who would be put to work in state parks.[50] In 1972, in a calculated publicity stunt, he donned a cowboy hat and rode a horse in Yosemite National Park to announce his opposition to a federal highway that would have cut through the Sierra Nevada.[51] By the end of his second term as governor, he had added 145,000 acres to the state park system.[52] In 1968, Reagan blocked the building of a massive dam—to be built with federal funds—on the Eel River.[53] The planned reservoir would have held more water than the two largest existing reservoirs in California—Shasta Lake and Lake Oroville—combined. Reagan blanched at the prospect of flooding a valley to create the reservoir, but his opposition was not merely about the environment. The dam also represented the kind of big-government project that conservative Republicans had come to loathe. By opposing the dam, Reagan undid some of the work of his Democratic predecessor, Pat Brown, under whom much of California's system of dams, reservoirs, and aqueducts was constructed. In November 1969, he pledged continued vigilance of that system, vowing that Brown's California Water Project must give "greater and earlier consideration" to "environmental factors."[54]

Reagan's most significant achievement in environmental reform was in improving California's air quality. Six months before Nixon created the Council on Environmental Quality, Reagan created the California

Environmental Quality Study Council.[55] In January 1970, he proposed a state clean air law nine months before Congress passed the Clean Air Act.[56] In 1971, in an effort to reduce smog in Los Angeles, he signed legislation creating state automobile emission standards that were tougher than federal standards. The legislation had been sponsored by a conservative Republican in the state assembly: air quality in southern California in 1971 was a bipartisan issue.[57] Indeed, environmental quality was such a bipartisan issue that it drew one of the most prominent conservatives in the United States into support for environmental protection. So long as environmentalism appeared to be a potent political force—and, at least until the first oil crisis in late 1973, it appeared to be just that—it stemmed the conservatism of a Republican such as Reagan. So long as voters demanded bipartisan solutions to environmental problems—a demand that meant that opponents of environmental protection from both parties would suffer at the polls for their intransigence—the Republican moderates could count on voters' environmental concerns to bolster their support, while conservatives such as Reagan had to trim their sails to the prevailing political winds.

The Rise of Conservatism and the Emergence of Partisan Environmental Politics

In the early 1970s, environmentalists' string of surprising successes—the creation of the EPA, Earth Day, and far-reaching congressional environmental laws—appeared differently to conservatives: they saw in the rise of the environmental regulatory state one more front of a growing attack on American business interests and the free enterprise system. In 1971, Eugene Sydnor, the education director of the U.S. Chamber of Commerce, asked a friend, Lewis F. Powell, a corporate lawyer in Richmond, Virginia, and a member of the board of the tobacco company Philip Morris, to draft a memorandum to the Chamber of Commerce. The subject of the memo was, as Powell put it, "that the American economic system is under attack." He bewailed the "stampedes by politicians to support almost any legislation related to 'consumerism' or to the 'environment.'" It was time for business interests to turn the tables.

Powell urged that "Business must learn the lesson, long ago learned by labor and other self-interest groups. This is the lesson that political power is necessary" and it "must be used aggressively and with determination." Following Hayek and other conservative economists, Powell argued that the "threat to the enterprise system is not merely a matter of economics. It is also a threat to individual freedom." The United States, he warned, had already "moved very far indeed toward some aspects of state socialism."

The assault came, Powell argued, not simply from liberal politicians or other traditional advocates of "some form of statism," but rather, more chillingly for Powell, "from perfectly respectable elements of society." He singled out two irritants to free enterprise in particular: Ralph Nader, a graduate of Harvard Law School, whose 1965 book, *Unsafe at Any Speed,* had catalogued the indifference of General Motors to the safety of the customers who bought its vehicles and who was, while Powell was writing his memo, engaged in research on a similar exposé about DuPont Chemical; and Charles Reich, a Yale law professor whose bestselling 1970 book, *The Greening of America,* argued that "America is dealing death," not only in Vietnam, but at home, where "uncontrolled technology" spelled "the destruction of the environment."[58] To Powell, Reich was merely the most prominent of a host of left-leaning academics busily criticizing the American free enterprise system. University campuses, he wrote, in a refrain that echoed decades of anti-intellectualism in America, were "the single most dynamic source" of the critique of capitalism. Liberal faculty members, Powell lamented, tended to be "personally attractive and magnetic" as well as "stimulating teachers." Their charisma gave them an influence that Powell judged to be "far out of proportion to their numbers."[59]

In contrast to the liberal critics of the free enterprise system who had seized the public imagination and influenced policy, Powell characterized business leaders as naively devoted to efforts to "improve the standard of living, to be community leaders, to serve on charitable or educational boards, and generally to be good citizens," and ill-equipped for "hard-nose [*sic*] contest." To combat the assault on the free enterprise system, Powell recommended that, beyond expanding corporate public relations departments, the Chamber of Commerce should establish a "staff of highly qualified scholars" who would publish studies favorable to business; be available as speakers, especially on college campuses; and vet textbooks to ensure that they were sufficiently pro-business. It was "essential," Powell wrote, "to establish the staffs of eminent scholars, writers, and speakers . . . who are thoroughly familiar with the media, and how most effectively to communicate with the public." Beyond media appearances, Powell wrote, "it is especially important for the Chamber's 'faculty of scholars' to publish" in order to counter the publications of "liberal and leftist faculty members." Finally, Powell, as a lawyer who would, a few months after writing the memorandum, be nominated to the Supreme Court by Nixon, recommended that the Chamber of Commerce establish a public interest law firm, modeled on the American Civil Liberties Union, to pursue cases in which businesses believed they could win important precedents.[60]

Conservative advocates for the free enterprise system were not quite as cowed or inept as Powell made them appear in what has become known as the "Powell memo." The conservative movement's intelligentsia—in particular, the thinkers who surrounded William F. Buckley's *National Review*—were not shy about articulating their criticisms of environmentalism. Robert Moses, the city planner who had overseen the construction of New York City's highways, tunnels, and bridges between the early 1930s and the end of the 1960s, denounced environmentalism in the pages of the *National Review* in 1970. Comparing environmentalists' fears for the planet to Prohibition in the 1920s and the rage for bomb shelters in the 1950s, Moses predicted that the "ecological hysteria" would not last much past Earth Day. Like Powell, Moses believed that the primary instigators of this hysteria were liberal intellectuals in "their Ivory Tower." Although Moses himself had earned a doctorate in political science from Columbia, he condemned "ambitious PhDs" whose "illusions of grandeur" inevitably proceeded "to regimentation and control under the guise of super-planning and preserving the balance of nature." The result, he wrote, would be a "new tyranny."[61]

Nonetheless, Powell captured a growing sense among business leaders of the urgent need for business interests to intervene in the political process by lobbying government, advertising, and founding think tanks. In other words, they set out to institutionalize the public interest right.

According to the historian Kim Phillips-Fein, at the outset of the 1970s few Fortune 500 companies had public relations departments; by 1979, 80 percent of them did. Between 1971 and 1979 the number of companies who employed registered lobbyists rose from 175 to 650. The number of corporate political action committees grew from 89 in 1974 to 821 in 1978. (The shift came after a 1976 Supreme Court decision that allowed companies to solicit their employees for political donations. Justice Powell voted with the majority in the case.)[62] Wealthy corporate leaders poured money into think tanks in the 1970s that would fashion a conservative ideology and pro-capitalist policy initiatives. In 1973, the beer magnate and arch-conservative activist Joseph Coors founded exactly the kind of incubator of conservative ideas that Powell had called for when he provided $250,000 as start-up money for the Heritage Foundation. (That same year, conservative Republicans in the House founded the Republican Study Committee; it maintained a close relationship with the Heritage Foundation.) The billionaire Charles Koch and others founded the Cato Institute (first known as the Charles Koch Foundation) in 1974.

According to some of the scholars who populated these new think tanks, the gloomy predictions of environmentalists that increased pollution and rising populations would make the planet uninhabitable were groundless—as long as the innovative capacity of the free enterprise system could be unshackled from needless government regulations. Julian Simon, a University of Chicago-trained economist who became a fellow at the Heritage Foundation in 1983, epitomized this view. Since the early 1970s, Simon had, with increasing stridency, opposed Paul Ehrlich's view that a rising population on Earth would eventually exhaust resources. Instead, Simon maintained that entrepreneurship would find technological solutions for any depleted resources. Rather than restrain human populations and technologies to protect the environment, Simon argued that they should be unleashed. "Life on Earth is improving!" he declared in an opinion piece in the *Washington Post* in 1980. "Bad news about population growth, natural resources, and the environment," he wrote, "is based on flimsy evidence or no evidence at all." A rising population, Simon maintained, would lead not to poverty but to rising prosperity, because it increased the capacity for human innovation and entrepreneurship. An energy shortage? No need to worry: one need only have faith in "the propensity for scientists and business people to discover substitutes for the resource."[63] In short, Simon cheerfully prescribed for global environmental problems a conservative American set of ideals, derived from the principles of American exceptionalism, that were less policy proposals than they were articles of faith: natural resources were abundant; were they ever to be exhausted, preternaturally entrepreneurial people such as Americans would find alternatives.

Four years after creating the Heritage Foundation, Coors provided the money to create a public interest law firm, the Mountain States Legal Foundation (MSLF), based in Coors's home state of Colorado. The MSLF, intended as a kind of conservative analogue to the American Civil Liberties Union, enjoyed carte blanche to pursue cases that advanced the causes of limited government, free enterprise, and private property rights: the MSLF's first case was on behalf of an Idaho plumber who refused to admit health and safety inspectors to his business premises without a search warrant.[64] Yet James Watt, the MSLF president, quickly steered the organization toward what he knew best: opposition to the legal trumps that environmental protections imposed. Watt had earned his undergraduate and law degrees from the University of Wyoming; worked as a staffer for Republican senator Milward Simpson of Wyoming; lobbied on behalf of the U.S. Chamber of Commerce, where he specialized in advancing the interests of mining, logging, and ranching companies; and served as a deputy assistant secretary of the Interior in the Nixon administration and vice chairman of the Federal Power Commission in the Ford administration. In 1977, Coors tapped Watt to lead the MSLF. Watt told Coors and the other members of the MSLF's board of directors that "We need to establish a special expertise in the law concerning the energy issues—oil, gas, coal, uranium, mining, underground and surface, agricultural, timber, livestock, crops; and particular attention to our state water rights and the federal encroachment on them as well as management of the public lands."[65] What Watt had in mind was challenging the legal trumps embedded in environmental laws that tipped the balance toward environmental concerns and away from business interests.

The growing conservative resistance to environmentalism that Coors, Watt, and others were trying to advance had already begun to emerge during the brief presidency of Nixon's successor, Gerald Ford. Ford was a Midwestern Republican who, in the tradition of Robert Taft, abhorred government bureaucracy. "Agencies don't fold their tents and quietly fade away after their work is done," Ford wrote in his 1979 memoir, *A Time to Heal*. "They find Something New to Do. Invariably that Something New involves more people with more power and more paperwork—all involving more expenditures." According to Ford, one such costly and cumbersome creature of the federal bureaucracy was the EPA. In a telling sign of the nascent partisanship on environmental issues, Ford effectively disowned the EPA, using sly elision to attribute its creation not to Nixon, but to Lyndon Johnson. "By the time Lyndon Johnson instituted his Great Society," Ford wrote, "the perception was ingrained in Washington that the solution to every problem was to create a new federal regulatory agency to write and enforce rules. Thus we saw the creation of the Equal Employment Opportunity Commission in 1965, the Environmental Protection Agency and the Occupational Safety and Health Administration in 1970, and the Consumer Products Safety Commission two years later."[66] As Ford well knew, the last three of those agencies were created during Nixon's presidency.

Not just costly, such agencies restrained businesses—at just the moment when the American economy was faltering. In October 1973, in retaliation for U.S. support for Israel during the Yom Kippur War, the Organization of Arab Petroleum Exporting Countries implemented an embargo on oil exports to the United States, driving up the price of oil from $3 to nearly $12 per barrel by January 1974. The result in the United States was rapid and crippling inflation: the average annual inflation rate rose from 3.2 percent in 1972 to 6.2 percent in 1973 to 11 percent in 1974. By the summer of 1974 about 20 percent of American gas stations had no fuel to sell. At remaining stations, motorists endured long lines and government-imposed rationing (see Figure 1-1). Frustrated by the limited supplies of fuel, truckers embarked on a brief, violent strike in December 1973. To curb gasoline consumption, the federal government imposed a national speed limit of 55 miles per hour.[67]

The 1973–1974 energy crisis, with its high prices and long lines at the pump, marked an important turning point in American environmental

Figure 1-1   One of the many service stations in the Portland, Oregon area carrying signs reflecting the gasoline shortage. June, 1973. *Source:* David Falconer, photographer, EPA. DOCUMERICA, Records of the Environmental Protection Agency, 1944–2006 (Record Group 412), U.S. National Archives and Records Administration.

politics. Environmentalists' calls for limits on consumption and regulations on production seemed to increasingly conservative Republicans like unnecessary austerity. What was needed, instead, was to loosen strictures on business—particularly the energy industry. Congress agreed: in the fall of 1973, as the oil crisis was unfolding, Congress tipped the balance from environmental protection back toward economic development, authorizing the Trans-Alaska Pipeline despite environmental protest and ongoing legal suits. The 800-mile-long pipeline was designed to funnel petroleum from new oil fields on Alaska's northern coast to the southerly port of Valdez. Construction began in 1974. The hasty congressional action exempted the pipeline from the trumps that put environmental quality ahead of economic interests. In the midst of the 1970s energy crises, lawmakers decided, in effect, that domestic energy production trumped the environment.

Ford grudgingly signed two environmental protection bills in 1976: the Resource Conservation and Recovery Act, which regulated hazardous and solid waste, and the Toxic Substances Control Act. In the interest of spurring domestic energy production no matter the environmental cost, however, he vetoed a bill in 1974 that would have regulated strip mining for coal. In May 1975, he castigated Congress for having passed "a strip mining bill which would have decreased domestic coal production." Congress, he lamented, "has concentrated its attention on conservation measures such as a higher gasoline tax." He called for opening up more of coastal California and Alaska to petroleum production.[68] The Republicans' 1976 party platform reflected this growing ambivalence about environmental protection and the consequences for energy production and economic growth. Only four years after Nixon's pro-environment platform, the 1976 platform downplayed the need for environmental protections and instead called for balancing protection with growth. "Public land areas should not be closed to exploration for minerals or for mining," it read. Further, "Americans are realistic and recognize that the emphasis on environmental concerns must be brought into balance with the needs for industrial and economic growth so that we can continue to provide jobs for an ever-growing work force."[69]

Ford narrowly lost the 1976 presidential election to Jimmy Carter. One of Carter's first acts was to sign the bill regulating strip mining that Ford had vetoed. (In the waning days of his administration, Carter also signed into law two landmark bills: the Comprehensive Environmental Response, Compensation, and Liability Act—better known as the Superfund Act—which gave the EPA new powers to go after producers of toxic waste; and the Alaska Lands Act, which protected over 100 million acres of land as wilderness areas, national parks, or wildlife refuges.) In office, Carter set a tone of frugality and environmentally sensitive retrenchment, installing solar panels on the roof of the White House (Reagan later had them removed) and turning the thermostat in the White House down to 65 degrees. Carter spent much of his four years in office fumbling toward an energy policy, highlighted by a stunning national address in July 1979 in which he stated that the United States was suffering from a "crisis of confidence," largely owing to the lingering effects of the energy crisis. In the months after that address, Carter finally settled on an energy plan: a phased deregulation of oil prices, gas rationing, and the development of alternative energy sources. As one historian put it,

Carter wanted Americans to pay more for the energy they consumed—and consume less of it.[70] Carter's ambitious plans were overtaken by the Iranian Revolution, which disrupted oil production in one of the world's largest oil-producing nations, thus reducing oil output and causing the price of a barrel of oil to more than double to nearly $40. Inflation in the United States rose to 11.3 percent in 1979 and 13.5 percent in 1980.[71]

While the oil crisis was a critical component of the rise of conservatism, there were other important parts of the conservative coalition that emerged in the late 1970s. Evangelical and fundamentalist Protestants, courted by business interests since the 1930s, finally emerged in the late 1970s as an electoral force. Yet the leaders of this new evangelical voting bloc were a far cry from James Fifield in the 1930s. Fifield's radio show reached a relatively small number of listeners. As late as the early 1970s, only about 12 percent of Americans watched religious broadcasts on television or listened to them on the radio. By the end of the 1970s, that number had doubled. The rise of cable television and a tweaking of a rule by the Federal Communications Commission that permitted television stations to count paid religious broadcasting as public service programming caused "televangelism"—a new term in the early 1980s—to mushroom. By 1980, 90 percent of religious broadcasting on television was commercial.[72] While Fifield had been a mainline Congregationalist, the new televangelists were primarily anti-modern Pentecostals, charismatics, and fundamentalists who believed in the literal truth of the Bible and anticipated the return of Christ.[73] The televangelists' dramatic support for conservative causes transformed evangelical Protestants—who at the start of the 1970s had been largely uninvolved in politics and unlikely to be registered to vote—into a highly active political bloc more likely to vote than non-evangelicals.

Since the 1940s, evangelical business leaders in the energy industry had supported evangelical groups and politicians who advocated limited government, private property, and the development of natural resources. Jerry Falwell, a televangelist who founded the Moral Majority in 1979 to advance his political agenda, once declared that "the free enterprise system is clearly outlined in the Book of Proverbs."[74] Robert Billings and Paul Weyrich, who had helped found the Heritage Foundation, helped get the Moral Majority off the ground as well.[75] Yet in the late 1970s and early 1980s, the televangelists focused less on economics than on an array of social issues: the absence of prayer in public schools and the presence instead of "humanism," Darwinism, and sex education; feminism; pornography; abortion; and homosexuality.[76] To the extent that evangelicals gave attention to environmental issues, they were divided on the issue. James Watt, who celebrated free enterprise and resource development, was an evangelical. Yet so too was Calvin DeWitt, who in 1979 founded a center for evangelical environmentalism, the Au Sable Institute of Environmental Studies. DeWitt and like-minded evangelical environmentalists believed that pollution and resource exhaustion were demonstrations of human sinfulness; they maintained that people were called to be stewards of the Earth.[77] In short, evangelicals were of many different types; in the late 1970s and early 1980s they had not yet articulated a consensus on environmental issues. But even if environmental issues remained secondary to the emerging Moral Majority, Reagan's successful election bid, which enjoyed strong support from evangelicals, made clear how important the religious right would be to the emerging conservative coalition.

During his two terms as governor of California, Reagan had learned that he could, at times, solidify his support among conservative, pro-business Republicans by opposing environmentalists without paying much of a price at the polls. The pattern began during his campaign for governor, when, in a speech before the Western Wood Products Association in San Francisco in March 1966, Reagan said "We've got to recognize that where the preservation of a natural resource like the redwoods in concerned, there is a common sense limit. I mean, if you've looked at a hundred thousand acres or so of trees—you know, a tree is a tree, how many more do you need to look at?"[78] Shortly after taking office, he had opposed the creation of Redwood Park in northern California, on the grounds that withdrawing land from development would have a negative effect on the state economy. His resistance helped to reduce the size of the park from the 90,000 acres that the Sierra Club had proposed to one that was less than half that size.[79] In April 1972, Reagan introduced a state environmental protection plan but at the same time he lambasted environmentalists for their "exaggerated rhetoric" and vowed that they would not bring "economic development to a sudden and catastrophic halt." He also stated his opposition to Proposition 9, the so-called "Environment Initiative," that would have regulated oil and gas drilling as well as the composition of gasoline and chemicals—the initiative was defeated in June.[80]

Reagan was always careful to wrap his opposition to environmental regulation in a cheerful assertion that, despite what experts might say, the environmental regulations that he opposed were unnecessary because conditions were not that bad. He told a group of graduating high school seniors from Wayne, New Jersey, that "a consortium of doom-cryers made up of journalists, commentators, writers, and yes, a goodly portion of the educational and intellectual community, have conspired together to paint a picture of a sick society in a polluted land." In a sign of his growing anti-intellectualism, Reagan emboldened the students to "check the doom-cryers' pronouncements against the facts." What, exactly, those facts were, Reagan never explained. It was enough to assert that environmentalists were pessimists and pessimists could never be true patriots. Instead, Reagan urged them to contemplate progress. "Each generation stands on the shoulders of the one that has gone before, and as a result, each succeeding generation can see farther and more clearly," he wrote to the students. "Man has known only a few moments of freedom in his entire history, and most of those moments have been ours. Half of the economic activity in all history has taken place in America."[81] Sunny and upbeat, the letter to the New Jersey high school students crystalized Reagan's political creed. He conflated economic progress with freedom, and cast intellectuals as the doom-crying enemies of both.

Drawing on those anti-intellectual themes, Reagan revolutionized the Republican posture on the environment in his campaign for the presidency in 1980. He projected a blithe nonchalance not only toward environmental problems, but toward the scientific facts about them. Instead, he mocked both environmental laws and the perspective of environmentalists. In May 1980, he told the *Chicago Tribune* that there had been a "resurgence" of deadly insect-borne diseases around the world because the federal government had "prematurely outlawed" the pesticide DDT. (In truth, DDT continued to be used to combat malaria and other insect-borne diseases where necessary outside the United States after it was banned in the U.S. in 1972. Outlawing the pesticide in the U.S. was not premature: DDT is a carcinogen that moves readily through the food chain. By the time it was banned it had worked its way into the bodies of many Americans.)[82] In an interview with *Time* in October 1980, he attributed acid rain to the eruption of Mount St. Helens earlier that year: "I have a suspicion that one little mountain out there, in these last several months, has probably released more sulfur dioxide into the atmosphere than has been released in the last ten years of automobile driving." (In truth, the cumulative emission of sulfur dioxide by American vehicles in the 1980s was over 80,000 tons per day, dwarfing the volcano's release of 2,000 tons a day.) In September, he told *Sierra* magazine that "80 percent of our air pollution stems from hydrocarbons released by vegetation." In October, he said that "I didn't say 80 percent. I said 92 percent, 93 percent, pardon me. And I didn't say air pollution, I said oxides of nitrogen." (In truth, industrial sources account for no less than two-thirds of nitrogen oxides emissions.)[83] Reagan's flouting of facts made sense for a conservative who had dismissed the "intellectual elite" since he had burst on the national political scene in 1964: deference to facts implied a deference to the intellectuals whom he regarded as subversives and defeatists. His campaign demonstrated many of the facets of the emerging conservative politics of the environment: a defiance of fact-based science and a reflexive view that government regulation was both laughably ineffective and, in its restraint of the market, an affront to property rights and entrepreneurialism. Reagan paid no price at the polls for his hostility to the concerns of environmentalists: he received 51 percent of the popular vote for president.

Reagan's ascendancy marked a turning point in environmental politics: it was the beginning of the Republican reversal and the party's gradual disavowal of the laws and institutions of environmental protection it had helped to craft. From the time of environmentalism's emergence— whether it was the publication of *Silent Spring* in 1962 or the celebration of the first Earth Day in 1970—the movement seemingly swept up everything in its path. From the Wilderness Act in 1964 through NEPA and the Clean Air Act in 1970, the Clean Water Act of 1972, Endangered

Figure 1-2   Ronald Reagan often dismissed environmental concerns during his presidential campaigns. *Source:* Steve Greenberg, "My fellow environmentalists," *Los Angeles Daily News*, July 19, 1984. Reprinted by permission of the cartoonist.

Species Act of 1973, and the Superfund Act and Alaska Lands Act that Carter signed in the eleventh hour of his presidency in 1980, environmentalism had remade the landscape of public health and environmental protection in a relatively sudden and surprisingly far-reaching way. The same can be said of the ascendancy of modern conservatism: in 1964, the conservative candidate for the White House was decidedly defeated, and many members of the Republican Party rejected conservatism as a dead end; yet in 1980, another conservative swept into power. Environmentalism emerged not alone but alongside conservatism in postwar America. Until the 1970s, the two movements proceeded in parallel. With the start of the Reagan administration, they were soon to collide.

2

Visions of Abundance

IN 1980, when Ronald Reagan won the White House by a landslide, he claimed 51 percent of votes nationwide, and beat the incumbent, Jimmy Carter, in all but four states. In an already resounding victory, one group of states fell especially hard for Reagan: those in the American West. Reagan won by an astonishing margin—claiming 61 percent of the vote—in the western states that were home to most of the nation's parks, wildlife refuges, and public lands.[1] That same year, Republican candidates defeated Democrats in Senate races in Alaska, Washington, and Idaho; as a result, the Senate delegation from the West to the 97th Congress in January 1981 consisted of seventeen Republicans and seven Democrats. What explains Reagan's and the Republicans' success in the West? In no small part, it was Reagan's promise to end what many westerners had begun to describe as the "War on the West." In the 1970s, "conservation" had become a watchword for environmentalists and Democrats—in their view, conservation of energy, resources, and the public lands were all essential to the nation's economic and ecological health. But for conservatives, such a mindset cut to the quick: in "conservation" they saw a license for government meddling in local affairs and a recipe for national weakness. Indeed, as the economy lagged during the late 1970s, western businessmen, ranchers, and developers chafed at a widening array of environmental laws that seemed to hold up everything from grazing permits to oil pipelines to timber harvests, all in the name of environmental protection. For them, Reagan represented change. "The emerging philosophy is one of Western thought," Senator Ted Stevens of Alaska crowed after Reagan's election in 1980. "Less government, wise use of lands, and movement toward the private sectors." With Republican control of the White House and Senate, now was the time to start "dealing with problems, rather than government."[2]

In the 1980s, as conservatives gravitated toward the Republican Party and set in motion what would become the Republican reversal, they gave new life to an old theme in American history: the nation's freedom depended on aggressively developing its abundant, God-given natural resources, not exercising conservation and restraint. Such a vision of abundance was a potent tonic for the emerging coalition that helped propel the Republican Party's conservative ascendancy in the last quarter of the twentieth century: it appealed to loggers, ranchers, and executives in oil, gas, and coal whose operations often depended on access to government-owned resources; it appealed to states' rights advocates who resented the growing power of what they perceived as an overbearing federal government; it appealed to people of faith who believed the nation's natural resources were of divine provenance; and it appealed to rural citizens and working-class individuals whose welfare often depended on agriculture and the natural resource industries and who had witnessed firsthand the consequences of tightening environmental and public health regulations. Often it seemed it was social concerns such as right-to-life activism, school prayer, or gun rights that entwined conservatives and the Republican Party after the 1970s. But in the West, where this emerging coalition had strong roots, the management of the nation's public lands, natural resources, and fossil fuels was not simply a matter of economics or jobs; how the nation managed its resources was also a matter of faith, freedom, and, ultimately, the nation's future.

To champion such visions of abundance, Reagan tapped James Watt as his secretary of the Interior in 1981. Watt was a western booster and devout evangelical Christian, who launched a crusade to expand natural resource development and "restore balance" to the management of the nation's public lands. Although neither Reagan nor Watt would bring this agenda to full fruition, the Reagan administration's approach offered a template that conservative Republicans would pursue with varying degrees of success through Gingrich's Contract with America, George W. Bush's administration, and into the Trump administration. First, with the effects of the 1970s energy crises still being felt in the U.S. economy, the Reagan administration pursued policies to open up public lands in the American West and on the nation's continental shelves for coal, oil, and gas exploration, establishing the framework for an "all of the above" energy strategy that Republicans and Democrats alike would come to support. Second, it marshaled the powers of the federal government to try and weaken or roll back the environmental policies that constrained natural resource development, such as the laws that governed grazing and logging on the public lands. One of the policies that would come to frustrate conservative Republicans the most was the Endangered Species Act, which they considered an ineffective law that put concerns for species such as spotted owls and gnatcatchers before those of loggers, farmers, and their families. As Republicans learned time and time again, weakening the laws that protect the public lands and their ecological values was difficult, in the face of the sustained and well-organized opposition of the nation's environmental community. But for Watt, and the conservatives who succeeded him, the deregulation campaign was not just about national parks, natural resources, or endangered species. As Watt explained, "They are battling me on a philosophical war zone."[3]

What Was at Stake in the American West?

All told, the federal government owns roughly one-third of the nation's public lands, 93 percent of which are located in the twelve western states, plus the nation's continental shelves. In 1980, the federal lands produced enough lumber to build 86,000 three-bedroom houses annually. Twenty-one thousand ranchers grazed 4.5 million head of livestock on federal lands. And the public lands and continental shelf were a storehouse of fossil fuel reserves, containing an estimated 30 percent of the nation's coal, 80 percent of its oil shale, and 10 percent of the nation's oil and gas reserves.[4] Many western boosters believed that the region's abundant re-

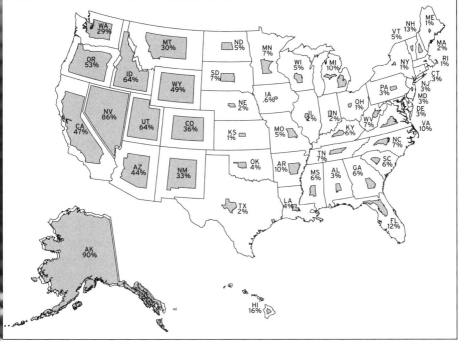

Figure 2-1   Federal landholdings by state in 1979. The federal government owned a significant percentage of the land in western states, which has contributed to western opposition to federal environmental policy. *Data source:* Bureau of Land Management, U.S. Department of the Interior, *Public Land Statistics, 1980.*

sources could help the nation pull itself out of the economic malaise of the late 1970s. As Reagan's transition team reported, "If the national economic pie does not grow—and it cannot grow without energy—those at the bottom of the economic ladder cannot rise without pulling someone down from the top."[5] (See Figure 2-1.)

While conservative Republicans viewed the West as an underutilized source of abundant and inexpensive resources, environmentalists saw a western landscape defined by fragility and scarcity. In 1980, the public lands included some of the largest tracts of unlogged forests that remained in the United States—what environmentalists described as the Ancient Forests of the Pacific Northwest. The public lands included the coastal plain of the Arctic National Wildlife Refuge, among the nation's largest and most remote wilderness areas. And the public lands included the deserts of the Southwest, many of which were hot spots for biological diversity. Although few public lands advocates denied the need for natural resources, they argued that the best use of much of the nation's public lands was not to prop up oil and gas or timber companies but to protect a broader public interest that valued parks and refuges, wildlife and biodiversity, and the health of the nation's wildest and most unique landscapes.

To many environmentalists, however, it seemed that rural westerners of the early 1980s wanted to turn back history. In the nineteenth century, after the United States had wrested control of the western lands from Mexico and Native Americans by treaty, purchase, and force, it gave away the public lands to white homesteaders and ranchers by the hundreds of acres and to railroad and timber companies in parcels measured by the square mile. Such policies encouraged western settlement and development, but growth came at a cost, including deforestation, industrial pollution near mining areas, the near extinction of the bison, and overgrazing.[6] Responding to the concerns of early conservationists such as John Muir and Gifford Pinchot, it was Progressive-era Republicans who put the federal government in the business of protecting the nation's public lands. President Theodore Roosevelt consolidated the federal government's role as steward of national parks, national forests, wildlife refuges, and other public lands in the West at the start of the twentieth century. As the chief proponent of the new conservation movement, Gifford Pinchot, explained in 1905, public resources should be managed "for the permanent good of the whole people and not for the temporary benefit of individuals or companies." When conflict over use arose, Pinchot's principle was that "the question will always be decided from the standpoint of the greatest good of the greatest number in the long run."[7]

Westerners were of mixed minds about the conservation movement from its inception. Many westerners, Democrats and Republicans alike, worried that the tightening grip of the federal government on the West's public lands meant fewer opportunities for homesteading and mining, a disregard for established local land management practices, and the beginnings of public control of vital industries, such as irrigation and electricity. In the 1930s, for instance, leaders such as Democratic senator Pat McCarran of Nevada fought fiercely against federal control of public grazing lands. Many westerners believed that a western ethos of independence and entrepreneurialism rooted in the nineteenth century was being edged out by government oversight and bureaucracy in the twentieth century. Yet western ranchers, miners, and loggers had never been as independent of the federal government as many of them liked to believe; they had always relied on a federal government that made resources available to them at well below market rates. It was a series of ecological disasters in the 1930s—notably the dust bowl in the southern Great Plains—that encouraged New Deal policymakers to take a more active role in regulating land use in the West.[8] Despite such catastrophes, many westerners came to believe that although it made sense for the federal government to protect the most exceptional resources, such as national parks and wildlife refuges, the greatest good would best be served by putting other public lands in private hands. As the historian Andrew Needham has explained, some westerners, upset with the legacies of the New Deal and increasingly allied with the Republican Party, believed that conservation policies "that regarded public lands as federal property in perpetuity did more to stymie economic growth than to protect the national interest."[9]

Such concerns gained new urgency in the 1960s and 1970s, as conflicts over the public lands were increasingly decided in favor of conservationists and environmentalists. Indeed, since the 1960s, environmental advocates had succeeded in advancing a series of laws that transformed the management of the nation's public lands. The Wilderness Act of 1964 led to the protection of millions of acres of public land from almost all uses, including motorized vehicles. The National Environmental Policy Act of 1970 meant considering the environmental impact of new oil pipelines, grazing permits, and other activities on public lands. The Endangered Species Act of 1973 created an explicit goal of not just protecting, but restoring endangered species on both public and private lands. And other laws created new processes, open to public comment, to ensure proper stewardship and planning for the public lands. Laws such as the National Forest Management Act of 1976, the Federal Land Policy and Management Act of 1976, and the Federal Coal Leasing Amendments Act of 1976, appeared to westerners—and the timber and mining companies allied with them—like so many hurdles they had to jump as they tried to fell timber, run cattle, or develop mines in the West. As James Santini, a Democratic representative from Nevada who later became a Republican, remarked, "the entire swing and orientation" of federal decision making since the 1960s, "has been to exclude, restrict, or limit use."[10]

By the late 1970s, many resource industries and westerners allied with them were fed up with the federal government, a slow economy, and what they saw as burdensome environmental regulations. With the support of western industries and politicians, westerners made their concerns known: drawing on western grievances that dated to the early twentieth century, they organized themselves into a loose-knit political movement, known as the Sagebrush Rebellion, and positioned themselves as "modern day freedom fighters who were going to liberate the western states from the federal government."[11] Their central claim was that the western states, not the federal government, should hold title to western lands. In 1979, the Nevada assembly passed a law asserting "a strong moral claim" over the federally owned public domain within Nevada's boundaries. The territory, most of which was administered by the Bureau of Land Management, amounted to roughly 86 percent of the state. The Nevada legislature believed federal land ownership "works a severe, continuous, and debilitating hardship upon the people of the state of Nevada."[12] Arizona, New Mexico, Utah, Wyoming, and Colorado followed suit with similar laws. Legally, these state laws had no effect: every western state had, as a condition of its admission to the federal union, disclaimed authority over federal lands within its boundaries. Yet, as symbolic politics the Sagebrush Rebellion captured the rising tide of frustration in the West among citizens, industry, and politicians.[13] The Sagebrush Rebels directed much of their ire at the Carter administration and Democrats, who had championed sweeping programs to protect public lands on the national forests, public domain, and in Alaska in the late 1970s. Ronald Reagan saw his opportunity. "Count me in as a rebel," he proclaimed on the campaign trail in the summer of 1980.[14]

As secretary of the Interior, Watt was unabashed in his embrace of Reagan's commitment to strengthening the nation's economy by easing environmental regulations and opening up the nation's public lands for development. Watt was a westerner, raised and educated in rural Wyoming, who had learned the ways of Washington, D.C., as a congressional staffer and as a bureaucrat in the Department of the Interior, Bureau of Outdoor Recreation, and Federal Power Commission. Watt was also an evangelical Christian, who saw in public service his opportunity to fulfill his Christian duty in the fight between good and evil. Watt had earned his spurs as a champion of free enterprise as the president of the Mountain States Legal Foundation in the late 1970s, a public interest law firm founded by the conservative beer magnate Joseph Coors in 1977 to "fight in the courts for individual liberties and economic freedoms."[15] In practice, under Watt's leadership, much of the foundation's work focused on advancing conservative arguments on public lands issues, including giving preference to local management, challenging environmental regulations, and protecting water rights.[16]

In these ways, Watt represented a new generation of conservative activist that began to come to power in the decade after Lewis Powell's 1971 memo: he was a staunch Republican, aggressive in his commitment to free enterprise, and eager to do battle with those he deemed leftist activists who threatened the nation's traditional values. Supporters from agriculture and extractive industries in the West applauded Watt's nomination: in Watt they saw one of their own—a trusted westerner who could bring much-needed balance to the management of the public lands. A representative from Rocky Mountain Oil and Gas described Watt as a "true environmentalist" who "grew up appreciating the values of the land and water, and most of all, the people in our part of the country." As secretary of the Interior, Watt oversaw a vast swath of the nation's public lands, including the national parks, wildlife refuges, and public domain, and all the coal, oil, timber, and forage they contained. From the start, environmentalists protested that Watt was too cozy with western industries. Their opposition only goaded Watt into action. He knew his policy agenda rankled environmentalists. Indeed, he invited the controversy. Watt saw himself as the champion for a necessary and sensible campaign to reform management of the nation's public lands and stave off crisis. In his words, "Unless we have such a program" of expanded resource development, "economic, social, and political pressures will grow to such an extent that the Federal Government will be forced, in a crisis situation, to mount a crash program to develop coal, uranium, oil shale, tar sands, and oil and gas." In his view, such emergency action would be far more costly and destructive than a sensible program for energy development.[17]

Those moves made Watt the lightning rod for the environmental movement's opposition to the Reagan administration. The Wilderness Society, a leading public lands organization, helped compile a two-volume "Watt Book" that detailed the secretary's ties to private industry, highlighted the pro-industry policies he pushed, and raised questions about the administration's agenda. Upon introducing the volume, the Wilderness Society's executive director commented, "It is both incredible and tragic that a cabinet officer can go astray so quickly that he prompts production of a four-pound book on his actions during his first six months."[18] The Sierra Club, the Wilderness Society, and other groups gathered one million signatures for a petition to "Dump Watt," focusing on Watt's proposals to mine in protected areas and sell off public lands, and his disinterest in expanding the national parks. As Doug Scott, a Sierra Club lobbyist noted, Watt served as a "unifying thread through many of our otherwise segmented and defensive political efforts."[19] Membership at national environmental groups soared, doubling between 1979 and 1983, giving the national environmental movement new resources in its fight against the Reagan administration. But the fight against the Reagan administration also demonstrated the limits of American environmental concerns. While many Americans increasingly cared about the environment, and strongly supported efforts to protect existing environmental laws like the Endangered Species Act, many Americans also strongly supported the gospel of more, which started with a steady supply of abundant and inexpensive energy.

Republicans, Energy, and the Gospel of More

In 1977, President Jimmy Carter announced that the American dream was running on fumes. Carter warned that a new era of scarcity "will test the character of the American people and the ability of the President and the Congress to govern this Nation." A series of energy crises in the 1970s, including the 1973 Arab oil embargo and a 1977 natural gas shortage,

Figure 2-2   James Watt, Reagan's first secretary of the Interior, was viewed as a threat by environmentalists. *Source:* Steve Greenberg, "When I'm Secretary of Interior. . . ," *Los Angeles Daily News*, January 8, 1981. Reprinted by permission of the cartoonist.

suggested that the era of scarcity had arrived. Carter characterized the energy crises as "the moral equivalent of war"—a rhetorical technique numerous presidents have employed since World War II to rally Americans to wars on poverty, crime, and drugs, among other domestic social and economic problems.[20] Yet instead of celebrating American productivity and enterprise as a source of strength in the face of this challenge, Carter instead chided Americans for overconsumption. "Ours is the most wasteful nation on Earth," he said. Such warnings were not new from Carter. Since the early 1970s, he had been giving voice to concerns about natural resource scarcity that underlay the environmental movement.[21]

That made Jimmy Carter the sobering Eeyore to Ronald Reagan's Tiggerish optimism about the future of the American economy, its resources, and the environment. Ronald Reagan's vision hinged on unleashing America's productivity. Where Carter saw conservation as an imperative, Reagan believed the United States could produce its way out of its energy problem. Reagan's transition team commissioned a report on energy, which optimistically predicted that the United States could produce as much oil and gas in the future as it ever had in the past. A key piece of that puzzle would be the public lands—both onshore and offshore—where the potential was "enormous" but so too was the "threat of excessive environmentalism."[22] Not surprisingly, the American Petroleum Institute had made much the same points in a preelection publication titled *Two Energy Futures: A National Choice for the 80s*. It called for regulatory relief and emphasized that "The rich energy resources on federal lands are indispensable in any effort to regain American energy security."[23]

Advancing the Reagan administration's and, by extension, the energy industry's agenda became James Watt's mission and his passion. Watt laid out the Reagan administration's goals in 1982, aiming to produce 85 percent of crude oil, 40 percent of the natural gas, and 35 percent of the coal produced in the United States from the public lands. There was no energy shortage, he claimed. "The American people own sufficient raw energy resources to meet our needs for hundreds and hundreds, if not thousands, of years."[24] It was a plan that would improve the nation's energy independence, generate new revenue to help close the budget gap, and create jobs. Although Watt rarely referred to his religious beliefs in public, and Christian leaders did not often testify in Congress on matters of energy policy, the Reagan administration's zeal for developing the nation's resources tapped into an evangelical Christian belief in human-kind's obligation to develop its God-given natural resources for the betterment of all. As the historian Darren Dochuk has argued, such beliefs were influential among conservative business leaders engaged in extractive industries, especially oil and gas in the Sunbelt, who helped propel conservative Republicans to positions of power in the post–World War II era. It was little coincidence that the American Petroleum Institute had hosted an annual prayer breakfast since 1971.[25] For such Christian-minded businesspeople, the politics of land-use and energy policy were, Dochuk argues, "just as vital to the Christian conscience as Court rulings on prayer and the unborn child." They were the ones who praised James Watt's "crusade" at the Department of the Interior.[26]

Watt launched a fusillade of policy initiatives aimed at opening up the public lands for energy development at the start of the Reagan administration. The most consequential of those policies aimed to expand coal production in the West and oil production from the outer continental shelves. In 1973, when the American energy crisis began, coal produced in the American West contributed just 10 percent to total U.S. production, in part because of the large reserves and high productivity in the privately owned coal mines in the Ohio Valley and Appalachia, and in part because of shortcomings in the federal government's coal leasing program. In 1973, the Nixon administration put a moratorium on new leases until Congress enacted a law, the Federal Coal Leasing Amendments Act, in 1976, that charged the Department of the Interior with systematically planning the development of federally owned coal reserves and then auctioning off mining rights through competitive leasing and development of coal fields at fair-market values. Environmentalists also worked to curb the coal industry's most destructive practices, such as strip mining, in the 1970s. In the East, hundreds of thousands of acres had been strip mined and then abandoned, which heightened concerns about expanded coal mining in the West. Despite the strong bipartisan support for environmental reform more generally in the 1970s, legislation to regulate strip mining was slow in coming due to fierce industry opposition. Once Congress passed legislation, Gerald Ford vetoed it twice. It was not until 1977, when Carter took office, that the Surface Mining Control and Reclamation Act finally became law. It imposed new taxes on coal to reclaim abandoned mines, required new environmental regulations to limit pollution from strip mining and require landscape restoration, and it created an Office of Surface Mining to coordinate permits and enforcement with the states.[27]

Thus, when Watt assumed office in 1981, he inherited a set of federal coal policies and regulations that had been modernized in the previous decade, but which retained a strong element of government oversight and planning. At the urging of the coal industry, Watt moved quickly to undermine the implementation of the new mining law and weaken the regulations it mandated. "If you knock down a hill because there was coal underneath it," Watt remarked, communities should use the resulting "flat area for a hospital or a school or a playground or whatever, a housing development or the like."[28] His first budget proposed downsizing the Office of Surface Mining's staff by 40 percent, closing key offices, and farming out its responsibilities to smaller offices managed at the state level. Watt set in motion rulemaking processes to roll back regulations that had been developed during the Carter administration pertaining to citizen participation, restoration standards for mined lands, and requirements for dams impounding waste on strip mines. The Department of the Interior also turned a blind eye to existing violations, declining to collect fines on coal companies that had violated the law in the early 1980s. Such moves drew enthusiastic support from coal operators, small and large. Coal operators believed their industry had been unfairly singled out by environmentalists for "drastic" regulation in the 1970s, which made the new direction of the Reagan administration a welcome relief. As one Kentucky coal operator explained, "I believe that a balanced program, as projected by Secretary Watt, is our way in this country." Indeed, without such a balanced program he warned, "we cannot feed the 42,000 people of Harlan County, Kentucky . . . because there are no other industries there."[29]

But Watt's efforts to weaken the new mining law faced challenges at every turn. Legal resistance, spearheaded by environmental groups such as the National Wildlife Federation, slowed any changes to the mining regulations, forcing Watt to comply with the National Environmental Policy Act's requirement of environmental reviews.[30] In the case of enforcement, Watt maintained he had "absolute discretion" as to whether the Department of the Interior collected fines for noncompliance with the Surface Mining Control and Reclamation Act. But the federal courts disagreed. In October 1984, a federal district court ordered the Interior department to begin collecting the fines that had gone unassessed during Watt's tenure.[31] Despite these legal setbacks, which had been orchestrated by environmental groups, Watt had successfully undermined the new Office of Surface Mining, reducing its staff and its authority. It never gained the power originally envisioned by the 1977 mining law.

Where Watt's agenda succeeded most fully was in reorienting the geography and economy of the nation's coal industry to the West. In place of the selective and deliberate pace of coal leasing outlined in the 1976 coal leasing law, Watt adopted a strategy meant to reduce government oversight and unleash market forces: he directed the Department of the Interior to offer extensive tracts of public lands for energy development simultaneously. The first parcels to go up for bid were in the Powder River Basin, which was the world's largest known reserve of fossil fuels (besting even the natural gas and oil fields of the Middle East). Unlike eastern coal fields, where the thickness of coal seams is measured by the foot, in Wyoming, according to one energy economist, coal seams are "as tall as eight-story office buildings."[32] Moreover, Powder River coal was low in sulfur, which gave it new value in the 1980s, as efforts to address sulfur dioxide emissions and acid rain from coal-fired power plants mounted. At the direction of Watt, the Department of the Interior put up the largest federal leases in history in 1982, offering tracts holding an estimated 1.6 billion tons of recoverable coal reserves. In setting both the size of the lease offering and adopting startlingly low minimum bid requirements, the Department of the Interior ignored advice received from advisory boards meant to guide the coal leasing process. The Powder River coal leases went for a total of a mere $67 million.[33] Watt described the coal leases as a resounding success. "I want to open as much land as I can," Watt told the *New York Times*. "The basic difference between this Administration and the liberals is that we are market-oriented, people-oriented. We are trying to bring our abundant acres into the market so that the market will decide their value."[34]

The problem was that, as the Government Accountability Office later estimated, the fair-market value of Powder River Basin coal leased in 1982 was at least $167 million. Instead of generating a robust and competitive bidding market as promised, only a handful of coal companies bid, most leases attracted only one bidder, and they bid low.[35] Some pinned the blame on poor timing: when the leases were offered, coal prices, along with other energy prices, had finally retreated from historic highs of the late 1970s. But critics blamed the Reagan administration's zeal for resource development, the amount of coal put up for lease simultaneously, and the irregularities in how the Department of the Interior established and advertised the minimum bid requirements—indeed, environmentalists believed it was evidence of Watt's allegiances to the energy industry. Although the controversy led to congressional investigations, an administratively appointed independent commission, and a lawsuit led by environmental groups, all of which would contribute to a hiatus on additional coal leases between 1984 and 1987, none of these strategies succeeded in reversing the 1982 leases.[36] The 1982 leases marked the beginning of a series of decisions, most made by Republican administrations, which would favor low-cost sales of western coal. In 1990, George H. W. Bush's administration reclassified the Powder River Basin through a process of "decertification" which strongly favored existing coal operators, allowing them to nominate tracts of land adjacent to their existing mining operations to be put up for bid. Although those lease sales were meant to be at fair-market value, roughly 90 percent of the sales attracted only one bidder (almost always the company that nominated the tract), and those bids remained low.[37] In 2015, environmental groups estimated that the low-cost leases added up to a $3 billion subsidy annually for coal companies.[38]

From the perspective of the industry and many westerners, this was not a sweetheart deal for the coal industry, however. It was an example of how pro-growth, market-oriented natural resource policies could benefit the West and the nation. As the chairman of the National Coal Association explained in 1982, developing the vast reserves of coal in the United States was the best way to protect the country's energy independence and provide for future economic growth.[39] Since the mid-1980s, coal companies had aggressively expanded in the Powder River Basin, increasing production 5 percent annually, compared to less than 1 percent annually for other coal regions. By 2008, power plants in thirty-eight states burned Powder River coal, providing electricity that was on average 12 percent cheaper than the national average. A resource economist at the University of Wyoming argued in 2013 that the Powder River Basin coal industry "is a good example of how dramatic improvements in productivity of a basic industry like coal production translate into downstream benefits."[40] Many conservatives, especially evangelical Christians, justified such policies not only in terms of economics, but in terms of belief. As one eastern miner explained in 2008, God "give us the coal so that . . . we can provide electricity for people. If God didn't want us to get that coal, he wouldn't have made means for us to get it."[41]

Despite Republicans' emphasis on the value of a free market, in their view, such benefits more than justified policies that gave coal companies low-cost access to public lands. Although the goal of the 1976 coal leasing act was that coal leases should return fair-market value to the federal government, instead the low-cost leases in the early 1980s in the Powder River Basin led to a flood of subsidized coal on the market, even after transportation from the West was factored in. By 2001, the inflation-adjusted price of coal had fallen steadily to one-third of its peak price in 1975. As a government audit reported in 1994, "the [national] decline in coal prices can be attributed to the increasing amounts of less-expensive coal produced from Powder River Basin mines."[42] The uneven application of environmental laws also worked to the advantage of strip mining in the Powder River Basin. The coal industry benefited from weak enforcement of the Surface Mining Act and also, somewhat ironically, from the 1990 Clean Air Act amendments, which increased demand for low sulfur coal. Thus, cheap coal both generated economic benefits and helped make the 1990 Clean Air Act amendments a success. Yet it also played an important role in ensuring the United States remained beholden to coal, even as concerns about the social and environmental costs of strip mining, particulate pollution, and global warming all mounted in the 1980s and 1990s. Indeed, by 2013, emissions from Powder River coal alone would have made Wyoming the seventh largest emitter of greenhouse gases in the world, right behind Japan, Russia, and Germany. In the United States, Wyoming coal accounted for 13 percent of the nation's greenhouse gas emissions.[43] And by helping to keep the nation's coal prices low, the coal boom slowed efforts to transition to cleaner sources of energy, such as natural gas or renewable energy technologies.[44] In 2014, the Center for American Progress estimated that the real cost of Powder River coal, factoring in the consequences for human health and climate change, was $62 per ton, four and a half times the market price.[45] (See Figure 2-3.)

The Powder River Basin is but one example of the many ways in which Republicans and their allies tilted the policy landscape in favor of fossil fuel production and away from conservation or renewable energy sources. Similar to the coal leases, the Reagan administration also helped set in motion policies that would expand offshore oil development.[46] When Watt assumed office in 1981, he inherited a federal offshore oil program that had, over the course of the previous decade, tried to expand domestic oil production in response to the 1970s oil crises without risking the kind of poorly regulated drilling that had led to the 1969 oil

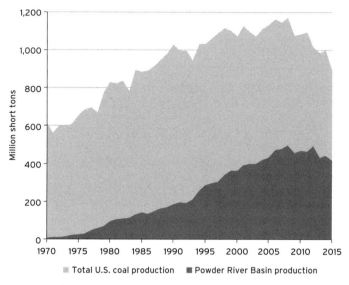

Figure 2-3   Powder River Basin coal as a percentage of total U.S. coal production. After 1980, Powder River coal production increased dramatically, accounting for 46 percent of U.S. coal production in 2015. *Data source:* U.S. Energy Information Administration / EIA.gov.

spill off the coast of Santa Barbara, California. Beginning in 1978, Interior secretaries were authorized to propose five-year plans in which they spelled out which offshore acreage would be available for leases. In 1982, when Watt had his first opportunity to propose a plan, he abandoned the balanced approach, gleefully announcing at a National Ocean Industries Association meeting, "We will offer one billion acres for leasing in the next five years." Rather than having the Department of the Interior select particular tracts for oil companies to bid on, Watt threw open large areas and allowed oil companies to select their own tracts. "I know of no company in the industry large or small which does not wholly support Secretary Watt's objectives of opening up more Federal lands onshore and off, for oil and gas leasing," said Charles Di-Bona, president of the American Petroleum Institute. "The industry has been crying out for decades for expanded and accelerated lease sales."[47]

In seven sales between 1983 and 1985—many of which took place after Watt had been forced from office but adhered to the leasing plan

Figure 2-4   As secretary of the Interior, James Watt championed policies aimed at opening up public lands for energy development. *Source:* Steve Greenberg, "Surf's up!" *Los Angeles Daily News*, June 5, 1981. Reprinted by permission of the cartoonist.

he had set out—the Department of the Interior leased over 2,600 tracts, nearly as much as all the lease sales since 1962 combined.[48] Those leases helped set the stage for a dramatic expansion in oil production in the Gulf of Mexico in the 1990s and 2000s. Although Republicans most often championed such policies, Republicans and Democrats (especially those from the Gulf Coast) alike supported expanding production from the Gulf. In 1995, during the Republican-led 104th Congress, Republicans and Democrats joined forces to further encourage offshore development in the western Gulf, passing the Deep Water Royalty Relief Act. In recognition of the risk and sizable capital investment involved in offshore exploration, the act waived royalty payments to the federal government valued at upward of $80 billion between 1996 and 2000. A decade later, as the market price of oil increased, the subsidies remained the same even as oil companies' profits soared. The Government Accountability Office questioned to what extent such generous royalty relief had actually served taxpayer interests.[49]

Although conservative Republicans and their allies continued to champion expanded offshore oil production in the western Gulf, Democrats and moderate Republicans (often from coastal states) also moved to block expansion in other areas, such as coastal California, Florida, New Jersey, and Massachusetts. Beginning in 1982, legislators from coastal states added stipulations to the annual appropriations bills for the Department of the Interior that prohibited funding for leasing activities on the Atlantic and Pacific coasts. In June 1990, President George H. W. Bush endorsed Congress's effective ban on drilling outside Alaska or the western Gulf, instituting moratoriums on coastal drilling anywhere but in those two areas. President Clinton extended the moratorium through 2012. Thus, at the outset of the twenty-first century, most offshore drilling was confined to the western Gulf of Mexico, which alone accounted for 25 percent of U.S. oil production.[50] And, as long as gasoline prices remained relatively stable, as they did in the 1990s, there was little incentive to open up new areas to production.

When George W. Bush's administration took office in 2001, however, it did so with a promise to expand the nation's domestic energy supply. As one political cartoon put it, "James Watt Days are Here Again!" The cartoon showed Bush dancing with his first secretary of the Interior, Gale Norton, a westerner who got her start working for Watt at the Mountain States Legal Foundation. Their tune? "The Reagan Era Once More!!"[51] In 2001, Vice President Dick Cheney released a national energy assessment, which urged expanded production of domestic oil and gas on federal lands, including the Arctic National Wildlife Refuge, and reexamination of offshore areas under moratorium. Environmentalists successfully defended the Arctic Refuge during the Bush administration, highlighting its unique ecological values and importance to Native Alaskans. But the Bush energy plan also emphasized the industry's outstanding offshore safety record and recommended a reconsideration of the moratoriums on offshore drilling outside the Gulf of Mexico. The opportunity to do so came in the summer of 2008, when gasoline prices surged above $4 per gallon and natural gas prices peaked at a historic high. In response, Bush lifted the presidential moratorium on offshore drilling in the Atlantic, Pacific, and eastern Gulf and persuaded Congress to do the same.[52]

During the 2008 campaign season, when Republican candidate John McCain faced Democrat Barack Obama, conservative media pundits joined Republican politicians in calling for increased domestic oil production. In August 2008, the conservative blogger Erik Rush coined the phrase "Drill, Baby, Drill" in a blog post.[53] Michael Steele, the chair of the Republican National Committee, and Sarah Palin, the Republican vice-presidential nominee, repeated it. Around the same time, the former Speaker of the House and Georgia Republican representative Newt Gingrich published a book titled *Drill Here, Drill Now, Pay Less: A Handbook for Slashing Gas Prices and Solving Our Energy Crisis.* "For decades anti-energy, left-leaning politicians have advocated higher prices and less energy," Gingrich wrote. "Viewing energy usage as a moral failing, they aim to save the environment by punishing Americans into driving less and driving smaller cars."[54] In the view of prominent evangelical Christian theologian Wayne Grudem, such leftist teachings advocating conservation were an affront to God's plans. Grudem believed that Americans should not be made to feel guilty about using fossil fuels, as environmentalists advocated, for fossil fuels were "God's good gifts" to be used with "thanksgiving."[55]

On the campaign trail, Obama had opposed lifting the moratorium on offshore drilling outside the Gulf of Mexico and Alaska. Yet, as the nation struggled to pull out of the 2008 economic crisis, Obama embraced many Republican energy policy positions, eventually describing his energy policy, which combined domestic fossil fuel production with alternative energies such as wind and solar, as an "all of the above" approach. Various Republicans had called for an "all of the above" energy program for at least a decade, and Palin had used the phrase together with "Drill, Baby, Drill!" during the 2008 campaign.[56] Through most of his first term, Obama's support for offshore drilling remained relatively strong. On April 2, 2010, speaking in Charlotte, North Carolina, Obama explained his all-of-the-above approach, noting specifically that "oil rigs today generally don't cause spills."[57] Eighteen days later, a blowout occurred on the *Deepwater Horizon,* an oil rig fifty miles off the Louisiana coast operating in water nearly a mile deep. The explosion killed eleven workers and injured seventeen more, resulted in $8 billion in losses in the fishing industry, and killed thousands of marine mammals and millions of seabirds.[58]

In the aftermath of that spill, and as Obama began to advance efforts to address climate change in his second term, his administration scaled back its offshore oil offerings considerably: Obama's five-year plan for 2012–2017 listed only fifteen sales, the fewest since 1978. The amount of acreage they opened for development was a mere 6.5 million, far below the average of 22 million acres offered in the six plans between 1982 and 2012.

In short, the Republican reversal helped transform U.S. energy policy, with significant consequences for the environment and the nation's geography of energy production. Although Democrats and some moderate Republicans often advocated stronger environmental regulations and opposed the development of domestic energy resources in specific areas, such as off the Atlantic seaboard or in the Arctic National Wildlife Refuge, the long shadow of the 1970s energy crisis deterred most Democrats and moderate Republicans from challenging the ramped-up domestic energy program that Reagan and Watt had initiated. Indeed, they tacitly endorsed the basic premise that developing domestic energy resources in places such as the Gulf or the Powder River Basin was in the national interest. In contrast to this grudging acquiescence, conservative Republicans rallied their supporters in an unbridled embrace of the gospel of more, with little regard for the environmental consequences. That was on full display in 2016, as Donald Trump made an "America First" energy plan a centerpiece of both his policy agenda and his efforts to cultivate support among working-class and rural Americans. As he reminded the nation, "This is your treasure, and you—the American People—are entitled to share in the riches."[59] In January 2018, Ryan Zinke, the secretary of the Interior, announced that roughly 90 percent of the Outer Continental Shelf—virtually the entire Atlantic and Pacific coastlines—would be opened to oil and gas lease sales. Within days, however, in a gesture to the Republican candidate for governor in Florida, Zinke exempted Florida from the new lease plan, a retreat that encouraged both Republicans and Democrats in other coastal states to press for exemptions as well.[60]

Logging at a Loss and Welfare Cowboys

The Reagan administration's and the Republican Party's fiscal strategy not only hinged on privatization, increasing productivity, and reducing taxes, but also on reducing unnecessary federal expenditures. Often that strategy posed a threat to the goals of environmentalists, since it meant proposals to drastically reduce budgets for the Department of the Interior and the Environmental Protection Agency—proposals that Congress, with the support of environmentalists, succeeded in blunting in the 1980s. But underlying many such proposals was one of the Reagan administration's key goals: reducing or eliminating government subsidies. As Reagan put it, "government will not continue to subsidize individuals or particular business interests where real need cannot be demonstrated."[61] That priority plunged the Reagan administration into sharp debates as it tried to curb a wide range of domestic programs, including social welfare programs, such as food stamps and housing assistance, and economic programs, such as price support for the dairy industry and subsidies for research into both fossil fuel and alternative energy.[62] But that strategy also opened up an opportunity for environmentalists. Although the timber industry and ranchers counted on the Reagan administration to relax restrictions on forests and grazing lands, the environmental community was able to take one of the Republican Party's core fiscal priorities—reducing subsidies and federal expenditures—and turn it to their advantage, especially in debates over the public lands. Indeed, many of the activities on the public lands, including logging, mining, and grazing, operated at below fair-market value or at a net loss to the federal treasury.

In the 1980s, instead of just describing these activities as an ecological threat to the public lands, environmentalists began emphasizing that they were a fiscal drain on the federal government too. Before then, the key strategy that environmentalists had adopted, usually with strong bipartisan support in Congress, was protecting specific parcels of the public lands. The high-water mark of that strategy came in 1980, when Congress passed the Alaska National Interest Lands Conservation Act just before Ronald Reagan took office. That law, which Carter championed, set aside more than 100 million acres of wilderness areas, national parks and other protected lands in Alaska, putting those lands largely off-limits to extractive industry. But in the 1980s, scientists increasingly realized that protecting biodiversity, water quality, and other environmental values could not be accomplished just by protecting specific areas—in effect, zoning the public lands. Just as important was changing how the public lands were managed overall. New laws, including the National Forest Management Act of 1976—which pertained to the national forests—and the Federal Land Policy and Management Act of 1976—which pertained to the public domain—established new procedural requirements, including resource inventories, long-term planning, and public input, all of which were meant to ensure that management of the public lands balanced resource extraction with recreation, preservation, species protection, and other values in both a fiscally and environmentally responsible manner.[63]

Thus, in the early 1980s, as the Reagan administration and James Watt put their support behind loggers, ranchers, and miners and opposed proposals for additional wilderness areas or national parks, environmentalists went on the offensive, seizing the opportunity to reshape the debate over the nation's public lands. It was a strategy made possible by the influx of support for environmental groups at the start of the Reagan administration: organizations such as the Natural Resources Defense Council, Sierra Club, and Wilderness Society expanded their staffs to include more economists, geographers, and scientists, which gave them new leverage in debates over public lands policy. For instance, in 1984, the Wilderness Society released a study that indicated that over the previous decade, the federal government had spent $2.1 billion more administering logging sales than it received in payment from logging companies. In an op-ed published in the *Wall Street Journal,* its resource economists argued: "national forests are managed uneconomically, at best, to the detriment of taxpayers, the environment, and the timber industry."[64] Environmentalists argued the story was much the same with ranching on the public lands. A government study indicated that ranchers paid one-fifth market rates to graze their cattle on public rangeland.[65] Not only did that revenue fail to cover the cost of administering the leases, most of the federal grazing lands were overgrazed. That set off Edward Abbey's indignation like a pistol. "Western cattlemen are nothing more than welfare parasites," the western writer opined in 1985. "They've been getting a free ride on the public lands for over a century, and I think it's time we phased it out."[66]

Such economic arguments succeeded in unsettling the status quo on the public lands in the 1980s, but not always in changing it. Reagan's Office of Management and Budget threw its weight behind such proposals, explaining that "This administration is committed to the philosophy that those who benefit from a specific federal service should pay the costs of providing that service where charges can reasonably be applied."[67] In the mid-1980s, Congress and the administration considered proposals to end below-cost logging and raise grazing fees to market prices, much to the consternation of timber and ranching interests. Even with strong support from environmentalists, however, those proposals went nowhere. Despite the Republican Party's emphasis on fiscal responsibility, it argued that activities like logging and grazing benefited the West in ways not accounted for by critics. In their view, logging activities funded road construction, habitat improvements, and pest management; grazing supported property values and communities in the West. Moreover, in the context of the federal government's budget, the funds at stake were modest. Senator Alan Simpson of Wyoming put that point more colorfully. In his words, even tripling the grazing fees "would be about like a fart in a tornado."[68] In 1986, it fell on President Reagan himself to decide whether to raise grazing fees from their historic lows and stop subsidizing ranchers. Simpson made clear that western senators were calling in a favor. "I told him it was the Western Senators who carried the water [for the party] and we would sure appreciate his help."[69] In February 1986, Reagan sided with his western allies and signed an executive order that extended the below-cost grazing fee on the federal lands indefinitely.

The opportunity to press the below-cost argument came again at the start of the Clinton administration. President George H. W. Bush promised on the campaign trail in 1988 that he would not revisit the grazing issue, and although his administration did consider curbing below-cost logging in 1989, those efforts fared no better in Congress than did earlier proposals to increase grazing fees. But when Bill Clinton won the White House in 1992, at the top of the administration's environmental agenda in 1993 was public lands reform. Clinton's secretary of the Interior, Bruce Babbitt, a native westerner and former governor of Arizona, argued that if the nation was going to solve its fiscal challenges, it was "unreasonable" to ask the American people to pay their "fair share" but exempt "miners, timber companies, ranchers, and reclamation water users." He promised, "we will bring old and true economic values to a new and urgent cause: the imperative to live more lightly and productively on the land—our land."[70] In the same 1993 budget proposal in which the Clinton administration proposed its ill-fated energy tax, it also included proposals to increase fees on public lands activities such as mining and grazing and to reduce below-cost logging. But the proposal faced near uniform opposition from Republicans, who largely sided with rural westerners and extractive industries. They were joined by Democrats representing the rural West, who proved to be a crucial swing vote in the budget debate. Those western Democrats forced Clinton to pull all of the proposed public lands reforms from the bill almost as quickly as they had been introduced.[71] At the time of Trump's inauguration, Reagan's 1986 executive order on grazing fees remained in force.

The Clinton administration's environmentally minded public lands agenda—of which the budget proposals were but the tip—became the focal point of what westerners again began describing as the "War on the West" in 1993. In the lead-up to the 1994 midterm elections, rural westerners trained their sights on Republican efforts to retake the House of Representatives. Although the Contract with America was the rallying cry for Republicans nationally, its emphasis on deregulation, property rights, and jobs resonated powerfully in the rural West, which had seen jobs in agriculture, the timber industry, and mining decline steadily since the early 1980s. Many of these westerners considered themselves a part of the Wise Use movement, which described itself as "a new balance, of a middle way, between extreme environmentalism and extreme industrialism." Much of this activity took place under the banner of People for the West!, a western organization that promised "to keep America strong by keeping public lands open." Corporate interests supported People for the West! as they did other public interest groups on the right. People for the West! described itself as a grassroots movement, but it openly acknowledged the support it received from the mining industry. It urged its members to vote. "Wherever elections are being held this year, VOTE FOR PUBLIC LANDS ACCESS, JOBS, RURAL COMMUNITIES AND A RESOURCEFUL AMERICA—don't accept anything else."[72] That support helped Republicans pick up House seats in Arizona, California, Idaho, Nevada, Oregon, Utah, and Washington, and to consolidate a Republican majority in the House and Senate.

With control of Congress, conservative Republicans quickly put environmentalists and the Clinton administration on the defensive in the 104th Congress, attaching numerous riders to budget bills, including language to open up the Arctic refuge to oil exploration, reduce royalties on mining on public lands, and mandate more logging from national forests in Alaska. With the strong support of environmentalists, the Clinton administration forced Republicans to abandon most such proposals through vetoes and subsequent negotiations. One exception was the so-called "salvage rider," which temporarily exempted logging activities from environmental review to expedite logging in areas that had suffered damage from wildfire, over the objections of environmentalists. Despite that legislative success, to many Republicans, especially conservative westerners, it seemed Clinton was thwarting Congress's ability and responsibility to redress "the devastating impact of federal regulations and environmental laws on the states."[73] But as the legislative gridlock deepened in Congress, the Clinton administration demonstrated the growing power of the presidency to shape environmental policy, using tools both old and new.

In 1996, Clinton ignored the strident objections of Utah's congressional delegation, and exercised the powers vested in him by the Antiquities Act of 1906. With the stroke of a pen, Clinton set aside 1.7 million acres of spectacular canyon lands in southern Utah as the Grand Staircase-Escalante National Monument—shoring up his environmental credentials amid his 1996 reelection campaign. It was the first of nineteen new national monuments Clinton created, most of which came during his second term. It was a legacy that infuriated many westerners, who viewed the Antiquities Act as an egregious infringement on states' rights—frustrations Donald Trump would appeal to two decades later. The Clinton administration also set in motion rulemaking processes aimed at addressing the below-cost management issues raised since the early 1980s. Of those, the most far-reaching was the management of the national forests. In close coordination with environmentalists, Clinton directed the Forest Service to develop an administrative rule to manage the remaining roadless areas—which harbored biodiversity and protected watersheds—to comply with the requirements of the National Forest Management Act. The rule was developed over three years, included extensive economic and scientific analyses, consultation with industry and states, and opportunities for public comment. It was adopted in the final days of Clinton's administration, giving new protection to 58.5 million acres of national forest roadless areas.[74]

Westerners fumed at what they saw as a pattern of administrative actions that usurped Congress's role in managing the nation's public lands. They had a point. Since the 1980s, Utah's congressional delegation had blocked legislation to protect the Escalante canyonlands, only to see Clinton swoop in at the behest of environmentalists and create the national monument. Since the early 1990s, Congress had failed to act on proposed wilderness protections for the national forests, only to see Clinton push through the roadless rule, which accomplished much the same goal, only on a far larger scale. Much the same could be said about efforts to reform grazing, mining, and other aspects of forest management. George W. Bush played to these western objections on the campaign trail in 2000. He made it clear that he opposed "command and control" policies handed down "unilaterally" from Washington, D.C., pointing to the roadless rule as an example.[75] Upon taking office, the Bush administration launched what would be an eight-year campaign to align public lands management with conservative western values and undo many of the Clinton administration's accomplishments. Behind much of the Bush administration's public lands agenda was Mark Rey, a former timber industry lobbyist and congressional staffer, whom Bush appointed as undersecretary of natural resources and environment in the Department Agriculture. Although Bush successfully advanced administrative policies that favored logging to curb wildfire risk, emphasized local decision making (in grazing for instance), and expanded access for energy development, the administration failed to overturn several key policies, including the roadless rule. The Bush administration's replacement rule, which it started pursuing in 2004, was deemed illegal after a protracted court battle that ended in 2011. That decision left the Clinton-era roadless rule largely intact, protecting more than 50 million acres of national forest from most forms of development. Although the roadless rule enjoyed broad public support, to conservatives with a stake in the public lands, the decision was only further evidence of a longstanding pattern of executive overreach by Democratic presidents meddling in western affairs.[76]

The Endangered Species Act at Risk

When Republicans gained control of the House of Representatives in 1994, at the top of their environmental hit list was the Endangered Species Act (ESA). Leading the charge was Richard Pombo, a second-term representative from rural California, who liked to wear his cowboy hat in Washington, D.C. and described himself as "a farm kid from Tracy."[77] Pombo jumpstarted the process to reform the law by organizing a series of hearings on the ESA in rural communities across the United States. Although many of the major debates over endangered species in the 1970s and 1980s hinged on the fate of public lands, the hearings in 1995 focused on how private landowners—farmers, ranchers, and developers—had been affected by the law. Indeed, a 1994 government report estimated that 90 percent of listed species depended upon habitat on nonfederal land and 37 percent of listed species were located entirely on nonfederal land.[78] Across the country, witnesses related their anger and frustration at limitations on their abilities to farm, graze, or develop properties because of seemingly insensible rules meant to protect species such as the kangaroo rat, the Delhi sands flower-loving fly, the spotted owl, or the red-cockaded woodpecker.[79] Robert Smith, at the Competitive Enterprise Institute, was one of the law's most outspoken critics. In his view, as with other groups on the public interest right such as the Heritage Foundation and the Pacific Legal Foundation, the law was fundamentally flawed. "The better steward a landowner is, the more wildlife habitat one maintains on one's land, the more likely it is that you will be rewarded by the loss of the use of or the economic value of your lands and property."[80]

No one foresaw such opposition to the ESA when Richard Nixon signed it into law in 1973. Like a whole series of foundational environmental laws, including the Wilderness Act, the Wild and Scenic Rivers Act, and the Marine Mammal Protection Act, Congress passed the ESA with nearly unanimous votes. It passed 390–12 in the House and 92–0 in the Senate. But the passage of the law generally went unnoticed. There were no protests either for or against the legislation. It drew almost no newspaper coverage. In what attention it did draw, it was usually described as a tool for protecting imperiled wildlife, such as wolves, whooping cranes, or brown pelicans—species that had drawn considerable public attention. Surprisingly, considering conservative Republicans' outspoken opposition to the law in the mid-1990s, it was shepherded through Congress by the Nixon administration, which in March 1973 had brought to a successful culmination multiyear negotiations on an international wildlife treaty that affirmed the role of the United States as a leader on global wildlife protection. On signing the ESA, Nixon praised Congress for giving the federal government the "needed authority to protect an irreplaceable part of our national heritage—threatened wildlife."[81]

In practice, the ESA went far beyond just protecting iconic wildlife. The law called on the federal government to establish a list of threatened and endangered species—including mammals, fish, birds, amphibians, reptiles, mollusks, arthropods, or other invertebrates—based on scientific considerations without regard for economic concerns. An endangered species was one "in danger of extinction throughout all or a significant portion of its range." It protected species from a wide variety of threats, including harassment, pursuit, hunting, and killing, and degradation or loss of habitat—restrictions that applied to private citizens, corporations, and the state and federal governments. Not only did it provide strict protection for endangered species, it also required recovery plans to provide for the reintroduction and restoration of endangered species. To accomplish that, it also included provisions for protecting habitat. The law gave the federal government—specifically, the Fish and Wildlife Service (FWS) and the National Oceanic and Atmospheric Administration (NOAA)—new responsibilities. It required other government agencies to consult with the FWS and NOAA regarding projects that might jeopardize a species or its habitat. It prohibited private land-owners from harming such animals or the habitat upon which they depended, even if the land was privately owned. For many of these require-ments, the ESA legislated specific timelines for when decisions about listing and critical habitat had to be made. And, like other foundational environmental laws, such as the Clean Air Act and Clean Water Act, the ESA gave citizens the right to petition for the protection of species—a right that became a powerful tool for environmental groups seeking to protect species and habitat.[82] Ultimately, the power of the ESA stemmed from the way in which it was written: as the historian Peter Alagona has observed, the law is uncommon in that it is "so clearly written, straight-forward, general, and concrete." In the decades ahead, that would afford little flexibility to judges, who would interpret the law expansively to the frustration of those who thought the ESA went too far.[83]

Even in the early 1980s, the Reagan administration, James Watt, and industry allies believed that the ESA had already begun to swing too far in the direction of preservation. Watt urged, "We have to put people in the environmental equation."[84] The highest profile and most controver-sial endangered species cases of the late 1970s exemplified the reach of endangered species protection. In 1976, environmentalists succeeded in halting the $115 million Tellico dam project in Tennessee to protect the snail darter—a three-inch long fish discovered in 1973. In 1980, envi-ronmentalists interrupted a residential development project worth more than $500 million and including 3,300 homes in San Bruno, California, just south of San Francisco to protect two species of listed butterflies. In the case of the dam, the Supreme Court upheld an injunction halting construction in *Tennessee Valley Authority v. Hill*, a pivotal legal case, explaining that the law's plain language made it clear "Congress intended to halt and reverse the trend toward species extinction—whatever the cost."[85] Indeed, in the decades to come, the plain language of the ESA, which put the fate of species before economic considerations, would prove decisive. The Tellico Dam only proceeded when Congress acted to exempt it from the Endangered Species Act in 1979.

Watt tried to put the brakes on the endangered species program in the early 1980s, just as he did with other environmental policies, rec-ommending drastically lower budgets for species listings, enforcement activities, and land acquisition and changes to the law, which was due for renewal in 1982. But as was true of most of Reagan's efforts to weaken existing environmental law, it made little headway in Congress. With moderate Republican senator John Chafee (Rhode Island) in the lead, Congress steered away from any dramatic reforms. Russell Train, a moderate Republican who had led Nixon's Council on Environmental Quality and then the Environmental Protection Agency in the 1970s, railed against efforts to lessen protection for those species or limit the types of species eligible for listing—proposals that industry and the Reagan administration had floated. As he explained in his testimony, "I regard these proposals as tantamount to a repeal of the Act." Senator Alan Simpson (R-Wyoming) praised Chafee's leadership and success in crafting a compromise that would provide for a "more workable and credible framework for wildlife protection."[86] The 1982 amendment included provisions for experimental populations, which made it easier to reintroduce species into their historic ranges (by adding flexibility to the protections for reintroduced populations). The amendment also legitimized Habitat Conservation Plans, which were pioneered in the San Bruno case. These plans allowed landowners to proceed with a project even if it threatened or harmed a species, but only after the development and implementation of a plan to protect the species or habitat elsewhere. But the 1982 amendments left the core of the ESA intact, as champions such as Senator Chafee knew: all species were still eligible for listing; decisions to list were still based solely on scientific criteria (economic considerations only came into play when designating critical habitat); and the broad prohibitions against harming species remained.

The case of the northern spotted owl thrust the ESA back into the national limelight in the late 1980s. The small bird nests in old-growth forests, primarily in Oregon and Washington. A century of industrial logging on private and public lands in the region had decimated the region's mountains—more than 85 percent of the old-growth fir and hemlocks had been clear-cut, jeopardizing the owl's habitat and its future. Yet, the Forest Service had been resisting efforts to protect the region's forests since the 1960s, whether the aim was to protect specific areas as wilderness or manage logging to protect biological diversity (a requirement under the National Forest Management Act of 1976).

Indeed, in the 1960s and 1970s, the alliance between the Forest Service, the timber industry (which employed more than 120,000 people and accounted for one-quarter of the economic activity in Oregon and Washington), and the region's politicians formed a seemingly unstoppable juggernaut. In 1987, a Boston-based environmental group petitioned the Reagan administration to list the Northern spotted owl, which would have far-reaching implications for the future of the region's forests.[87] The Reagan administration rejected the petition, despite the advice of government scientists in 1988.[88] The Sierra Club Legal Defense Fund challenged that decision in the courts, which sided with the environmentalists and ruled that the agency had been "arbitrary and capricious" in its decision. In 1990, the FWS listed the owl as threatened, and a year later proposed 11.6 million acres of critical habitat. It was a stunning turn of events, for it threw into uncertainty the timber industry's access to millions of acres of federally owned forests in the Pacific Northwest.

Logging companies and their employees saw themselves not as villains in a story about the beleaguered spotted owl, but as victims of environmental extremists. When the federal courts initially blocked logging in 1989, 125 logging trucks paraded through the streets of downtown Seattle in protest. Opponents of restrictions on logging organized as part of the Oregon Lands Coalition, which argued for legislation to protect endangered communities, much as the ESA protected endangered species. In 1992, the organization's representative, Evelyn Badger, testified that "the people I know and love are suffering. These people are suffering from an unyielding ESA which is strangling the western way of life." She urged Congress to change the law to recognize that "people are part of the environmental equation."[89] It was a point that the timber industry and the union echoed, warning that the law might save the owl, but at the risk of endangering loggers and their families. But, as was often the case in debates over environmental policy, the spotted owl was a convenient scapegoat for a changing industry: overcutting on privately owned timber land, increased mechanization and efficiency in the timber industry, and an increase in exports (meaning less domestic processing) had all contributed to declining employment in the timber industry— trends that had started well before the spotted owl controversy. Recognizing this, some environmentalists had tried to push a broader reform agenda in the late 1980s, working through Congress to balance support for workers, the timber industry, and the need to protect the region's forests as part of a sustainable economy. Despite those efforts, the debate over the future of the region's forests boiled down to "cute birds vs. sobbing mill workers' children," as one environmentalist lamented.[90]

The spotted owl controversy became an issue in the 1992 presidential election. Running for reelection, George H. W. Bush played to growing frustrations with the ESA, despite his moderate stance on environmental issues during his first term. In his words, the law was "intended as a shield for species against the effects of major construction projects like highways and dams, not a sword aimed at jobs, families, and communities of entire regions like the Northwest." Speaking to timber employees in Oregon, he put it simply: "The law is broken, and it must be fixed."[91] Loggers and their families also traveled to Washington, D.C. to press their case in Congress, reflecting the growing mobilization of conservative citizens. As part of the emerging Wise Use movement, the Oregon Lands Coalition helped sponsor week-long "Fly-in for Freedom" rallies in Washington, D.C. in the early 1990s. Borrowing tactics that environmentalists had often used in the 1970s and 1980s to drum up support for environmental legislation, those conservative rallies brought together conservative activists in "an intense lobbying effort" to challenge laws related to wetlands, endangered species, mining, grazing, and "takings" of private property. Although Republicans had helped pass the Endangered Species Act in 1973 and key Republicans stood by it in the early 1980s, it was no longer clear they would do so again in the mid-1990s.[92]

Republicans' hopes to reform the ESA were thwarted the following year. Bill Clinton won the election and when he arrived in the White House, he quickly delivered on a campaign promise: he convened a Northwest Forest Conference in Portland, Oregon to break the gridlock over the Ancient Forests. Out of that process, which was meant to balance the economic, ecological, and social issues at stake, came the Northwest Forest Plan. The plan limited logging to 74 percent of historic levels, protected 76 percent of forest land, created a system of reserves to protect owls, and included programs and funding to support timber communities.[93] After decades of clear-cutting and unsustainable logging in the Pacific Northwest, the plan promised a measure of protection for the spotted owl and the Ancient Forests on which it depended. In December 1994, the courts ruled that the plan was sufficient to meet the federal government's obligations to balance protection of species and biological diversity with logging and other economic activities. To rural westerners, the Northwest Forest Plan was but another example of how the Clinton administration had strengthened the hand of the federal land agencies at the behest of environmentalists. Indeed, Washington and Oregon were hotbeds of Republican support during the 1994 midterm elections that put Congress back in Republican hands.

For that reason, when Representative Richard Pombo launched his effort to reform the ESA in the 104th Congress, he had a strong base of support, especially among rural Americans. Many environmentalists viewed it as the most potent threat the law had faced. Pombo's efforts advanced quickly in the House of Representatives. In October 1995, Pombo and Representative Don Young (R-Alaska) successfully pushed a rewrite of the ESA through the House Committee on Natural Resources that would have fundamentally changed the law. It required weighing economic considerations in decisions to list species, eliminated provisions that applied to private individuals and private lands, and required the government to compensate landowners for reductions of property values.[94] The proposed reforms drew strong support from farmers, ranchers, and those in the extractive industries. But nationally, Republicans came to realize that the anti-environmental crusade being spearheaded by westerners like Pombo was not playing well with more moderate Republicans nationally (and that anti-environmental agenda faced overwhelming opposition from Democrats in Congress and the Clinton White House). The issue even rallied an emerging group of evangelical Christians, organized under the banner of the Evangelical Environmental Network, who supported protections for the nation's environmental laws, particularly the ESA. Disagreeing with Christians who subscribed to dominion theology, these evangelicals saw in the Bible a mandate to steward all of God's creation. In 1996, they ran television ads, sent out mailers, and organized a campaign of "Noah congregations" across the nation to defend the ESA. Such positions put the Evangelical Environmental Network at odds with other groups in the Christian

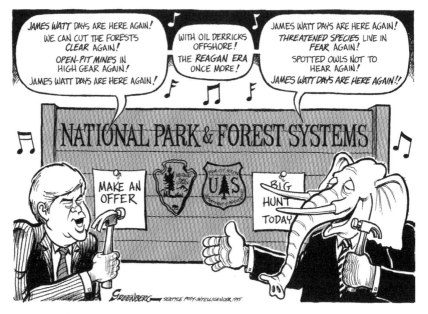

Figure 2-5 In part, the Contract with America spearheaded by Newt Gingrich represented an effort to advance Reagan-era environmental policies. *Source:* Steve Greenberg, "James Watt days are here again," *Seattle Post-Intelligencer,* February 13, 1995. Reprinted by permission of the cartoonist.

Coalition and their conservative Republican allies. Representative Young voiced his frustration, saying "Americans expect religious leaders to abide by a higher standard . . . don't use the pulpit to mislead people."[95] Such opposition from moderate Republicans and evangelicals played a key role in blocking Pombo and Young's efforts to gut the ESA. Their proposal died in the 104th Congress; Speaker Newt Gingrich refused to bring the legislation to the full House.

With legislative action dead in Congress, the Clinton administration moved forward with an agenda it had initiated in 1993 to improve the implementation of the act. With Secretary of the Interior Babbitt in the lead, it actively worked to expand the role of habitat conservation plans, which had been included in the 1982 amendment but little used since, as a cooperative strategy to balance endangered species protection with the interests of private landowners. Two new administrative rules proved crucial to this strategy. The Clinton administration first promulgated a "no surprises" rule, meaning once a plan was adopted—and plans often had durations of decades up to a century—the agreement was grandfathered in no matter what new information, research, or threats to the species arose. A second rule guaranteed a "safe harbor" for landowners, meaning if a private landowner attracted endangered species to their property through good management under a habitat conservation plan, they would not face further restrictions on their property as a result. Of the two rules, the no surprises rule would be particularly consequential. It made habitat conservation plans a central part of the implementation of the ESA, transforming it from a punitive law, focused on individual species, to a more proactive law, encouraging long-term planning for ecological conservation. Although environmentalists challenged the validity of such plans, the collaborative approach proved popular with private landowners, such as logging companies and developers, and cities and municipal planners, who gained a measure of long-term security in exchange for moderate concessions to protect species and fund restoration efforts.[96]

But those reforms did little to defuse tensions over endangered species policy, especially among conservative, rural Americans who looked to the Republican Party for change. Despite the efforts of groups like the Evangelical Environmental Network to mobilize support for the Endangered Species Act, the law became an important target in George W. Bush's environmental agenda. The precipitating event was the fate of several species of listed fish, including the Lost River sucker, the shortnose sucker, and the coho salmon, that lived in the Klamath River Basin in Oregon and California. In response to drought conditions in 2001, the Fish and Wildlife Service and National Marine Fisheries Service issued biological opinions under the Endangered Species Act that upended management of the Klamath River and the lives of local farmers. To avoid jeopardizing the fish, the agencies determined it was necessary to withhold irrigation water from 1,400 farmers cultivating 200,000 acres of wheat, potatoes, and other crops—a decision upheld by a federal district court.[97] In April 2001, George W. Bush's secretary of the Interior, Gale Norton, complied, cutting off water to farms that had depended upon the irrigation water since 1907.[98]

Delivering water to fish rather than farmers quickly thrust the ESA back into national news. From an environmental perspective, farming in the Klamath River Basin never made ecological sense; it was an arid region, wholly dependent on federal subsidies and water. Recognizing that reducing irrigation water to farmers put their enterprises at risk, some environmentalists urged the federal government to buy farmers out at premium prices and return the land to more fiscally and ecologically sustainable forms of wildlife management. The *Wall Street Journal*'s editorial staff described that proposal as tantamount to "rural cleansing" aiming to "expunge humans from the countryside."[99] That May, farmers and their friends formed a bucket brigade to pass water from a nearby lake to the irrigation canal. The event drew 15,000 participants.[100] In July, angry farmers took matters into their own hands, using a blowtorch to open up the irrigation gates themselves. After that, the government began guarding the gates around the clock, leading to a standoff with protesters that lasted until September. By the fall of 2001, local agricultural losses exceeded $150 million.

Determined to see the local farmers control water resources, Norton pursued a strategy that became characteristic of the Bush administration—questioning the underlying science.[101] Secretary Norton asked the National Research Council to assemble a scientific committee to review the biological opinions that justified withholding irrigation water to manage water levels in Klamath Lake and the Klamath River. It was the first time the government had commissioned an after-the-fact scientific audit. Four months later, the committee's interim report issued conclusions that, to the Bush administration's delight, largely vindicated the farmers' position.[102] Although it was only an interim report and some scientists raised concerns about the preliminary findings, the Bush administration restored irrigation levels in the spring of 2002 despite the continued drought. Secretary Norton traveled to Oregon to personally open the gates. The decision was ill-timed. That fall, the biggest recorded fish kill in the Klamath River struck—more than 30,000 fish, including Chinook salmon, steelhead, and several hundred endangered coho died.[103]

Although environmentalists succeeded in securing a legal decision to provide more water in the Klamath for the coho in 2006, by then the controversy had become "Exhibit A" in conservatives' calls for reforming the ESA.[104] Since the early 1990s, they had been arguing that protecting species often unfairly burdened private property owners, in this case farmers. Riding herd on that effort was none other than Richard Pombo, who had gained a key committee post in 2003 and co-sponsored the Threatened and Endangered Species Recovery Act of 2005. It included provisions similar to those in the 1995 proposal: it elevated economic considerations in decision making, eliminated critical habitat requirements, weakened requirements for interagency consultation, and, especially controversial, required compensating private landowners for any loss of property value. But the centerpiece of the proposal was the seemingly unassailable commitment to using the "best available scientific data." The Congressional Budget Office estimated that implementing the proposed legislation, including new financial assistance programs for private landowners, nonprofits, and states, would double the cost of implementing the ESA between 2006 and 2010, adding $2.6 billion in costs (almost certainly guaranteeing the law would not be fully implemented).[105]

Yet, with the support of some rural Democrats, most Republicans, and the Bush administration, Pombo succeeded in doing what he had not accomplished in the mid-1990s.[106] The House passed the bill on a largely party-line vote of 229 to 193. But environmentalists tarred the bill, arguing that it "guts" the ESA by eliminating its enforcement provisions, requiring unreasonably short timelines for action (after which activities would be exempt from species protection) and creating unworkable procedural hurdles (such as barring consideration of results from population models, a key tool for ecologists, and requiring peer review of all data). In their view, the compensation for private landowners amounted to "an endless slush fund for private developers."[107] And, despite their opponents' claims to the contrary, they argued that the existing ESA worked: 99 percent of the species ever listed were still alive. When the House moved the legislation, it was the first time legislation to amend the Endangered Species Act had been passed since 1988. But, as was the case in the mid-1990s, moderate Republicans—this time, Senator Lincoln Chafee (R-Rhode Island) who chaired a key committee in the Senate—kept it from ever moving in the Senate.

Conservatives, unable to change the law in Congress and stymied in the courts by its unyielding language, turned to the Bush administration to pursue their agenda through executive action. Indeed, between 2003 and 2007, substantial evidence arose to suggest that Vice President Dick Cheney and Bush policy advisor Karl Rove may have personally intervened in the Klamath case, urging the Department of the Interior to pursue actions that favored the farmers (a key constituency in a state Bush lost by fewer than 7,000 votes in the 2000 election).[108] The leading government fisheries biologist, Mike Kelly, who had been charged with analyzing the impact on the coho salmon for the National Marine Fisheries Service, sought whistle-blower status in 2002, describing how the agency had cut short the biological analysis to push through the irrigation plan that favored farmers without fully considering the impacts on the coho.[109] What the Bush administration learned from the Klamath case was that science was a powerful lever by which to affect the reach of the ESA—change the science and one could undermine the case for listing species, establishing critical habitat, and restricting activities that could affect listed species. In 2007, the Department of the Interior's inspector general released a damning report that detailed the role of Julie MacDonald, Norton's deputy assistant secretary for Fish, Wildlife, and Parks, who oversaw the Endangered Species Program, for "editing, commenting on, and reshaping the Endangered Species Program's scientific reports from the field" and leaking confidential information to lawyers at the Pacific Legal Foundation, which spearheaded conservative challenges to the ESA.[110] MacDonald resigned her post within months and in July 2007 the Fish and Wildlife Service announced plans to review and, potentially, reverse decisions in eight cases where MacDonald had put politics first.[111] As the inspector general concluded, "MacDonald's zeal to foster her agenda caused significant harm to the integrity of the ESA decision-making process, along with potential harm to FWS's reputation among its state and local sister agencies."[112]

The Bush administration's track record on implementing the ESA was one of overt and covert resistance from its start to its very end. Despite the efforts of moderate Republicans and some Christians aligned with the "creation care" movement to blunt the Bush administration's agenda, it took its cues from the ranchers, miners, developers and their allies on the public interest right who urged Congress and the administration to weaken the law or, at least, its implementation.[113] Just over a month before leaving office in 2008, the Bush administration finalized a rule substantially scaling back the circumstances in which federal agencies had to consult with agency scientists in the Fish and Wildlife Service regarding potential impacts on listed species. Such a policy would have significantly weakened the power of the ESA in ways that conservatives had long advocated. But, once in office, the Obama administration moved almost as quickly to reverse the rule (which was vulnerable to reversal, due to its last-minute adoption). That meant, despite two decades of growing opposition, the ESA remained the most powerful law for protecting the nation's wildlife and the habitat it depended upon, with the power to "trump" entrenched economic interests and large-scale government projects, much to the chagrin of the mining, farming, logging, and development interests who opposed it.

When the law's fortieth birthday was celebrated in 2013, it provoked assessments of its successes and failures. As the historian Peter Alagona observed, "The truth is that it has really been a mixed bag to date, and 'to date' is a really short time." In his assessment, the act has done "a really good job" of preventing extinctions, but "it's done a really poor job promoting the recovery of species that are on the list."[114] Although the ESA played an instrumental role in protecting key species such as the gray wolf, bald eagle, brown pelican, American alligator, Louisiana black bear, and Oregon chub—all of which are among the thirty species delisted thanks to successful recoveries—1,361 listed species remained at risk. But equally true, the law has directly affected citizens around the country, especially in hotspots of biological diversity, such as the West Coast, Florida, and the Appalachians, where it has imposed on the interests and rights of private landowners. In 2013, House Republicans once again began laying the groundwork for an effort to reform the ESA. In their view, "with less than 2% of species removed from the ESA list in 40 years, the ESA's primary goal to recover and protect species has been unsuccessful."[115] After the November 2016 election, with Republicans in control of Congress and a sympathetic Republican in the White House, Representative Rob Bishop of Utah announced the time had come to "repeal and replace" the Endangered Species Act.

Conclusion

The Republican reversal cast a long shadow over the nation's public lands. Put simply, the Progressive-era Republican Party of conservation became the modern Republican Party of extraction. This transformation had been underway well before James Watt and Ronald Reagan took office and, at the same time, they did not see it through to its completion. Three years into the Reagan administration's first term, Watt was forced to resign as secretary of the Interior, in part because of his own political missteps—he made offensive and discriminatory comments regarding the individuals appointed to the commission investigating below-cost coal leases—but also as a result of sustained public opposition.[116] Upon his resignation, one colleague lamented privately that Watt's "crusade" at the Department of the Interior was over.[117] But that was hardly true. Watt had played a key role in consolidating the Republican Party's identity as the party of extraction in the early 1980s, which laid the groundwork for the nation's commitment to domestic energy production, affirmed that many conservative Americans put resource development and economic growth ahead of environmental protection, and helped drive a wedge between rural Americans and the Democratic Party that would last into the twenty-first century.

While Republicans had much success in pushing an all-of-the-above energy strategy, expanding coal, oil, and gas development both onshore and offshore after the 1980s, efforts to transfer public lands to the states or roll back the scope of environmental laws had largely fizzled. At the behest of environmentalists, between 1964 and 2015 the amount of protected wilderness grew from 9 to nearly 110 million acres of public lands, almost all of it in the West. Logging on the national forests fell by over 60 percent from 1986 to 2015, as forestry rules tightened. And key laws, such as the Endangered Species Act, remained potent tools for environmental protection. Other activities, from renewing grazing leases to building pipelines, could not proceed without formal consideration for environmental impacts, endangered species, and effects on the "human environment." If westerners needed a reminder of the nation's enthusiasm for environmental protection and the power of the presidency, President Obama set aside another 5.1 million acres of western lands as national monuments between 2013 and 2016, capping it off with the 1.4 million acre Bears Ears National Monument designation less than a month before he left office.

One way to explain the transformation of the Republican Party's agenda is to follow the money. If one looks at the record of campaign donations, this Republican zeal for energy development is hardly surprising. Between 2010 and 2016, oil and gas, mining, and agribusiness interests gave 72 percent of their political contributions to Republicans. The coal mining industry led the pack, directing 90 percent of its support to Republicans.[118] But big money alone does not fully explain the Republican embrace of the gospel of more. As the Powell memo had recommended in 1971, extractive industries also organized lobbies and supported firms on the public interest right, such as the American Petroleum Institute and the Mountain States Legal Foundation, to advance their interests in Washington, D.C. and the courts. Yet, what the Powell memo did not foresee was the important role that conservative citizen groups, such as People for the American West!, the farmers in the Klamath River Basin, or the local Utahns who protested the creation of Bears Ears National Monument, would play in supporting the Republican reversal. The Republican commitment to policies favoring extractive industries attracted support from workers and their families: for farmers, truckers, or miners, easier access to natural resources meant lower energy costs, job security, and a sense of freedom. And for many conservatives, the gospel of more dovetailed with a belief in the nation's providential future, which was rooted in their Christian faith.

Republicans did not sweep the West in the 2016 presidential elections, as they had in 1980, however. Where their stronghold remained intact was in the rural West, where people had lost jobs and seen communities collapse, and deep-seated resentment over "rural cleansing" festered. Despite these frustrations, recent public polling in the West has consistently shown strong support for environmental protection. Overall, westerners strongly favor retaining federal oversight of the public lands, generally approve of their management, support strengthening environmental protections, and oppose expanding energy development. In fact, 80 percent of westerners favored keeping the national monument designations in place and they prioritized protection over expanding energy development by a margin of three to one—preferences that Trump ignored in December 2017, when he dramatically reduced the size of Bears Ears and Grand Staircase-Escalante National Monuments.[119] The western preference for protection is not surprising, considering that protected public lands have been an engine for growth in the West. An economic study of nonmetropolitan counties in eleven western states found that between 1970 and 2015, the counties with the most federally owned land experienced more economic growth than those with less federal land. The gains were even greater for counties with high percentages of federally protected lands, such as national parks, wildlife refuges, or wilderness areas.[120] While federal ownership and protection of public lands has benefited the western economy in the aggregate, the accumulation of environmental regulations over fifty years has worked to the detriment of some rural communities in the West where extractive industries once reigned, such as Sweet Home, Oregon, where people scrambled to protect their jobs and the communities that depended upon minerals, timber, and forage from the public lands. Of course, trees are still logged and coal is still mined in the West—but changes in extractive industries, such as automation in logging and mining have reduced jobs. For many people in those communities, they seemed to have little choice but to peg their hopes on a mythic past and the possibility that a rising tide of rural, anti-federal populism could help "make America great again."

In this way, the West reflected a broader shift that has come to define the twenty-first century American political landscape: the widening divide between rural and urban counties. In part, this is partisan. Whether in Georgia, New Hampshire, Wyoming, or Oregon, rural communities had become a hotbed of political resentment in twenty-first century America. As Katherine Cramer, a political scientist, put it, these are people who "felt like they were on the short end of the stick."[121] In part, this was structural. Scholarly analysis indicates a form of structural gerrymandering is at work. It is a geographic reality that strongly favors the Republican Party. In regions where Democrats cluster in cities, Republicans have a sizable electoral advantage in more rural regions. Indeed, since the start of the twentieth century, that gap has widened, not just in the West, but nationwide.[122] Heavily populated counties have moved leftward in their politics, throwing their support almost exclusively behind Democrats. Lightly populated counties have moved rightwards in their politics; throwing their support almost exclusively behind Republicans.[123] The West has long been viewed as an exceptional region in American history. By 2016, instead of being an outlier, it had come to represent the norm in American politics, which suggested a rocky road ahead for environmental reform.

3

The Cost of Clean Air and Water

SHORTLY AFTER ITS CREATION IN 1970, the Environmental Protection Agency commissioned Project Documerica to capture the state of the nation's environment. More than one hundred photographers produced 81,000 images over six years. Some produced photographs of mountain wilderness and pastoral farmland. Others captured an America where polluted air and water was an everyday fact of life. The photos captured images of dirty factories, polluted waterways, and abandoned dumps: the smokestack of a lead smelter towering over a family of five playing in the yard of their Tacoma home; a woman with a jar of nauseatingly dark well water in Ohio; a Navajo herding sheep downwind from a coal-fired power plant; a boater near signs forbidding swimming, diving, and boating in the polluted Potomac.[1] This was an America where urban centers suffered through smog alerts once every third day on average. It was an America where most municipal sewage was dumped into rivers, lakes, and bays largely untreated. It was an America where cars, factories, and power plants had minimal, if any, pollution control technology. In such a landscape, President Nixon's claim in 1970 that we "have too casually and too long abused our natural environment" resonated powerfully.[2]

That sense of urgency and shared vulnerability provoked an unprecedented response. Within a decade of its creation, the Environmental

Figure 3-1   Pollution was poorly controlled in the 1970s, as seen in this photograph in Detroit, Michigan, July 1973. *Source:* Frank J. Aleksandrowicz, photographer, EPA. DOCUMERICA, Records of the Environmental Protection Agency, 1944–2006 (Record Group 412), U.S. National Archives and Records Administration.

Protection Agency had a $1 billion budget and employed more than 10,000 people. It was charged, in partnership with the states, with implementing the nation's foundational environmental laws, which had been enacted with overwhelming bipartisan majorities in the 1970s: the Clean Air Act, the Clean Water Act, the Toxic Substances Control Act, and the Safe Drinking Water Act, among others. Each of those laws empowered the federal government to set strict standards—based first and foremost on the goal of protecting human health—that required municipalities, manufacturers, utilities, automakers, and farmers to adopt new technologies and practices to clean up the environment and protect public health. With the EPA in the lead, the nation accomplished goals that had seemed nearly impossible in 1970. Automakers implemented pollution controls that cut some pollutants from new cars by more than 90 percent. Oil refiners phased out leaded gasoline. State and federal governments invested more than $30 billion in public funds in wastewater treatment plants. By the early 1980s, studies credited the Clean Air Act alone with extending the life of the average American by a full year.[3]

Yet, the passage of a law is never the end of the story. The Civil Rights Act of 1964 and the Voting Rights Act of 1965 hardly marked the end of the civil rights movement.[4] The Americans with Disabilities Act of 1990 hardly resolved the question of who might be considered disabled. And the passage of the Affordable Care Act in 2010 did not close the books on health care reform. In every instance, political and legal contestation continued. So, too, the passage of the major environmental laws of the 1960s and 1970s neither marked the end of the environmental movement nor solved, in the case of the Clean Air Act and Clean Water Act, the complex problems of air and water pollution. Within a decade of their passage, environmentalists argued that both laws, while important advances, were also inadequate. As scientists' understanding of environmental and public health issues evolved, advocates pressed to strengthen and expand the laws. At the same time, business interests and, increasingly, conservative Republicans interested in rolling back government regulations of all kinds, pushed back against the laws as the Republican reversal gained momentum. In short, the "Environmental Decade," as Nixon once described the 1970s, became the opening chapter in an ongoing political contest.

For that reason, the success of the nation's environmental laws was not a given in the early 1980s at the start of the Reagan administration. Even for those who cared deeply about the future of the nation's environment and public health, there were reasons to be concerned with the scope and effectiveness of the 1970s environmental laws. The health-based technology standards they adopted often imposed one-size-fits-all standards on complex industries. Top-down regulations overseen by federal agencies often resulted in legal suits over enforcement and stifled innovation. Inefficiencies in administration and uncertainty for industry resulted in billions of dollars wasted annually. By the 1980s, even sympathetic critics argued it was time to "stop celebrating the statutory revolution of the 1970s" and set about the urgent task of refining the nation's environmental laws and institutions to make them more flexible, more efficient, and, ultimately, more effective.[5] At the start of the 1980s, with nearly a decade of experience implementing the Clean Air Act and the Clean Water Act, and both laws up for reauthorization, it was a golden opportunity to draw on the lessons learned and improve the nation's environmental laws: streamlining regulations, improving compliance, and—for some Republican environmental leaders—introducing new market-based environmental policies.

The Reagan administration chose a different course. Ronald Reagan broke with the nation's bipartisan commitment to environmental protection and ushered in the beginnings of the Republican reversal, pursuing a conservative, anti-regulatory, pro-business agenda that dismissed environmental expertise, gave new emphasis to economic costs, and aimed to roll back the nation's environmental laws. "I haven't heard any talk that the administration position will be just a fine-tuning," explained one Reagan official in 1981. "The administration is looking at basic, fundamental change."[6] That approach put the nation's two most fundamental anti-pollution laws—the Clean Air Act and the Clean Water Act—squarely in the Reagan administration's sights. Reagan's anti-environmental agenda, shaped by conservative interests, including industry, farmers, and developers, became characteristic of conservatives, putting Reagan, Newt Gingrich, and George W. Bush, among others, at odds not just with many Democrats, but more moderate Republicans too. Since the 1980s, those Democrats and moderate Republicans have had only fitful success in making much-needed improvements to anti-pollution laws. Yet at the same time, it has proven equally difficult for conservative Republicans and their allies to roll back the nation's environmental laws. And, at times, despite the Republican reversal, effective environmental advocacy, careful legal maneuvering, and the support of moderate Republicans have aligned, leading to advances, often incremental, sometimes substantial, that have measurably improved the nation's environment and public health.

Reagan's Attack on the Environmental Protection Agency

Although Reagan railed against environmental regulations on the campaign trail, when his administration took the reins in Washington, D.C., its approach to environmental policy remained unclear. Norman Livermore, the conservationist who had been Reagan's secretary of resources in California and who had steered Reagan toward pro-environment positions on dams, highways, parks, and air quality in the late 1960s and early 1970s, led Reagan's transition team for the EPA. During the transition, moderate Republicans, who had played a key role in developing the nation's environmental laws in the 1970s, including former EPA administrators William Ruckelshaus and Russell Train, urged the incoming administration to seize the opportunity to reform the nation's environmental laws. Yet, when Reagan chose his nominee to lead the Environmental Protection Agency, he signaled his intent not to reform, but to roll back the nation's environmental laws. Reagan nominated Anne Gorsuch, a thirty-eight-year-old Denver lawyer and legislator, who came to Washington eager to rein in an agency that she, along with many conservative Republicans, believed exemplified the problems of a swollen federal regulatory bureaucracy.

For such a large task, Reagan tapped someone who was neither an experienced administrator nor an environmental policy expert. What experience Gorsuch had she gained during four years as a Colorado state legislator in the late 1970s, where she sponsored legislation related to the Clean Air Act and oversaw an interim committee on hazardous waste. But during her Senate confirmation hearings in 1981, Gorsuch made clear her commitment to advancing Reagan's agenda. She embraced "New Federalism" and its promise of shifting responsibility for policymaking and implementation back to the states. "No greater opportunity exists for implementation of that new federalism than" at the EPA, she told the Senate. The "EPA must be non-confrontational in its approach, leading by action and encouragement." She emphasized the need to "improve the scientific and technical basis for the standards and regulations developed," including relying more on peer review and cost-benefit analyses. And she promised a program of "regulatory reform" that prioritized reducing costs.[7]

That last promise aligned with an agenda that conservative business interests had been pushing since the early 1970s. Many conservatives believed that the proliferation of regulations—on everything from auto efficiency standards to food quality to clean air—had become a stranglehold on the nation's industries and its economy. Since the early 1970s, regulatory reform had been a priority for the Business Roundtable, an elite organization founded in 1972 that was made up of the CEOs of the nation's Fortune 500 companies. Following the playbook laid out in the 1971 Powell memo, the Roundtable aimed to ensure that the likes of Exxon and DuPont had as much say in federal regulatory activities as did environmentalists or unions. It was not that corporations opposed pollution controls, food safety standards, or other social regulations. Their chief concern was that when such standards were administered by bureaucratic federal agencies, the resulting regulations were often inefficient, unnecessarily expensive, and, in some cases, cost more to comply with than they returned in social benefits. Four years before, the Business Roundtable had pressed their case with President Carter, but with little consequence. By contrast, when Reagan arrived in the White House, he made it clear that acting on big business's agenda was a priority for his administration.[8]

Reagan moved swiftly to rein in the federal regulatory state. He too saw its growth as the root of the nation's economic malaise. "It is no coincidence that our present troubles parallel and are proportionate to the intervention and intrusion in our lives that result from unnecessary and excessive growth of government," Reagan explained during his inaugural address.[9] The following day, Reagan created the Presidential Task Force on Regulatory Relief, and appointed his vice president, George H. W. Bush, to lead it. Nine days later, Reagan put a sixty-day hold on all unimplemented federal regulations. And in February, Reagan issued Executive Order 12291, which charged the Office of Management and Budget with reviewing all major regulations issued by administrative agencies. It required the agencies to undertake cost-benefit analyses (when not prohibited by law) to justify any regulation with an impact of more than $100 million on the economy. These actions aligned with the agenda pushed by the Business Roundtable, the U.S. Chamber of Commerce, and the Heritage Foundation. Since the New Deal, the scope and power of the federal agencies had steadily expanded, accelerating in the 1970s with the array of new environmental laws. But, as the historian Benjamin Waterhouse put it, Reagan's actions in 1981 "turned the tables on the entire regulatory regime, shining the critical spotlight not on regulated companies, but on government regulators."[10]

Gorsuch worked feverishly to advance this regulatory reform agenda at the EPA, attacking both the agency itself and the laws it administered.

She moved most quickly to weaken the EPA. She proposed slashing the agency's budget by 44 percent and staff by 29 percent, taking her cues from the Reagan administration's goal of reducing discretionary spending government-wide. The EPA's budget shrank by 21 percent and staffing by 26 percent during her first two years.[11] She nearly eliminated the agency's enforcement division, urging negotiation and settlements with polluters instead. Newspapers reported "open warfare" in the halls of the agency. One staffer noted, "morale is so low that there currently is no known scientific method to measure it."[12] Yet such drastic cuts only began to meet the goals set forth by David Stockman, the young policy wonk Reagan had chosen to oversee his Office of Management and Budget. As a member of the House, Stockman had acquired a reputation as a "vitriolic opponent" of the EPA. Upon joining Reagan's administration, he described the agency as part of a "ticking federal regulatory time bomb" that required "swift, comprehensive, and far-reaching regulatory policy corrections."[13] During Reagan's first term, Stockman was a constant presence, watchdogging the EPA's budget and its regulatory activities, as he wielded his budgetary powers like an axe across the federal government.

More challenging for the Reagan administration was overhauling key environmental laws, such as the Clean Air Act or the Clean Water Act. These laws were emblematic of the "command-and-control" approach to regulation that characterized most 1970s federal environmental law and frustrated conservative critics. These laws empowered federal regulators to set strict standards to protect public health and the environment and to work closely with states to hold industries and other stakeholders accountable. For instance, in the 1970 Clean Air Act, Congress required automakers to reduce emissions of hydrocarbons, carbon monoxide, and nitrogen oxides from new cars by 90 percent by 1976—ambitious standards that forced automakers to quickly develop and deploy new technologies such as catalytic converters. Failure to comply could lead to civil or, in egregious cases, criminal penalties. But critics saw "command-and-control" regulations as a recipe for inefficiency and waste. Environmental regulators, no matter how thorough or well intentioned, only had limited knowledge of the challenges and possibilities for implementing pollution control technologies that were specific to each industry. Enforcing such standards was time-consuming and expensive, and penalties often led to litigation and delay that could slow or halt pollution reductions. Such an approach was all "stick" and no "carrot"—in theory, it could guarantee a certain level of environmental compliance, but it did nothing to encourage polluters to exceed those standards.

But any substantive reforms of the nation's environmental laws required a cooperative Congress. And in the early 1980s, even with Republicans controlling the Senate, Congress proved deeply skeptical of the Reagan administration's environmental agenda. In 1981, a series of leaks indicated that the administration planned to propose legislation that would rework the Clean Air Act along the lines recommended by the Edison Electric Institute (EEI), the trade group representing the nation's independent utility industry. The EEI had been founded in the 1930s to fight the Franklin Roosevelt administration's plans for the Tennessee Valley Authority, which put the federal government in the business of generating and distributing electricity during the New Deal.[14] In the 1980s, EEI continued to defend the industry against government intervention, but now among its chief concerns were the consequences of the 1970s environmental laws. It argued that overbearing environmental regulations risked compromising the reliability and affordability of the nation's electricity supply. When the Reagan administration floated potential changes to the Clean Air Act, it seemed to be doing EEI's bidding. The Reagan administration called for giving states the power to set clean air standards and requiring that regulations be justified by a cost-benefit analysis, rather than developed to protect public health irrespective of costs.

It was this latter point that was particularly important to conservative proponents of regulatory reform. While cost-benefit analysis had been used in the making of public policy since the 1930s, it had notably been omitted from most environmental and public health laws. While it made sense to weigh the costs and benefits of deregulating industries such as telecommunications or trucking, how could one put a price on the benefits of reducing the incidence of cancer, making a polluted lake swimmable, or alleviating urban smog? And while cost-benefit analysis could weigh the aggregate consequences of a policy, it had no regard for issues of justice and fairness—how did health benefits that accrue to a senior citizen compare to those that benefit a poor child? Environmentalists and their allies worried that mandatory cost-benefit analysis would benefit industrial interests, because the costs of complying with regulations were seemingly quantifiable and precise, compared to quantifying the benefits of extending lives, avoiding disease, or protecting vulnerable populations.[15] Most 1970s environmental laws required regulatory agencies to adopt science-based standards that put protecting public health (including vulnerable populations) and restoring ecosystems first, allowing consideration of costs only when weighing options for meeting those standards. But when the costs of complying with laws such as the Clean Air Act ran into the billions of dollars, critics argued it was essential to give more consideration to costs. As the *New York Times* reported in 1981, "American industrialists and Reagan administration economists argue that the progress to date may have been worthwhile, but that each additional dollar from here on in is buying fewer benefits."[16]

In the early 1980s, however, proposals to overhaul the nation's environmental laws, return standard-setting to the states, and institute cost-benefit analysis were nonstarters in Congress. Senator Robert Stafford (R-Vermont) described the Clean Air Act as "one of the major public health laws of this country." The moderate Republican, who chaired a key Senate committee, warned that such fundamental changes would face a "bloody struggle" in Congress.[17] The Reagan administration's Clean Air proposal never saw the light of day. Similar legislative proposals in 1982 to weaken the Clean Water Act fared little better. Most concerning to environmentalists, in place of the strict national standards that aimed to make all the nation's water swimmable and fishable—a hallmark of the command-and-control approach—the EPA proposed giving states flexibility to determine local water quality standards. As a representative of the National Association of Manufacturers explained, "We urge that the states be allowed flexibility to adjust water quality standards and uses to meet realistic conditions and needs of each particular state."[18] But old-guard Democrats, including Jennings Randolph (West Virginia), and moderate Republicans, including Stafford and John Chafee (Rhode Island), made clear they saw no room for renegotiating the goals of the Clean Water Act. In a letter to the EPA, they explained that the law's ambitious goals were not "intended to be a hollow promise when it was established in 1972. It is a goal that we take seriously."[19] They chastised Reagan's EPA for trying to promulgate regulations, justified by cost-benefit analyses, that would allow states to downgrade water quality standards.

When the conservative efforts to rewrite the Clean Air Act and Clean Water Act failed in Congress, the Reagan administration aimed to circumvent legislative gridlock by turning to an alternative policymaking pathway: executive action. Laws such as the Clean Water Act, Clean Air Act, and others, are implemented through administrative rules, which agencies develop through a multistep process governed by the Administrative Procedure Act. That process—whether to develop a new rule or rewrite an existing rule—generally takes one to three years, and includes provisions for public notice, comment periods, and judicial review. Rulemaking offers presidents a powerful tool for aligning the implementation of existing laws with their priorities. Scholars have credited Reagan with being the "quintessential practitioner of the administrative presidency, wielding its tools with a comprehensiveness, vigor, and relentlessness unparalleled in his predecessors."[20] But such administrative rules have to comply with existing law, and the Reagan administration often struggled to advance its administrative reforms when it was being watchdogged by concerned legislators and environmental groups.

Some of the rules the Reagan administration had to address were holdovers from the Carter administration. For instance, one of the rules caught up in Reagan's sixty-day rule freeze was a final rule for the pretreatment of industrial waste under the Clean Water Act. The rule, which had been in development since the Clean Water Act was amended in 1977, required industry to treat hazardous wastes before releasing wastewater into municipal sewers. Events in Louisville, Kentucky, demonstrated the importance of such policies. The month after Reagan was inaugurated two miles of sewer lines running through working-class neighborhoods in Louisville exploded in flames just before dawn. A factory dumping its waste had released hexane, a toxic and flammable waste product from soybean processing, into the city's sewers untreated.

Yet the Reagan administration nonetheless bridled at the national, uniform standards for pretreating industrial waste under development at the EPA. In the administration's view, such standards exemplified the problem with command-and-control regulations. Such standards were more appropriately set at the local level, where industry and municipalities could tailor the program to reflect local conditions, costs, and priorities. In 1981, the administration delayed the pretreatment rule along with other key regulations under the Clean Water Act, including pollution standards for twenty-three major industries.[21]

Reagan also moved quickly to make good on his campaign promise to work with industry to develop "reasonable rules" to implement the Clean Air Act. A chief frustration for big utility companies with coal-fired power plants were rules meant to restrict the use of "tall stacks." After the Clean Air Act became law in 1970, many utilities had responded by doubling or tripling the height of their smokestacks. It was a cheaper strategy than switching to cleaner fuel sources or installing scrubbers, which at the time were a new, uncommon, and not always reliable technology.[22] Tall stacks helped bring nearby areas into compliance with Clean Air standards, but only by sending pollution downwind, where it could contribute to acid rain and smog. In the mid-1970s, the EPA, the courts, and, ultimately, Congress acted to limit the practice, with Congress including restrictive language in the Clean Air Act amendments of 1977. Those amendments allowed tall stacks to supplement, not replace, other pollution control strategies. But implementing those provisions required a new administrative rule, and industry lobbied vigorously to delay and weaken how the law was implemented. The EPA not only missed a congressionally mandated 1978 deadline, it had still failed to finalize the regulations when Reagan took office. And under Gorsuch's direction, the EPA effectively reworked the rule to align with industry's priorities. The final rule largely circumvented the Clean Air Act amendments of 1977 and lifted the restrictions on tall stacks.

The Reagan administration also developed a new rule to govern how pollution from power plants, factories, and other so-called "stationary sources" was counted under the Clean Air Act. Under existing air pollution rules, oil refiners, auto plants, and other industries had to play by particularly strict rules in areas of the country that did not meet federal clean air standards—so-called "nonattainment areas." In such areas, if a company made a change to a plant that affected its overall emissions, the company was required to install "best available control technology" to reduce pollution. The goal was straightforward: if a plant underwent renovation or expansion, it had to implement technology that would lower the plant's emissions and, in doing so, help bring the area's air quality closer to compliance. In March 1981, the Reagan administration relaxed that requirement, adopting the so-called "bubble approach." In their interpretation of the law, companies should have the flexibility to make changes at a plant or factory, so long as the changes did not increase the plant's overall air pollution.[23] That meant instead of the EPA monitoring every smoke stack and every change made at a plant, a requirement industry chafed at and which drove up compliance costs, a company could undertake as many upgrades or expansions as it wished, as long as the overall pollution from the facility's "bubble" did not increase.

In the early 1980s, environmental groups were well prepared to keep watch on the Reagan administration's activities: membership, staff, and budget at many environmental groups had soared as public concern about environmental issues mounted. In 1982, *Fortune* magazine described the greatly strengthened environmental movement as a "super-lobby," in large part due to its success in challenging the Reagan administration's agenda. Indeed, by March 1982, environmental groups, including Friends of the Earth and Sierra Club, had tallied thirty-seven specific steps the administration had taken to weaken the Clean Air Act and Clean Water Act, not counting steps taken to unwind other regulations for drinking water, hazardous waste, or pesticides. In most cases, the environmentalists believed that the Reagan administration's activities were illegal, because they failed to fully implement or they ignored provisions of existing law. And in many cases, the courts agreed. Environmentalists won a lawsuit reversing the hold on the water pretreatment rule in 1982. The court declared that the EPA "must be pushed to work harder" and reinstated the Carter-era rules finalized in 1981. In 1983, in response to a Sierra Club lawsuit, the courts declared a major rule that allowed replacing pollution control technology with taller smokestacks "arbitrary and capricious" and sent it back to the agency for rewriting.

But regarding the "bubble approach," the case, which ultimately went to the Supreme Court, was decided in favor of industry and the Reagan administration in 1984. It was a precedent-setting ruling.

In siding with the administration's "bubble approach," the Supreme Court established what is now known as the Chevron doctrine. The case, *Chevron USA, Inc. v. Natural Resources Defense Council,* established the circumstances under which the courts will defer to an agency's interpretation and implementation of a law. Under the Chevron doctrine, the first consideration is whether the legislation is ambiguous or vague on the issue in question. If that is the case, then the second consideration is whether the agency's interpretation of the law is reasonable. In the case of the "bubble approach," the court agreed with the agency on both counts. First, it agreed that the Clean Air Act was unclear on what constituted a "stationary source." Second, it agreed that the EPA's interpretation, which regulated overall pollution from the facility, rather than monitoring each individual smokestack within the facility, was reasonable. It was a victory for both industry and the Reagan administration. But it was also a decision that affirmed the powers of the federal agencies and, by extension, the presidents who oversee them. The courts were giving a new level of deference to administrative agencies to decide how the nation's laws were implemented, and that would make administrative rulemaking an even more important battleground in debates over environmental policy in the decades to come. To the frustration of conservatives, it turned out that it was a battleground that often seemed to tilt in environmental advocates' favor.[24] Ironically, the Chevron doctrine would be an important issue at the start of the Trump administration, when Neil Gorsuch, son of Anne Gorsuch, was nominated to the Supreme Court. Gorsuch's skepticism of the Chevron doctrine earned him praise from conservatives concerned about the powers it invested in administrative agencies.[25]

Despite the bluster of Reagan's anti-environmental rhetoric on the 1980 campaign trail and his administration's anti-regulatory agenda, by the end of his first term, he had surprisingly little to show for it. In part, the administration's failures were a product of Anne Gorsuch's inexperience. As her third-in-command wrote upon resigning, Gorsuch had two irredeemable flaws: first, she "could not evoke any vision of the future—she focused instead on dismantling prior regulations," and second, "she could not engender the support and loyalty of the professional staff" at the EPA.[26] Indeed, EPA staff began "abandoning a wallowing ship" as quickly as they could in the early 1980s and key positions remained unfilled, hampering the agency's ability to move its regulatory agenda forward.[27] Gorsuch's troubles mounted when Democrats in Congress began scrutinizing irregularities in the agency's hazardous waste program. As questions mounted about Gorsuch's leadership, actions of her subordinates, and mismanagement of government funds, scandal began to swirl around the EPA and its political leadership. Under growing pressure, both from within and outside the agency, Gorsuch resigned her position in March 1983. Another Reagan EPA appointee, Rita Lavelle, was convicted of perjury before Congress, and sentenced to six months in prison. Between firings and resignations, the EPA lost twenty-two political appointees. Gorsuch had come to the EPA with hopes of bringing her no-nonsense sensibilities to an agency in need of streamlining. She left the agency in shambles and the nation's environmental laws weakened, but largely intact.[28]

Following Gorsuch's departure and the resignation of Secretary of the Interior James Watt that fall, the Reagan administration took stock of its environmental strategy. For almost three years, it had mounted a headlong attack on the nation's environmental laws at the behest of conservative interests like the Business Roundtable, the National Association of Manufacturers, and EEI, with zealots like Gorsuch and Watt in the lead. Yet, as the Heritage Foundation would later lament, the Reagan administration had "squandered" what it described as "a rare opportunity to reform America's flawed environmental protection programs."[29] Considering the Reagan administration's ambitions for environmental reform, what explains its failure? First, any fundamental legislative reform had been blocked by Congress, where moderate Republicans and Democrats still called the shots on environmental issues. Second, despite Reagan's electoral success, the public remained vocal in its support for environmental laws. A majority of Americans favored strengthening the pollution abatement laws, even if it increased costs or meant closing factories.[30] And, third, environmental groups, which enjoyed a significant uptick in funding and membership in the early 1980s, had proven adept at challenging much of the Reagan administration's agenda both in the public arena and in the courts.

With an eye on his reelection campaign, Reagan adjusted course in 1983. To replace Gorsuch, Reagan chose the most experienced, well-regarded, and moderate Republican he could find: William Ruckelshaus, a Republican who had served as the EPA's first administrator from 1970 to 1973. Ruckelshaus was as near to a savior as the EPA's employees could hope for. Ruckelshaus had come back to the EPA with the apparent mandate from Reagan to rebuild the agency's credibility with the public and Congress.[31] He described the agency's staff as an "inspired, committed, and energetic group of public servants," charged with the formidable, but essential, task of protecting "human life and that which sustains human life, our natural environment." He lamented the agency's failure to enforce the nation's environmental laws evenly. When it comes to enforcement, he explained, the states needed support. "Unless they have a gorilla in the closet, they can't do the job. And the gorilla is EPA."[32]

Reagan's Opposition to Addressing Acid Rain

The Reagan administration's biggest victories for its industry supporters in the 1980s were often not what it achieved, but what it stopped. The highest-profile environmental issue of the decade was acid rain: pollutants, such as sulfur dioxide and nitrogen oxides, from vehicles and industry reacted with water, oxygen, and other atmospheric compounds to form acids which then returned to the planet's surface in rain or snow. Scientists first recognized the scale of the problem in the early 1970s. By the mid-1980s, research increasingly indicated that acid rain was undermining the ecology of lakes and rivers, stunting tree growth and weakening forests, threatening water supplies, and corroding buildings, bridges, and other structures. Ironically, acid rain was a problem the Clean Air Act had unintentionally worsened. In the 1970s, the "tall stacks" installed by coal-fired power plants and heavy industry to reduce local pollution in accordance with the Clean Air Act sent sulfur dioxide and nitrogen oxides—the precursors of acid rain—higher into the sky.[33]

Pollution drifted eastward across the country, especially from the Ohio River valley into the mid-Atlantic, New England, and even Canada, increasing the acidity of rainfall. In 1980, before Reagan took office, environmentalists proposed tighter regulations on sulfur dioxide under the Clean Air Act that would have forced industry to upgrade old plants to burn low-sulfur coal or add scrubbers to their smokestacks.

Industries' campaign against acid rain regulations showcased the growing sophistication and coordination of conservative interest groups in public debate. With EEI in the lead, the nation's electric utilities and other industries opposed such action, arguing it was too costly and would yield uncertain benefits. In their words, the regulations would be "extraordinarily expensive," requiring industry to invest billions of dollars in pollution control technology, raising the price of electricity by 20 percent for many customers. But industry opponents also pursued another strategy: they questioned the scientific research. They published informational pamphlets such as *Before the Rainbow,* which purported to provide an objective overview of the state of the science. They misconstrued scientists' research to downplay concerns about acid rain. And they emphasized the uncertain nature of the scientific knowledge. In their view, the existing scientific research on acid rain was limited and failed to clearly link sulfur dioxide emissions to "alleged increases in rainfall acidity."[34] Michael Oppenheimer, a leading atmospheric scientist with the Environmental Defense Fund, remembers they "challenged every possible link in the chain between emission and ecosystem effects."[35] This strategy, weighing seemingly certain costs against lesser understood benefits, proved effective with the Reagan White House. It was a strategy industry lobbyists would return to again during debates over other issues, including climate change, in the decades to come.

Even as alarm over acid rain mounted in the early 1980s, Gorsuch and the Reagan administration responded to calls for regulatory action with support, not for action, but for additional research—just as industry wished. When Ruckelshaus returned to the EPA in 1983, however, the window of opportunity for action on acid rain seemed to open. At Ruckelshaus's swearing-in ceremony, President Reagan specifically called on him to meet the issue of acid rain "head on."[36] Ruckelshaus promised a proposal by September. That June, three independent scientific groups—the National Academy of Sciences, an Interagency Task Force on Acid Precipitation, and an acid rain panel assembled by the White House's Office of Science and Technology Policy—each released independent reports which, when taken together, argued for swift action. Although scientists had begun to settle on a goal of reducing sulfur dioxide emissions by 40 percent, or 10 million tons annually, they acknowledged that questions remained about the relative roles of sulfur dioxide and other pollutants, local versus long-range transport of pollutants, and the consequences of reduced pollution. But, in light of the threat, immediate action was necessary.[37]

During an October 1983 meeting between Ruckelshaus and senior staff at the White House, Ruckelshaus made the case for reforming the Clean Air Act to take on acid rain. Environmental leaders considered it a test of Ruckelshaus's influence in the administration. It did not go well. Government estimates suggested industry compliance costs could range from $2.4 billion to $4 billion per year.[38] The utilities warned many customers would see rate hikes of 14 to 20 percent, with two utilities warning of rate hikes of more than 50 percent.[39] Reagan's senior advisors remained skeptical of the urgency of addressing acid rain. Stockman questioned the value of a program with such high costs and uncertain benefits. At the White House meeting, he concluded his report with a sharp rebuttal. He reported that, by his analysis, acid rain regulations would require investing $6,000 for every pound of fish saved in affected lakes and rivers.[40] It was that kind of hard-nosed reasoning that would have appealed to EEI, the Heritage Foundation, and their allies, who continued to question the science and opposed costly regulations.

Environmentalists and scientists may not have had the ear of the White House in the mid-1980s, but they did command attention in Congress. During the 1980s, Congress held some eighty hearings on acid rain and the Clean Air Act.[41] Those hearings revealed deeply entrenched interests. Addressing acid rain pit region against region, complicating efforts to draw the broad bipartisan support that had made the environmental victories of the 1970s possible. The utilities with the greatest sulfur emissions served residential and industrial customers in the Ohio River valley, where electricity rates would increase the most. High-sulfur coal mining regions, concentrated in northern Appalachia and the mid-

West, stood to lose mining jobs to lower-sulfur coal fields like those in the Powder River Basin if the law did not require utilities to install expensive scrubbers on their smokestacks. Democratic senator Robert Byrd of West Virginia, the minority leader, refused to allow any acid rain legislation onto the Senate floor that might weaken West Virginia's coal industry.[42] And, while the costs would be borne by states like Ohio and West Virginia, the benefits would accrue to downwind states in the mid-Atlantic and New England that suffered most of the effects of acid rain. In the 1980s, with so many divided interests, a legislative proposal to expand the Clean Air Act to address acid rain never gained momentum.

A Market-Based Strategy to Rein In Acid Rain

As the debates over acid rain continued with no end in sight, Fred Krupp—a rising environmental leader and the recently appointed executive director of the Environmental Defense Fund—saw an opportunity. The Environmental Defense Fund had been founded in 1967 and had emerged as a leading national environmental advocacy group, known for its legal talent and scientific expertise and its work on issues related to environmental and public health. Starting in 1984, under Krupp's leadership, Environmental Defense Fund gained a reputation for championing market-based solutions to environmental problems. In 1991, *The Economist* described Environmental Defense Fund as "America's most economically literate green campaigners."[43] In Krupp's view, the command-and-control approaches of the 1970s, while important, were spent: they had cast environmentalists as "relentlessly negative, opposing industry by reflex, standing in the way of growth and driving up costs." Writing on the op-ed page of the *Wall Street Journal* in 1986, Krupp laid out an alternative vision for the future of environmental regulations. He saw the potential for what he described as "third-stage" environmentalism, which hinged on the potential for market-oriented incentives to create win-win solutions, whereby environmental protections could be achieved at lower cost.[44] In 1988, Senator John Heinz III (R-Pennsylvania) and Senator Timothy Wirth (D-Colorado), two longtime friends whose spouses were on the board of the Environmental Defense Fund, took up Krupp's vision. They hoped to focus environmental discussions during the 1988 presidential election around the potential of markets to solve problems. They described the initiative as "Project 88" and hired a young Harvard economist, Robert Stavins, to assemble a series of case studies that made the case for market-based approaches to environmental policy.

Such ideas had been on the drawing boards in the early 1980s, but gained little purchase amid Reagan's anti-regulatory push. But Project 88 resonated with Vice President George H. W. Bush, as he actively worked to distance himself from Reagan's environmental record during his 1988 presidential campaign. It was not an easy sell. Bush had made his millions as a West Texas oil man. The League of Conservation Voters gave Bush's environmental record a D, largely based on his role challenging environmental policies as chair of Reagan's Task Force on Regulatory Relief in the early 1980s. But the League did acknowledge that when Bush represented Texas in the House of Representatives between 1967 and 1971, "he had a good progressive record on the environment."[45] Trailing Massachusetts governor Michael Dukakis in the polls in the summer of 1988, Bush tried to improve his reputation on several issues, including the environment. Bush described himself as the "environmental president," reminded voters of his passion for fishing, and criticized Dukakis's failure to clean up the Boston Harbor. Whereas eight years earlier, Reagan had described environmental regulations as a drag on economic growth, Bush argued that a sound economy and sound ecology went hand in hand. Bush did not pander to environmentalists: he supported nuclear energy, deregulating natural gas, and expanding domestic oil production, including in the Arctic National Wildlife Refuge. But he promised to clean up the oceans, host an international conference on global warming, and address acid rain at home. In his view, the time for more studies on acid rain was over.[46]

Despite Bush's efforts, national environmental groups rallied around Dukakis in the 1988 election, faulting Bush for his Reagan-era record. Once Bush won the election, however, environmentalists were quick to raise expectations for the incoming administration. For his part, Bush saw the environment as an opportunity for legislative success, especially with supportive Democratic majorities in the House and Senate, and key allies in the Republican Party, such as Senators John Chafee (R-Rhode Island) and Heinz, eager to advance a legislative agenda. Notably, the public interest right had less influence in the incoming Bush administration, compared to the Reagan administration, at least on environmental issues. C. Boyden Gray, one of Bush's key advisors, acknowledged the president's responsibility to follow through on his campaign promises on the environment. In a nod to Project 88, Gray suggested Bush would pursue "market incentives" to achieve those goals. Bush signaled his environmental agenda with the appointment of William Reilly, an environmental lawyer who had gotten his start as an environmental staffer in the Nixon administration and then gone on to serve as president of the Conservation Foundation and the World Wildlife Fund. It was the first time a career environmentalist had been tapped to lead the EPA.

When Bush took office, he quickly assembled a team to craft an amended Clean Air Act to address acid rain. Senator Heinz championed the Project 88 approach and urged swift action, warning that the Senate was prepared to move on yet another command-and-control bill.[47] That June, President Bush released the administration's proposal with the goal of "break[ing] the stalemate."[48] Although the bill included proposals to address other issues, such as reducing hazardous air pollutants and the question of vehicle fuel efficiency, the centerpiece was the Acid Rain Program. The proposal included surprisingly ambitious goals with strict timelines: it required industry to reduce sulfur dioxide emissions by 10 million tons and nitrogen oxides emissions by 2 million tons by 2000.[49] But the proposal was also flexible: instead of charging the EPA with setting performance standards or pollution limits that each facility would have to meet, as had previous iterations of the Clean Air Act, the proposal embraced a "cap-and-trade" approach to sulfur dioxide emissions—a strategy never deployed at such a large scale before. Under the proposal, each utility was allocated a proportion of a national "cap" on sulfur dioxide emissions. Each could then pursue what they deemed the most cost-effective pollution control strategy to meet their reduction goal: improving efficiency, installing scrubbers, purchasing low-sulfur coal, or retiring aging coal-fired power plants. If they chose not to reduce emissions, they could instead purchase sulfur dioxide emission allowance credits from other companies that had been able to lower their emissions more than required. The approach created a market in tradable sulfur dioxide emission credits, and each year the EPA would reduce the overall "cap" further to reach the final emissions goal. The only requirement was that at the end of each year, each company had to have enough sulfur dioxide emission credits to cover its emissions from the previous year. If it did not, the fine was $2,000 per missing credit. Bush described it as an "ambitious reduction target," but one that gave industry flexibility to choose "any combination" of compliance strategies, "just as long as it works."[50]

Passage of the amended Clean Air Act was hard won. The legislation faced significant opposition from the utility industry, eastern coal interests, and coal miners. If the utility industry was going to have to submit to new regulations, companies like Dominion Power signaled their preference for an approach that allowed them "flexibility and discretion" to "achieve emissions reductions at the lowest cost."[51] But others, like American Electric Power, signaled their concern that the savings from emissions trading were optimistic. The utility industry's research arm continued to raise questions about the urgency and scope of the acid rain problem and questioned the validity of the science. Mining interests, including the United Mine Workers, warned of "massive long-term unemployment" and "economic catastrophe" for high-sulfur mining communities. They saw few advantages in the market-based approach.[52] Although environmentalists embraced Bush's commitment to a 10 million-ton reduction, which was in line with scientists' recommendations, some remained uneasy about allowing utilities to buy and sell what they described as the "right to pollute." Barry Commoner, a longtime environmental leader and skeptic of the market, argued that by creating a market for pollution, "Mr. Bush's proposal not only fails to prevent pollution, but actually requires it."[53] Although other environmental groups like the Natural Resources Defense Council supported the proposal, only the Environmental Defense Fund championed it.[54]

But, most importantly, Bush's proposal broke the phalanx of industry opposition. Western coal companies, which were sitting on enormous reserves of low-sulfur coal in Wyoming and Montana, and railroad operators saw opportunity in a Clean Air Act that allowed utilities "freedom of choice." They eagerly anticipated supplying more eastern utilities with low-sulfur coal from places like the Powder River Basin. In the end, the final legislation was even stronger than what Bush had initially proposed, as a result of congressional amendments, with a shorter time frame for sulfur dioxide reductions. Final passage came over the persistent objections of the coal-fired electric utilities and the coal industry, which believed the legislation was too ambitious. Although the dirtiest utilities successfully negotiated for extra emissions credits to ease initial implementation, last-ditch efforts by Senator Byrd to secure financial assistance for displaced workers tax breaks for utilities that installed scrubbers failed when Bush's chief of staff, John Sununu, persuaded Joe Biden (D-Delaware) and Alfonse D'Amato (R-New York) to vote against the amendment, promising that Bush would veto the legislation if Byrd's amendment was included.[55] Although utility interests lobbied the Bush administration to block the final legislation, President Bush signed the Clean Air Act amendments into law on November 15, 1990, describing it as the "most significant air pollution legislation in our nation's history."[56]

Although it represented a tremendous political victory and a return (though a brief one, as it turned out) to bipartisanship on environmental issues, many observers thought it was a victory that came at a high cost and with uncertain benefits. Paul Portney, an analyst with the nonpartisan think tank Resources for the Future, explained: "we have a better understanding of the expenditures required to control SO_2 emissions at coal-fired electric power plants than for any other source of air pollution." Based on the available research in 1990, he estimated compliance would cost $4 billion annually, which was $2 to $3 billion less than if a command-and-control approach had been adopted. But Portney explained that the benefits of controlling acid rain—including impact on rivers and lakes, forests, human health, and visibility—were much harder to pin down. He guessed the benefits to be $2 to $9 billion annually.[57] History proved Portney, along with almost every other economist and analyst, wrong. He both overestimated the costs and underestimated the benefits.

The Acid Rain Program went into effect in two phases, starting in 1995, requiring compliance first of 263 most-polluting facilities, then another 2,800 facilities, starting with phase two in 2000. Sulfur dioxide emissions fell, millions of emission credits were traded on a stable market, and government involvement was minimal.[58] The annual cost to meet the goals of the program was $3 billion in 2010, less than half what had been projected in 1990, due to lower-than-anticipated costs for scrubbers, efficiency gains, and railroad deregulation, which made it cheaper to transport low-sulfur coal from the West. And electricity rates for consumers in most states, even those most dependent on coal, actually fell between 1990 and 2009 (measured in 2009 dollars) contrary to utility predictions.[59] And, conversely, new research revealed that the health benefits resulting from lowered sulfur dioxide emissions vastly exceeded those that had been anticipated in 1990. Sulfur dioxide is one among several contributors to particulate aerosols, which were shown by epidemiological research to contribute to chronic bronchitis, heart attacks, and death. Avoiding those health outcomes accounted for the vast majority of the benefits of curbing sulfur dioxide emissions. Economists estimated the benefits at 18,000 avoided deaths and $108 billion annually in 2010, or thirty-six times greater than the cost.[60]

After a decade of partisan wrangling, the Clean Air Act of 1990 signaled that Congress could still tackle major environmental challenges. Despite the objections of the electric utility industry, which remained fixed on the potential costs and continued to question the urgency of the science, President Bush's leadership and a novel market-based regulatory approach had made possible a bipartisan legislative victory on the scale of earlier 1970s environmental laws: the law passed with overwhelming congressional majorities. The opposition came from both Democrats and Republicans in coal mining states such as West Virginia, Ohio, and Illinois. Environmentalists hoped this success might oil the gears of legislative compromise to allow more such market-based strategies for other difficult issues, such as climate change. The success of the law offers another lesson too: the challenges of forward-looking cost-benefit analyses. Just as critics warned, detailed analyses of differing regulatory strategies were inaccurate. Industry significantly overestimated the cost of compliance (as it often does) and analysts underestimated the benefits of regulation (since knowledge about the human health impacts of pollution control was underdeveloped). Yet, both of these lessons would prove all too easy to forget, especially in future debates over addressing global warming.

Expanding the Market for Clean Air

The Clean Air Act amendments of 1990 did not solve another problem, however: smog. Nitrogen oxides, produced by power plants and vehicles, were a precursor to the summertime haze that choked cities nationwide. New research in the 1990s highlighted the particular role of nitrogen oxides in smog formation and the consequences for human health. Of the major pollutants regulated under the Clean Air Act, only nitrogen oxides emissions did not fall significantly between the 1970s and 1990s. For states to meet the Clean Air Act's health-based standards for ground-level smog, which were tightened in 1997, the problem was increasingly interstate transport of nitrogen oxides. Although the Clean Air Act amendments of 1990 included provisions to reduce nitrogen oxides, they had been less effective than the sulfur dioxide controls. In 1997, northeastern states petitioned the Clinton administration's EPA to tighten controls on utilities in the Midwest and Southeast, leading to new court-ordered regulations, including seasonal restrictions on nitrogen oxides emissions and a regional cap-and-trade program. But, in the late 1990s, those efforts became tangled in a series of complicated lawsuits challenging the ozone standards and undermining the new rules, which clouded the regulatory picture.[61]

President George W. Bush tried to take a card from his father's playing deck in 2001, proposing far-reaching market-based reforms to the Clean Air Act to simplify the law and improve its effectiveness in addressing problems like smog. Bush appointed Christine Todd Whitman, governor of New Jersey, to lead the EPA. Whitman was a capable administrator, sometimes criticized for accommodating industry, but also praised for leading New Jersey to strong positions on air pollution, climate change, and ocean pollution. Whitman took the helm of the EPA with enthusiasm and optimism. She called for "a new era of environmental policy" that moved beyond command-and-control regulations.[62] But Whitman quickly found herself out of step with the rest of the Bush administration.

Many of Bush's appointees, unlike his father's, were drawn from the ranks of the industries subject to regulation. Fossil fuel interests, led by electric utilities and the coal industry, had donated generously to Bush's campaign. In Washington, they had the ear of the administration, especially Vice President Dick Cheney, whose top priority was overseeing a task force to establish the Bush administration's energy priorities. Early in the administration's first term, one of Bush's appointees in the Department of Energy emailed a group that included energy lobbyists and legislative aides, asking them, "If you were King or Il Duce, what would you include in a national energy policy?" One respondent described his response as "obviously a dream list," reported the *New York Times*. "Not all will be done. But perhaps some of these ideas could be floated and adopted." But many of the priorities that lobbyists for groups like EEI, the American Petroleum Institute, and the Heritage Foundation pushed early in 2001 helped shape the administration's agenda.[63] Even before Cheney's energy task force released its report in May 2001, the Bush administration had reversed its pledge for mandatory reductions on greenhouse gas emissions. In its stead, the Bush administration geared up for the most sustained environmental policy initiative of the administration: overhauling the entire Clean Air Act following the market-based model of the Acid Rain Program.

Such an overhaul was at the top of the utility industry's wish list. As EEI's representative testified, it would address a maze of regulations that "are duplicative, contradictory, costly, and complex."[64] The Bush administration optimistically labeled its market-based proposal the Clear Skies Act. It called for significant reductions in air emissions: 73 percent cuts in sulfur dioxide emissions, 67 percent cuts in nitrogen oxides emissions, and, for the first time ever, 69 percent cuts in mercury emissions, in two phases by 2010 and 2018. "I'm absolutely confident," Bush argued, that a market-based approach modeled on the successes of the Acid Rain Program "will bring better and faster results in cleaning up our air."[65] But there was a catch: the Clear Skies Act paired the new pollution caps with far-reaching reforms meant to vastly simplify the Clean Air Act's regulatory requirements and implementation. This explained why the administration's approach drew enthusiastic support from almost every affected industry. The underlying rationale was that if power plants could cut these key pollutants, the numerous other, more specific provisions of the Clean Air Act pegged to human health, toxics regulations, and plant upgrades would become redundant and unnecessary. A case in point was the back-and-forth regulations and litigation over nitrogen oxides, which had stalled efforts to reduce smog in the 1990s. Whitman explained before Congress, by eliminating those specific provisions in favor of the broader, more efficient, multipollutant cap-and-trade approach proposed in the Clear Skies Act, utilities would be better able to meet more aggressive clean air goals with more regulatory certainty, less litigation, and, ultimately, at a lower cost.[66]

Environmentalists saw in the Bush administration's proposal an Orwellian agenda that appeared progressive, yet gutted essential provisions of the Clean Air Act. The Natural Resources Defense Council argued the proposal "would harm public health, weaken current pollution fighting programs, and worsen global warming."[67] The Clear Skies Act proposed rolling back key command-and-control provisions of the Clean Air Act, some of which had been in place since the 1970s: No longer would every utility be required to install "maximum available control technology" to prevent emissions of mercury and other hazardous pollutants by 2007, as scheduled. No longer would every utility have to upgrade pollution controls on plants when they underwent major maintenance or upgrades as required under existing New Source Review rules. No longer would states have the right to petition to reduce pollution from upwind states, as they had done to spur action to address acid rain and smog. And, most troubling, despite the administration's rosy label and optimistic claims, the Clear Skies Act did not actually establish more ambitious targets for pollution reduction. The analyses of environmentalists and the EPA demonstrated that actively enforcing existing Clean Air Act regulations would result in significantly more stringent and more consistent pollution reductions than those the Clear Skies Act proposed. Not even the Environmental Defense Fund, the most enthusiastic champion of market-based environmental policy approaches, supported the Clear Skies Act.[68]

How the Clear Skies Act approached mercury reductions explains the scientists' and environmentalists' opposition to the Bush administration's approach. Mercury, a potent neurotoxin, is present in minute amounts throughout the environment. It concentrates in coal deposits; when the coal is burned, 90 percent of the mercury is released as vapor. In 2001, coal-fired power plants emitted 40 percent of mercury emissions nationwide. That mercury fell back to earth contaminating waterways, lakes, fish, and, potentially, people. In 2001, forty-three states had consumption advisories in place to protect people from mercury exposure due to eating contaminated fish. Those most at risk were the poor and Native Americans, who more often relied on local fisheries for subsistence. Children were especially at risk.[69] A cap-and-trade approach made sense when it was the total amount of pollution, not the distribution of pollution, that mattered most. That was the case with easily dispersed pollutants such as sulfur dioxide, nitrogen oxides, or, especially, carbon dioxide—indeed, environmentalists and scientists strongly supported cap-and-trade for those pollutants. But that was not the case with mercury, much of which fell back to earth within sixty miles of the source. Under a cap-and-trade approach there was no guarantee that all utilities would reduce mercury emissions, since some could continue polluting, as long as they purchased emission credits from other utilities that overcomplied. If a cluster of utilities in one location chose that strategy, it would result in a mercury "hot spot," with significant local environmental and health consequences. For that reason, scientists and environmentalists strongly supported the existing command-and-control Clean Air Act regulations, which required all utilities to implement "maximum available control technology" to reduce mercury emissions by 2007. Industry chafed at such a uniform, inflexible, and ultimately expensive regulation. But that approach was projected to reduce mercury emissions to 5 tons per year, compared to the 15 tons per year target the Clear Skies Act proposed for 2018.

The energy and natural resource industries donated three times as much money to Republican candidates as Democrats in the 2000 congressional election campaigns—a significant shift from 1990, when donations were split almost evenly.[70] Yet, even with Republican control of the House and Senate at the start of the Bush administration, Bush could not wrangle the support needed to move the Clear Skies Act forward. The opportunity to do so vanished when Senator James Jeffords (I-Vermont), a strong proponent of clean air legislation that addressed greenhouse gas emissions, defected from the Republican Party in May 2001, flipping leadership of the Senate from the Republicans to the Democrats. Facing opposition from moderate Republicans and Democrats in Congress, the Bush administration did precisely what Reagan and, later, Obama did when faced with legislative gridlock: it aggressively pursued new administrative rules to change how the Clean Air Act was implemented. Between 2002 and 2005, the EPA developed rules to further reduce emissions of sulfur dioxide and nitrogen oxides using a cap-and-trade program, a separate rule to reduce mercury emissions using a cap-and-trade program, and a rule to substantially weaken the New Source Review program that ensured pollution upgrades when plants were built or refurbished. As the *New York Times* warned, "the administration has managed to effect a radical transformation of the nation's environmental laws, quietly and subtly, by means of regulatory changes and bureaucratic directives."[71] During the Reagan administration, the Supreme Court had given agencies, including the EPA, considerable deference when interpreting ambiguities in environmental statutes under the 1984 Chevron decision. The Bush administration tried to take full advantage of the Chevron doctrine. So too would the Obama administration. There was one major difference, however: almost every major reform the Bush administration pursued through administrative rulemaking under the Clean Air Act, each of which favored energy industry interests, was ultimately determined to be illegal.

Consider the Bush administration's proposal to revise the New Source Review program, which was a priority for the electric utility industry. The purpose of the program was to require utilities to meet new pollution standards when a new facility was built or an existing facility underwent upgrades or improvements, while excluding "routine maintenance, repair, and replacement" activities necessary to keep old power plants running. Indeed, it made sense to exclude routine activities like replacing worn-out turbine blades or coal pulverizers, but what if those parts were replaced with more efficient or more powerful technology? What distinguished routine maintenance from an upgrade was never clear, to the frustration of both industry and regulators.[72] The policy was poorly observed and little enforced until the late 1990s when the Clinton administration began to aggressively pursue litigation under New Source

Review, filing thirty-six suits arguing that utilities had undertaken major upgrades of old, dirty coal-fired power plants, while describing those activities as routine maintenance, to avoid the pollution-control upgrades a New Source Review would likely require. The courts often agreed with the EPA and the Justice Department. The largest settlement required a $1.2 billion investment and imposed a $5.3 million civil penalty on Virginia-based Dominion in 2000—a major coal-fired utility company.

But the government's approach to New Source Review changed quickly when Bush took office. Scrapping New Source Review was at the top of the wish list for the utility industry and its allies. Even before the Clear Skies Act stalled in Congress, the Bush administration stopped pursuing the lawsuits against the utilities over New Source Review. Whitman wrote privately to Vice President Cheney, warning that "We will pay a terrible political price if we decide to walk away from the enforcement cases; it will be hard to refute the charge that we are deciding not to enforce the Clean Air Act."[73] But at the behest of Cheney and his allies in the administration, the EPA went further: it initiated steps to promulgate a new administrative rule fundamentally changing the structure of the New Source Review program. The new rule defined routine maintenance as any project that cost less than 20 percent of the value of the plant, with no cap on the number of such projects a plant could undertake. With clever accounting, any project could be structured to avoid triggering New Source Review and the tighter pollution controls it would entail. "It's such a huge loophole that only a moron would trip over it and become subject to N.S.R. requirements," one environmentalist explained to the *New York Times*.[74]

Safeguarding the Clean Air Act fell to the ranks of environmental lawyers, at organizations such as the Natural Resources Defense Council and Earthjustice. It was a campaign they did not undertake alone: public health organizations, Native American tribes, and numerous states joined suits challenging each of the Bush EPA's new administrative rules. And the law was on their side. The courts decided that the New Source Review and mercury cap-and-trade rule were illegal in 2006 and 2008 respectively. In both cases, the agency failed the first step of the Chevron test—the language of the law was not ambiguous, meaning the agency did not have the leeway to interpret the law as it had. In the mercury

Figure 3-2   George W. Bush's administration weakened environmental enforcement at the EPA, often at the behest of Vice President Cheney. *Source:* Steve Greenberg, "Air quality enforcing," *Ventura County Star*, November 26, 2002. Reprinted by permission of the cartoonist.

case, the key word was "any"—in that the law required the agency to regulate "any" source that could pose a health threat, which a cap-and-trade approach could not guarantee. The D.C. Circuit Court of Appeals compared the agency's capricious reasoning to that of the Queen of Hearts in *Alice's Adventures in Wonderland*, faulting the agency for "substituting EPA's desires for the plain text" of the law.[75]

What caught the environmental community by surprise, however, was the court's decision on the Bush administration's 2005 Clean Air Interstate Rule. This rule extended the cap-and-trade approach for sulfur dioxide to include nitrogen oxides, which would help reduce smog. The Clean Air Interstate Rule, which applied to the eastern United States, required reducing sulfur dioxide emissions by 73 percent and nitrogen oxides emissions by 61 percent below 2003 levels by 2015. Although environmentalists sharply criticized the slow timeline for implementation and the modest reduction goals (they maintained that proper enforcement of the existing Clean Air Act would be more effective), they supported the final rule.[76] But in response to lawsuits filed by the state of North Carolina, which argued the rule was not stringent enough, and utilities, which argued the rule exceeded the agency's authority, federal courts vacated the law in a complex ruling in July 2008. The ruling left open to question whether the EPA could extend cap-and-trade to include nitrogen oxides without enabling legislation from Congress. One environmentalist described it as "without a doubt the worst news of the year when it comes to air pollution."[77]

What these decisions meant is that by the time the Bush administration left office, all of its major efforts to reform the Clean Air Act had failed. That left the core provisions of the Clean Air Act intact, thanks to the clarity of the original statute and the legal defense mounted by environmentalists. The law continued to put health-based standards for setting goals for ambient air pollution nationwide before cost considerations, the EPA was still the "gorilla in the closet" ensuring those standards were met, and market-based programs were limited to pollutants that posed no local health risks. And, in retrospect, it is clear that environmentalists were largely right—continued enforcement of the existing Clean Air Act yielded greater reductions in pollution than George W. Bush's failed proposals promised. The Obama administration vigorously pursued implementation of the Clean Air Act's command-and-control provisions during its first term, including implementation of strict standards for emissions of mercury and other hazardous pollutants at power plants nationwide. Although industry and conservative allies tried to challenge those rules based on the cost, they failed to reverse them. By 2014, reductions of sulfur dioxide and mercury already exceeded the goals Bush had proposed for 2018, while reductions of nitrogen oxides were on pace to match Bush's goals.[78] Although groups like the American Lung Association made clear that air pollution remains a challenge, especially in cities like Bakersfield, California or South Bend, Indiana, the Clean Air Act had made a tremendous difference: it is credited with preventing some 160,000 deaths per year. It is arguably the most successful environmental law in the nation's history—a legacy that moderate Republicans and Democrats alike can take pride in, especially considering the sustained efforts to weaken the law advanced by the utility industry and its political allies (see Figure 3-3).

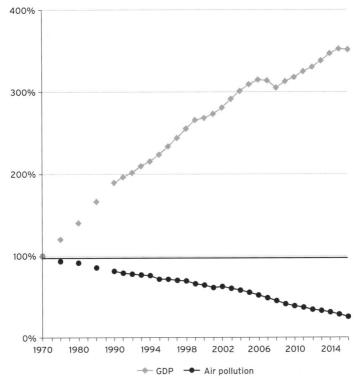

Figure 3-3 Even as key air pollutants regulated under the Clean Air Act have fallen by more than 50 percent since 1970, the nation's economy has expanded by more than 300 percent. *Data source:* Environmental Protection Agency / EPA.gov.

Clean Water Act: The Problem of Nonpoint Source Pollution

The Clean Water Act's record of environmental improvement is spottier than that of the Clean Air Act. When the law was written, it focused primarily on well-defined, easily identified pollution sources, such as municipal waste treatment plants and factories—so-called "point source" pollution. That meant it turned a blind eye to an equally large source of pollution, which was the runoff from storm drains, parking lots, construction sites, and farm fields nationwide. Although the Clean Water Act has helped reduce pollution from point sources, expanding the scope of the law to include such "nonpoint source" pollution has been a defining challenge for clean water advocates. The language of the Clean

Water Act has not made this task any easier: the Clean Water Act of 1972 applied to "navigable waters," which became a focal point of legal debate in the late 1990s and 2000s. Although navigable waters clearly include rivers and lakes, what about the tributaries, headwaters, and wetlands that support them? In large part, this legal debate and the failure of the Clean Water Act stem from the successful efforts of agricultural interests, developers, and other groups most affected by the law to keep it from fully tackling such nonpoint source water pollution. As a representative of the National Livestock Feeders Association explained in 1971, he saw "no justification for singling out agriculture along with mining and construction." He opposed language that addressed nonpoint sources, because in his view, it would give the government too much say in land use, an authority "that abounds with the potential for dictatorial misuse."[79] In the decades to come, farmers increasingly allied with miners, developers, and sympathetic politicians, most often conservative Republicans, to block efforts to strengthen the Clean Water Act and rein in one of the nation's most troublesome and widespread sources of pollution.

The strength of this opposition, rooted in farm states like Kansas, Nebraska, and the Dakotas—Republican strongholds, especially during presidential elections—became clear during the Reagan administration. Once Ruckelshaus began to right the EPA after Gorsuch's tenure, prospects for expanding the Clean Water Act's scope seemed to brighten. "The Clean Water Act is working," Ruckelshaus explained in 1983. "The control strategy formulated by Congress in 1972 and refined in 1977 has proven effective and successful." Ruckelshaus worked to curry support within the Reagan administration to strengthen the Clean Water Act: he supported retaining the pretreatment program for toxic waste, elevating purposeful violations of the Clean Water Act to felony crimes, and expanding the scope of the law to address nonpoint sources. In the case of the controversial pretreatment program, which industry had lobbied hard to weaken at the start of the administration, Ruckelshaus was unsympathetic: "I think the Agency, indirect dischargers, and affected [municipalities] need to get on with implementing the program in a reasonable, rapid, and effective fashion." Ruckelshaus also supported a commitment of $2.4 billion per year in grants to fund improvements and

expansions in municipal wastewater treatment plants through a re-
volving loan fund.[80] Ruckelshaus found eager allies, both within the
environmental community and Congress. The Natural Resources Defense
Council praised Ruckelshaus for being "faithful to the [act] and responsive to the public's concerns."[81] And in 1985, Congress moved forcefully
to strengthen the Clean Water Act, allocating $21 billion for water treat-
ment projects over nine years. Equally important was what the bill did not
do: it did nothing to weaken the existing command-and-control approach
to point sources, it maintained minimum standards for clean water
that applied nationwide, and it continued to require that industry meet
government-set standards for "best available technology."

Even with Ruckelshaus's support, however, the bill was not well received by Reagan, who remained focused on curbing government
spending. When the legislation landed on his desk late in 1986, Reagan
adopted the same strategy that Nixon had thirteen years before: he described the legislation as "budget-busting." With Congress in recess,
Reagan chose not to sign it into law, effecting what is known as a pocket
veto at the end of the 99th Congress. In its place, the Reagan administration pushed a bill with a smaller $12 billion budget at the start of the
100th Congress. But Congress again moved swiftly to pass the Clean
Water amendments, with a $20 billion budget over nine years. The law
passed with overwhelming majorities in the House (406 to 8) and Senate
(93 to 6).[82] Senator Chafee urged Reagan to "embrace it, claim credit,
have a marvelous signing ceremony, and move on." Instead, Reagan vetoed it again. But, even if the costs were high, one Republican member
of Congress explained, "we can't afford not to have it."[83] The House and
Senate quickly overrode the president's veto, making the Clean Water
Act amendments of 1987 law. It was a reminder that, despite Reagan's
conservative anti-environmental agenda, strong public support, an environmental "super lobby," and allied Democrats and moderate Republicans added up to the political might necessary to reaffirm the core approach to environmental protection, first set out in the Clean Water
Act of 1972.

But reaffirming that approach was different than building upon it.
And in the mid-1980s, conservative opposition to federal overreach did
leave one enduring mark on the final legislation. Since the 1970s, although

the Clean Water Act had made significant progress in reducing the most noxious types of water pollution from wastewater treatment plants, factories, and other point sources, the shortcomings of that approach were increasingly evident in the 1980s in places like the Chesapeake Bay, the Gulf of Mexico, and Lake Erie, where the accumulation of nutrient-laden runoff, much of which was from agriculture, resulted in large-scale algae blooms which then died, decomposed, and robbed the waterbodies of oxygen. Most of the dead zones started with the application of nitrogen- and phosphorous-rich fertilizers upstream on farmland, which then polluted streams, rivers, and lakes with runoff. The algae blooms and resulting "dead zones" led to beach closures, fish kills, and drinking water contamination. As the National Wildlife Federation testified in 1983, such pollution was an "enormous" problem "affecting some portion of all the Nation's waterways." And "existing voluntary programs and scattered demonstration projects" to address nonpoint source pollution were "simply not enough." The National Wildlife Foundation, Natural Resources Defense Council, and other environmental groups all urged Congress to adopt strong measures to curb nonpoint source pollution.[84]

Although the Clean Water Act amendments of 1987 expanded the scope of the law to include nonpoint sources, in doing so, Congress broke with the command-and-control tradition of the 1970s. Instead of making the EPA "the gorilla in the closet," as Ruckelshaus once put it, responsible for developing standards and enforcing the law in partnership with the states, the 1987 nonpoint source program cast the EPA squarely in a supporting role. During debates leading up to the legislation, groups such as the National Association of Homebuilders, the National Cattlemen's Association, and the American Farm Bureau Federation presented a united front, all emphasizing their commitment to addressing nonpoint source pollution, but limiting the government's role to "encouragement, not regulation." As Earl Sears of the National Cotton Council put it, "we believe more can be accomplished with a 'carrot' than a 'stick.' Teaching and demonstrating soil-conserving tillage methods that actually do the job can go a long way toward achieving the desired goals."[85] Republican legislators from the West and the Plains states, such as Alan Simpson (R-Wyoming) and Bob Dole (R-Kansas), backed them up, ensuring that efforts to address nonpoint source pollution did not become yet another "new full fledged regulatory program."[86] They succeeded. The 1987 provisions for regulating nonpoint source pollution required states to survey impaired waters and develop mitigation plans, but the EPA's role was limited to providing technical assistance and funding for approved plans. The agency had no power to demand updates to state plans, oversee enforcement, or to step in if states failed to act.

That approach did little to curb the runoff of pollutants into the nation's waterways. The results, as two scholars put it, was "fifty unique nonpoint source programs in the United States," most of which relied on voluntary and largely ineffective programs.[87] Indeed, in 1993, the hypoxic "dead zone" in the Gulf of Mexico reached a new peak, double the size of the late 1980s. An opportunity to rectify this shortcoming in the Clean Water Act came at the start of the Clinton administration, as expectations for environmental reform soared, especially with Democratic majorities in the House and Senate. In 1994, the administration released the Clean Water Initiative, a blueprint to strengthen the act, especially its provisions for addressing under-regulated sources of pollution, such as stormwater, sewer overflows, and nonpoint source runoff.[88] Clinton's EPA administrator, Carol Browner, described it as a "remarkable opportunity to create a second generation environmental law." The proposal recommended restructuring the Clean Water Act to make watersheds the unit of management, increasing funding for a state-revolving loan fund to support local and state infrastructure projects (the funds authorized in 1987 were due to expire), giving states more flexibility in implementing the Clean Water Act, and codifying a national goal of no net loss of wetlands. In place of the existing voluntary, state-level nonpoint source pollution program adopted in 1987, the Clinton administration recommended developing national guidance for "best available management measures" to control nonpoint source pollution, which could then be tailored at the local level. It would then be the responsibility of the state or, if necessary, the EPA to "ensure compliance" and meet water quality standards after a five-year implementation period.[89] In short, the strategies which had been brought to bear on point-source pollutants would be applied to nonpoint source pollutants.

Farmers, ranchers, and livestock operators argued vigorously against the Clinton administration's efforts to give teeth to the nonpoint source regulations. Even as they acknowledged the problem, and their role in creating it, they argued the best way to solve it was to maintain the status quo. In their view, the 1987 programs had not yet had time to be fully implemented; reform was premature. "We work hard to preserve the soil and keep our water clean," explained one Alabama farmer, speaking for the National Cotton Council. They viewed the Clinton proposal for best available management measures as ineffective, since government could never keep up with the innovations and changes in agricultural practice. The proposed timelines were both unrealistically short for implementation and, subsequently, measuring success. They called for an approach that remained at the state level and promoted "cooperative partnerships" and "voluntary programs" with "additional technical assistance and funding." In their view, nonpoint pollution was a highly local problem, related to specific agricultural practices and soil conditions. Since the early 1970s, they had voiced their opposition to the kind of top-down, federally driven regulations—often supported by environmentalists and Democrats—that would interfere with how they managed their land and drive up their costs.[90] Such frustrations with the inefficiencies of the federal government were once again on the rise in the mid-1990s.

The Contract with America and the "Dirty Water Act"

Any hope of strengthening the Clean Water Act dried up with the conservative Republicans' success in the 1994 mid-term elections. When 300 Republican congressional candidates had ceremoniously gathered on the steps of the U.S. Capitol that fall to sign the Contract with America, they promised to pass ten bills that would bring fundamental reform to the federal government. "You don't have to go out and beat up on President Clinton or beat up on the Congress. People get it," trumpeted Newt Gingrich, the architect of the Contract with America. "They are already fed up." He painted a dire picture of an America at risk: "The child abuse, the rape, the murders, the cocaine dealing, the problems of American life are unbelievable."[91] The Contract with America advanced "common-sense reforms" to rein in spending, improve crime fighting, advance welfare reform, reduce taxes, strengthen national defense, and roll back government regulations. Despite the Clinton administration's and Democrats' support for regulatory reform, the message resonated, especially in rural and agricultural communities across the country. In the 1994 elections, every Republican incumbent was reelected, many Democratic incumbents lost, and the Republicans took control of the House and the Senate for the first time since 1955. As the 104th Congress convened, Republicans believed they had a mandate not just to challenge the Clinton administration's initiatives, but to advance a sweeping conservative agenda for federal reform, including, they thought, of environmental regulations.

Even if the Contract with America made no specific mention of the environment, legislation introduced at the start of the 104th Congress took aim at the heart of the nation's environmental laws. Most troubling to environmentalists was the so-called "Job Creation and Wage Enhancement Act." The bill was the most far-reaching effort to reform federal policymaking in modern American history. It proposed giving the Office of Management and Budget veto power over major regulations—a significant expansion of the oversight Reagan invested in the office with Executive Order 12291 in 1981—and reducing the burden of existing federal regulations until it was less than 5 percent of national gross domestic product. It allowed citizens to seek compensation from the federal government if a regulation decreased the value of their property by more than 20 percent. And the bill required that all major rules include a cost-benefit analysis. In cases where existing legislation put other criteria, such as public health protection, before an economic analysis, the bill made clear that the new "decision criteria" it set forth would "supersede" existing law.[92] As the *Washington Post* reported, this was the "regulatory counterrevolution" that conservatives at the Heritage Foundation, Cato Institute, and other think tanks on the public interest right and their allies in industry had "spent years preparing for."[93]

Although the House of Representatives passed H.R. 9 on March 3, 1995, the sweeping proposal never gained traction outside of the rebellious House. The Natural Resources Defense Council, in a 121-page analysis of the ill-consequences of H.R. 9 summed it up pointedly: the legislation "effectively rewrites the nation's environmental laws."[94] Speaking on Earth Day, President Clinton said as much. Clinton supported regulatory reform—indeed, he had appointed a Regulatory Reform Commission and signed Executive Order 12866 in 1993, which overrode Reagan's 1981 executive order, somewhat lessening the oversight of the Office of Management and Budget, although maintaining the requirement for cost-benefit analysis for major rules, when permissible under existing law.[95] But Clinton rejected the Republicans' proposal outright. "One line in this proposed legislation overrides every health and safety standard on the books," explained President Clinton. "It says rather than our children's health, money will always be the bottom line."[96] Efforts to advance the legislation in the Senate failed in the face of a potential Democratic filibuster and President Clinton's promise of a veto. But the failure of their broader anti-regulatory reform agenda did not keep Republicans from trying to write similar provisions into other laws. Indeed, their most aggressive effort targeted the Clean Water Act.

Representative Bud Shuster (R-Pennsylvania) introduced a reform package that drew on provisions of H.R. 9 to overhaul the Clean Water Act. Not only did the proposal fail to strengthen nonpoint source regulations—as had been the focal point of Democrat-led efforts the previous year—it proposed weakening the point-source regulations, the foundation of the Clean Water Act since 1972, by elevating the role of cost-benefit analysis and risk assessment. In both cases, environmentalists argued such analyses led to misleading results which often favored those who opposed regulation and disadvantaged those concerned about public health and environmental consequences.[97] In a nod to the farmers and developers, the legislation also weakened protections for wetlands and required the federal government to compensate private landowners if wetland protections reduced a property's value by more than 20 percent—policy changes those groups had pushed for since the 1980s. In short, the proposal would make the cost of compliance the overriding factor in matters of public and environmental health and put the interests of private property owners before that of the public. "The subcommittee bill will make it much easier for polluters to pollute," editorialized the *New York Times*. "But that is no surprise. Polluters wrote the bill."[98] Indeed, many of the specific provisions of the legislation were the product of task forces composed of industry, business, and local government interests, which endorsed the legislation.[99]

Republicans, led by Shuster, tried to position themselves as the standard bearers of the environmental tradition. He argued the bill retained the most successful provisions of the Clean Water Act of 1972, while reducing the "EPA's dictatorial controls." He described the legislative task forces as inclusive of those most involved in keeping the water clean, not "professional Beltway environmentalists." And he faulted the campaign against the bill as one of "misrepresentations and deceit" stirred up by the "liberal extreme environmentalists."[100] The House passed what environmentalists had come to describe as the "Dirty Water Act" on May 16, 1995. The nickname stuck. Shuster's claims did nothing to sway environmentalists or the moderate Republicans, including Senator John Chafee who had long overseen Clean Water legislation in the Senate. As one California environmentalist summed it up that December, "1995 has been a terrifying year for water quality. . . . But Sen. John Chafee is the environmental hero of the year."[101] With no support from the Senate leadership and a presidential veto looming, this bill died in the Senate too.

But House Republicans and the interest groups who were banking on a "regulatory counterrevolution" did not relinquish their campaign easily. Faced with gridlock in Congress, House Republicans began to advance many of the proposals through the annual congressional appropriations process. In the arcane world of congressional legislation, appropriations bills are like legislative express trains that can bypass the gridlock—they get expedited treatment and must always reach their destination to provide funds for the government. Appropriations bills are meant to authorize funding for existing programs, however, not to change the implementation of laws. But legislators often try to add so-called riders to appropriations bills, which include just such language, betting those riders will slip through amid the urgency of the appropriations process. In 1995, House Republicans tacked on seventeen riders to the EPA's funding bill, affecting everything from regulations for lead pollution, arsenic in tap water, to the regulation of toxic emissions from the oil and gas industry—in hopes of advancing their agenda in the high-stakes budget process. One rider barred the EPA from enforcing the wetland protection program. Another barred the EPA from promulgating new standards on industrial pollution.[102] The appropriations legislation moved through Congress over the sharp objections of both Democrats and moderate Republicans, notably Sherwood Boehlert (R-New York). Overall, Republicans attached more than fifty riders to seven budget bills. With the strong support of Democrats and environmentalists, Clinton vetoed the appropriations legislation, including that for the EPA, leading to unprecedented federal government shutdowns between November 1995 and January 1996.

It became clear that the Republicans had misplayed their hand on the environment in 1996. In fact, something unusual happened that fall. The environment, which has rarely been the issue on which U.S. elections turn, topped the list of voter concerns about continued Republican leadership in Congress.[103] As the elections approached, Republicans tried to shore up their environmental credentials. Republican leaders in the House issued an internal memo, advising representatives on how to talk about the environment with their constituents, describing themselves as "stewards," and their goal of "improving" not rolling back environmental protections. One party strategist noted that what galvanized the party's conservative base in farm country and the rural West did not play with "our growing Republican majority—especially suburban women and young people."[104] Republicans began to backpedal on their legislative strategy. That summer, House Republicans pulled most of the anti-environmental riders from pending appropriations legislation. They even withdrew key demands, such as mandating cost-benefit assessments and risk analyses, from a set of amendments to the Safe Drinking Water Act. (That bill became law in the summer of 1996, making it one of the few bipartisan legislative accomplishments for the environment in the 104th Congress.) Despite several legislative successes ahead of the 1996 elections, for Gingrich's conservative Republicans, being on an environmental hit list during the 1996 election was "the most dangerous place to be." While more than 90 percent of Republicans held their seats, sixteen of the nineteen Republicans targeted for their anti-environmental positions lost, including two-thirds of those singled out by the Sierra Club.[105] Although Republicans maintained their majorities in the House and Senate, Senator John McCain (R-Arizona) acknowledged the party enjoyed no mandate on the environment. "We need to assure the public that in the 105th Congress the Republican environmental agenda will consist of more than coining new epithets for environmental extremists or offering banal symbolic gestures."[106]

Clean Water Act: Reform Deferred

Although Republicans had failed to roll back the Clean Water Act in the mid-1990s, just as importantly, the window of opportunity to meaningfully strengthen the Clean Water Act to address nonpoint source pollution was slammed shut. That did not change in the years to come. Congress continued to fund the Clean Water Act on a year-to-year basis without taking up any legislation to reauthorize the bill. But the importance of such reforms became even more apparent in the late 1990s. Citizen lawsuits forced the EPA and the states to follow through on one of the key commitments of the Clean Water Act of 1972 and establish "total maximum daily load" regulations that would govern the amount of various types of pollutants a water body could absorb and still meet water quality standards. Creating such "total maximum daily load" (TMDL) plans became a focal point of state and federal clean water activity in the late 1990s and early 2000s. Such planning required empirical assessment of each waterbody's chemical, physical, and biological health, data on point source and nonpoint source pollution entering the waterbody, and modeling to estimate the impact of pollution on the waterbody. With that information, in theory, state regulators could then allocate permits to regulate point source and nonpoint source polluters at levels that would protect water quality. Developing and then acting on these TMDL studies, however, posed a challenge for often understaffed and under-resourced state and federal environmental regulators. Most studies lacked clear goals, implementation plans, or assessment strategies. What the TMDL program did do was make painfully clear the ongoing challenges in realizing the Clean Water Act's goals. Although 83 percent of the programs achieved targets for point source pollution, only 20 percent achieved targets for nonpoint source pollution.[107]

The hurdles to reining in nonpoint source pollutants increased in the 2000s—only this time, the challenge emerged in the courts. The extent of the Clean Water Act's regulatory scope hinged on one crucial, yet ambiguous, phrase used throughout the Clean Water Act of 1972 and subsequent amendments: the law applied to "navigable waters," which Congress defined as "waters of the United States." Congress urged that the phrase be given "the broadest possible constitutional interpretation."[108] Between 1975 and 1985, the agencies and the courts, often at the behest of environmentalists, affirmed the law's scope, interpreting "navigable waters" to mean not just tidal waters or those used for interstate commerce, but the wide range of waters that contributed to the health and integrity of navigable waters, including tributaries, headwaters, and wetlands. Most important and controversial were the provisions for protecting wetlands. As scientists came to realize in the 1980s and 1990s, wetlands functioned as "nature's kidneys," moderating water flow, filtering nutrients and pollutants, providing habitat, and contributing to the health of downstream waters. If the nation was ever going to fully address nonpoint pollution, those efforts began with protecting wetlands. But the same research also revealed that wetlands were disappearing at the rate of 2.6 million acres per decade, much of the remaining wetlands were located on private property, and more than 50 percent of the wetlands loss was due to agricultural development.[109] In the 1980s and 1990s, the EPA and Army Corps of Engineers developed a complex and inconsistently enforced body of regulations meant to safeguard the nation's wetlands.

Those policies put the Clean Water Act on a collision course with farmers, miners, and developers, who often faced significant delays and costs, whether expanding a farm or building a shopping mall. In the new wetlands science, they saw a ploy to expand the government's say in how they used their land, complaining that the definition of wetland has "escalated to include even those areas that do not have standing water at any time during the year and do not exhibit wetlands characteristics."[110] They argued with increasing success in the 1990s and 2000s that the Clean Water Act's restrictions infringed on their property rights. In the early 2000s, the federal courts issued more than thirty decisions, including Supreme Court rulings in 2001 and 2006, related to the scope of the Clean Water Act. The upshot was general agreement that the existing rules governing the scope of the Clean Water Act and its applicability to wetlands were unsatisfactory. At stake in the 2006 Supreme Court decision was whether a particular stretch of wetlands, which were dry much of the year and located more than ten miles from the nearest navigable waterway, could reasonably be described as "waters of the United States." The Supreme Court split on the issue, leaving unresolved whether the scope of the act should be narrowly construed to mean only wetlands "adjacent" to navigable waterways—which would reverse what conservative justices described as an "immense expansion of federal regulation" of land use under the Clean Water Act—or whether it should be more broadly construed, including wetlands with a "significant nexus" to navigable waters, as had been the practice of the EPA and the Army Corps of Engineers historically. It was a question that neither Congress, George W. Bush's administration, nor the Obama administration was able to satisfactorily resolve, despite clarifying legislation being introduced in Congress, the Bush administration issuing new guidance in 2003 and 2007, and the Obama administration undertaking new rulemaking meant to clarify what constituted the "waters of the United States" in 2011. That has left the full extent of the Clean Water Act's regulations in an ongoing state of uncertainty. President Trump only heightened the uncertainty when he signed an executive order in February 2017 "paving the way," as he put it, "for the elimination of this very destructive and horrible rule."[111]

Conclusion

The Clean Air Act and Clean Water Act have been among the most important environmental and public health laws enacted in American history. But that outcome was not guaranteed. At key moments, such as at the start of the Reagan administration, during the Contract with America, and during George W. Bush's administration, it seemed the strength and scope of these laws would be rolled back amid the Republican reversal championed by economic interests and the public interest right. When conservative Republicans failed to weaken the laws in

Congress, they instead sought to undermine their implementation by trying to reduce their scope, dilute underlying health standards, give greater emphasis to costs, and relax protective requirements through administrative rulemaking processes. But over nearly fifty years such efforts have failed more often than they have succeeded, thanks to the careful and sustained defense of these laws by environmentalists, legislators, and environmental and public health lawyers. The result is what the political scientists David Sousa and Christopher Klyza have described as "green drift": despite the tumult of environmental politics, the overall trajectory of environmental policy has tended toward a strengthening of the nation's environmental laws, the expansion of their scope, and more effective and far-reaching implementation.[112]

But, for many people today, recognizing the significance of these laws requires an act of environmental imagination. The improvement in the nation's environment over fifty years has been so significant, few Americans remember just how dire the nation's environmental challenges were in the 1960s and 1970s, when cars spewed poisons from their tailpipes, industrial smokestacks were largely unfiltered, haze and smog regularly clouded skylines, and most sewage plants dumped wastewater into rivers and bays with minimal or no treatment. While challenges remain, the Clean Air Act and Clean Water Act have materially improved the health and safety of the nation's environment and its people. Between 1967 and 2006, the number of young children with high lead levels in their bodies—much of which was caused by burning leaded gasoline—dropped from more than 80 percent to fewer than 3 percent. By 2010, the benefits of the Clean Air Act were estimated at $1.3 trillion annually, largely through avoiding hundreds of thousands of premature deaths.[113] And the most comprehensive studies demonstrate that there have been significant declines in most major pollutants targeted by the Clean Water Act.[114] In some places the improvements have been dramatic. Sewage released to the Chattahoochee River in Atlanta has been reduced by 99 percent. The Boston Harbor has once again become a hub of urban activity, development, and recreation.[115] But the gains from these laws have not been uniform, either in their costs or benefits.

Conservative Republicans have been quick to respond to the frustrations of communities that, in their view, have borne the costs of these laws. Although the collapse of jobs in industries such as steel and coal has largely been the result of automation and globalization, environmental regulation has contributed too. Consider coal country in West Virginia. Between 1990 and 2000, coal production in the high-sulfur coal fields in Appalachia declined by half. Employment fell even further with the declining demand, as mines improved efficiency and they became more automated. By 2000, employment in the region had dropped by 70 percent, meaning 30,000 lost jobs.[116] Some of those miners got new work further south in the low-sulfur seams of Central Appalachia. But most new mines employed a radically different type of mining practice that involved far fewer workers: mountaintop coal mining removal. Instead of mining coal from beneath the mountain, explosives, oversize dump trucks, and monstrous draglines made it economically sensible to literally remove mountaintops in search of the low-sulfur coal beneath. The process devastated the region's mountains, streams, and public health, leaving behind valleys filled with mining waste and toxic settling ponds meant to control runoff.[117] After the Clean Air Act amendments of 1990, when mountaintop removal expanded, mortality rates in Central Appalachia remained high compared to trends nationally, and even compared to elsewhere in Appalachia.[118] Although there were few protests in the coal fields of Appalachia in the 1990s, these changes seeded the populist frustration that erupted in opposition to the "war on coal" during the Obama administration and rallied around Trump's "America First" energy plan.

Yet conservative Republicans have been much less concerned with another group of people: the communities that have not fully shared in the environmental gains of the past fifty years. Many communities, often including the poor, people of color, or Latinos, are disproportionately exposed to higher levels of air, water, and other forms of pollution and hazardous waste than the nation as a whole. In places like Kettleman City, California, Baltimore, Maryland, and Flint, Michigan, seeing the consequences of pollution requires no act of imagination, even today. Three-quarters of the people who live within three miles of a coal-fired power plant are people of color. Asthma rates of black and Latino children remain higher than those of white children. And, as the contamination of Flint, Michigan's public water supply with lead reminded the nation in 2016, protections for clean air and water are often more poorly implemented and enforced in communities of color.[119] Addressing these issues requires that issues of environmental justice be acknowledged, and environmental laws be implemented accordingly. Since the 1990s, however, when such legislation was first proposed, Congress has not acted to ensure that environmental justice is a core consideration in the implementation of environmental policies, such as the Clean Air Act and Clean Water Act. Instead, it has fallen to presidential administrations to take the lead, which the Clinton and Obama administrations did, while George W. Bush's administration let efforts to address environmental justice languish. At the start of the Trump administration, the agency's longtime director of environmental justice resigned in protest over proposed cuts to the agency and its environmental justice program.[120]

4

American Exceptionalism
in a Warming World

ON APRIL 5, 1988, Ronald Reagan signed a pathbreaking international emissions treaty. It committed the United States to deep cuts in industrial pollutants by 1999. In his words, the treaty was the "result of an extraordinary process of scientific study, negotiations among representatives of the business and environmental communities, and international diplomacy."[1] Despite the Reagan administration's antagonism to environmental regulations at home, it could take pride in the Montreal Protocol. During the negotiations, Reagan's EPA administrator, Lee Thomas, pressed his European and Japanese counterparts to adopt strict targets for emissions cuts. Reagan's secretary of state, George Shultz, urged an international commitment, despite scientific uncertainties about the scope and pace of the threat. And the president himself overrode antiregulatory skeptics in his administration and clered the way for an international agreement.[2] As a result, the international community made commitments that would successfully stabilize one of the dire environmental threats of the twentieth century: the stratospheric ozone hole. It was, as President Reagan described it, a "monumental achievement."[3]

That claim was especially true, given that the potential for a stratospheric ozone hole had been little more than a scientific hypothesis fourteen years before.[4] In 1974, scientists first theorized that trace pollutants, measured in the parts per billion, might, under the right conditions, serve as catalysts to chemical reactions that could destroy stratospheric ozone. Although early research confirmed the validity of the concerns, it was not until 1985 that the British Antarctic Survey actually spotted the "hole" in the ozone layer over the Antarctic.[5] Scientists described what they were seeing as "absolutely unprecedented."[6] From the start, coverage of the threat made it clear that human health was at risk: loss of stratospheric ozone, which blocks ultraviolet radiation from the sun, would mean higher rates of skin cancer, cataracts, and other health ailments—trends that already seemed to be accelerating in the 1980s. But curbing the threat would require regulating growing industries. Chlorofluorocarbons (CFCs) were important to refrigerators, air conditioners, and aerosol spray cans; bromines were common in fire extinguishers and flame retardants. And the ozone hole represented a wholly different kind of environmental challenge: it was a truly global issue. An act as simple as spraying a can of deodorant in the United States contributed to stratospheric ozone depletion above the Antarctic. Solving the problem would require the concerted action of the global community.

The Reagan administration, led by Richard Benedick, the deputy assistant secretary of state, threw its full diplomatic weight behind the international negotiations. Despite early resistance, by the mid-1980s, the domestic chemical industry largely accepted scientists' warnings about the threat CFCs posed. Leading companies, particularly DuPont, had begun to position themselves to profit from selling substitute chemicals. Anti-regulatory skeptics within the president's cabinet were overridden, in light of the gathering scientific consensus and economic analysis. The administration's own cost-benefit analyses suggested the benefits of action were more than 150 times greater than the potential costs.[7] And the administration had a visceral understanding of the consequences of inaction: the president had undergone surgeries to remove carcinomas in 1985 and 1987. The administration also knew that if it did not forge an international agreement, Congress and the federal courts would likely force action at home. In 1977, Congress had included language in amendments to the Clean Air Act which specifically required the EPA to regulate ozone-depleting substances if they "may reasonably be anticipated" to "endanger public health or welfare."[8] The Reagan administration's legal team fully anticipated that if it could not get the global community to take action, U.S. environmental groups and Congress would succeed in forcing the United States to act unilaterally. As Benedick explained, "industry preferred to face a stronger treaty, which would at least bind its foreign competitors, than unilateral U.S. controls with no treaty." Congress had already made it clear that it had no plans to relax the law. In 1987, as negotiations proceeded, the Senate passed a bipartisan resolution 80 to 2 in support of a global treaty.[9] With the Reagan administration in the lead, the Montreal Protocol on Substances that Deplete the Ozone Layer committed the world's industrial nations to a 50 percent reduction in the emissions of ozone-depleting substances by 1999.

The treaty not only protected the ozone layer, but was viewed as a template for international cooperation for addressing other emerging global environmental challenges. With the United States in the lead, such optimism seemed warranted. The United States had a long history of international environmental leadership. In 1911, it joined with other nations to create the North Pacific Fur Seal Convention to regulate the hunting of fur seals; in 1916, the United States agreed to the Migratory Bird Treaty with Canada; in 1946, U.S. diplomats played an important role in the International Convention for the Regulation of Whaling; and, in the early 1970s, the United States led the negotiations that resulted in the Convention on International Trade in Endangered Species.[10] As the political scientist Elizabeth DeSombre has observed, such actions followed a clear pattern: the United States aggressively pursued international treaties that built upon existing domestic environmental policies, especially when international agreements leveled the international regulatory playing field and protected domestic industry from competitive disadvantages.[11] Through the late 1980s, both Democrats and Republicans could take pride in the record of the United States in international environmental leadership. Indeed, just two years after Reagan signed the Montreal Protocol, George H. W. Bush's administration successfully pressed the international community to accelerate the timetable for reductions, with the goal of eliminating emissions of ozone depleting substances by 2000.[12]

This record of accomplishment explains why some observers were guardedly optimistic that the world was prepared to address another emerging environmental challenge in the late 1980s: global warming. Bush's own state department warned in 1989, "We can probably not afford to wait until all of the uncertainties have been resolved." In its view, if scientific assessments of climate change hold, "the consequences for every nation and every aspect of human activity will be profound."[13] Leading environmentalists, such as Gus Speth, president of the World Resources Institute, later recalled, "We thought we were on track to make real changes."[14] As we now know, such confidence was misplaced. Over the past three decades, marshalling support in Congress to address climate change has largely failed, often dramatically. As a result, the most meaningful efforts to address climate change have been channeled onto alternative policymaking pathways, including administrative action, court decisions, state-level initiatives, and international agreements never submitted to the Senate for ratification. Although those strategies have yielded notable successes—including a favorable Supreme Court decision in *Massachusetts v. EPA,* the Obama administration's Clean Power Plan, and the Paris climate accord—those strategies have also made the politics of climate change increasingly volatile, as has become apparent in the Trump administration's sweeping moves to dismantle the Obama administration's domestic and international climate agenda.

To begin to understand the checkered history of U.S. climate policy requires considering several underlying factors: The end of the Cold War emboldened some conservatives, who had always been skeptical of international agreements and organizations such as the United Nations, to urge the United States to retreat from such cooperation. Bipartisan support in the United States for domestic policies that maintained a supply of abundant and cheap energy continued unabated. Fossil fuel interests and the public interest right amplified uncertainties in both the related science and economics, often at key moments of policy action. But, ultimately, the debates over climate change also serve as a potent reminder that the Republican reversal has not just been about the power of special interests, well-funded scientific misinformation campaigns, or the fate of jobs in sectors like coal or oil and gas. Although all of those factors have been important, in the case of climate change, those factors alone cannot explain how climate change came to provoke such vigorous and heartfelt opposition from conservative interests and grassroots activists.

By 2010, opposition to climate policies had become a rallying cry among conservatives, aligning groups that included coal miners, evangelical Christians, and Tea Partiers, over concerns that policies to address global warming threatened deep-set conservative beliefs about American exceptionalism, the resilience of God's creation, and individual freedom. Taken together, all of these factors help explain how debates over climate change science and policy helped to harden a conservative strain of anti-environmentalism in the twenty-first century that—despite a long history of American leadership in international environmental policy—put a conservative Republican Party in opposition to the nation's leading scientists, the global community, and the majority of the American people.

George H. W. Bush and the "White House Effect"

Climate change first seized national attention in the summer of 1988, when temperatures spiked far above average, and a deep drought set in across the United States, killing crops on millions of acres of farmland, reducing the Mississippi River to its lowest level on record, and leaving forests tinder dry. Agricultural losses totaled $40 billion. Between June and September, fires scorched nearly one-third of Yellowstone National Park. Nationally, more than 5,000 deaths were attributed to the heat and drought.[15] While many in Washington, D.C. scrambled to assemble emergency relief funds for their districts that summer, the Senate's Committee on Energy and Natural Resources held hearings on "The Greenhouse Effect and Global Climate Change." The scientists testifying delivered an arresting message: they described global warming as a near certainty, they warned it posed a global problem on the scale of nuclear arms, and they recommended immediate action.

Testifying before Congress that June, James Hansen, a scientist from the National Aeronautics and Space Administration (NASA), reported: "We can state with about 99 percent confidence that current temperatures represent a real warming trend rather than a chance fluctuation." Michael Oppenheimer, an atmospheric scientist with the Environmental Defense Fund, warned of warming that was three to six times greater than the historical record. George Woodwell, director of the Woods Hole Research Center, called for a "single, simple signal policy that would lead the world—and we must lead the world." What would send that signal? Aggressive policies to reduce fossil fuel consumption and protect the world's forests. The day they testified, temperatures in the capital hovered around 100 degrees for the third day in a row, and with much of the nation stricken by heat and drought that would last into August, the scientists' warnings commanded public attention.[16]

Although the urgency of their warnings was new, the underlying theory of global warming had been established long before 1988. In 1896, Svante Arrhenius, a Swedish scientist, projected the potential consequences of increasing carbon dioxide concentrations for global temperature. In 1938, Guy Callendar, a British engineer and meteorologist, collected data on temperatures and carbon dioxide, and suggested industrial emissions might already be affecting the climate. In 1958, Charles Keeling, a scientist at the Scripps Institution of Oceanography at the University of California, began measuring atmospheric carbon dioxide levels continuously and the data showed that carbon dioxide levels were increasing nearly one part per million per year. In 1977, James Black, a senior scientist at Exxon, told the company's management committee that "there's a general scientific agreement that the most likely manner in which mankind is influencing the global climate is through carbon dioxide release from the burning of fossil fuels."[17] In the 1970s and 1980s, a series of reports from groups like the National Academy of Sciences and hearings in Congress, such as those convened by Senator Al Gore (D-Tennessee) in 1981, drew attention to global warming.[18] A 1983 report commissioned by the Reagan administration warned of an average warming of 1.5 to 4.5 degrees Celsius in the twenty-first century, but its chief author, William Nierenberg, explained, "We feel we have 20 years to examine options before we have to make drastic plans."[19]

Momentum toward action on global warming appeared to build quickly in the late 1980s. On the campaign trail in 1988, then vice president George H. W. Bush envisaged himself as the "environmental president" and promised to meet the "greenhouse effect with the White House effect." The same year, with the support of the Reagan administration, the United Nations Environment Programme convened the

Intergovernmental Panel on Climate Change (IPCC) to synthesize the state of the science. Edison Electric Institute's vice president warned his colleagues in the utility industry, "There is growing consensus in the scientific community that the greenhouse effect is real." If business as usual continues, "there is the possibility that such changes will disrupt the biosphere as we know it . . . even more disconcerting is the possibility of a destabilization of the earth's entire weather system."[20] In 1989, Mobil Oil publicly acknowledged that global temperatures had risen during the twentieth century, likely in response to increasing carbon dioxide emissions. "Mobil is very much aware that cleaner, more efficient, and more carefully used fossil fuels will cut the risk of global warming, and we're hard at work along all these fronts."[21] Widespread media coverage of climate change in 1988 and 1989 was near uniform in its emphasis on the role of humans in driving the change.[22] What was largely absent in the late 1980s, whether in congressional hearings, media coverage, or scientific testimony, was debate over the basic scientific premise of global warming or the potential threat. As researchers have documented, at the time, many scientists and researchers within the electric utility and fossil fuel industries acknowledged the basic science underlying concerns about global warming. In February 1989, with the State Department in the lead, the Bush administration signaled it could not wait for scientific certainty before taking action on climate change. The Bush administration seemed primed for action.

That changed quickly. In 1990, President Bush made good on his campaign promise to host and attend a global conference on climate change in Washington, D.C. But his opening remarks signaled a telltale shift. He described the state of climate science as fundamentally uncertain, noting that some scientists warned of doomsday scenarios and others suggested future changes were likely to be manageable and any "drastic reordering of our economy" was unnecessary. "What we need are facts," Bush emphasized.[23] At least in 1990, Bush's assessment of the science was reasonable. While the basics of greenhouse gas emissions, their sources, and their potential consequences were well understood, the role of humans in driving climate change, at what rate, and to what degree compared to natural factors was uncertain. Indeed, in 1990, the Intergovernmental Panel on Climate Change released its first report, which made clear that the concentrations of greenhouse gases were increasing due to human activity and those greenhouse gases would enhance the greenhouse effect, but that there was "no firm evidence that climate has become more variable" or that the warming observed to date exceeded "the magnitude of natural variability."[24] In short, while the scientific community was alarmed about the potential for human-caused global warming, it did not yet share Hansen's assessment that the observed warming could definitively be attributed to human activity—indeed, many scientists were frustrated with Hansen's bold claims and the media attention he drew. But, in the view of many scientists, such uncertainty was not reason for inaction: whether the warming was 1.5 degrees Celsius or 4.5 degrees Celsius, whether warming was detectable in 1989 or in 2010, the twenty-first century world faced potentially significant warming, rise in sea levels, and changing weather patterns. The danger warranted precautionary action. In anticipation of the 1990 conference, leading scientists, including half of the members of the National Academy of Sciences and forty-nine Nobel Prize-winners, urged the Bush administration to take a leadership role and adopt aggressive goals to curb greenhouse gas emissions. In their words, "Global warming has emerged as the most serious environmental threat of the twenty-first century."[25]

But those were not the scientists who had the ear of the White House in 1990, particularly Bush's chief of staff, John Sununu. Despite the mounting concerns about climate change within the EPA and the State Department, Sununu, who was an MIT-trained engineer and former governor of New Hampshire, appraised the science of climate change with the eye of a skeptic.[26] Starting in 1989, Sununu relied heavily on the guidance he received from a small group of scientists affiliated with the George C. Marshall Institute, which had begun to emphasize the uncertainties and potential economic costs of addressing climate change that had been brewing since the early 1980s.[27] The Marshall Institute was a D.C.-based scientific-policy think tank founded by Cold War physicists with the support of prominent conservative foundations (it did not accept corporate donations until the late 1990s). It had originally been created to support President Reagan's Strategic Defense Initiative. But, as Naomi Oreskes and Erik Conway explain in their book *Merchants of*

Doubt, after the Cold War ended, the Marshall Institute "didn't go out of business. Instead, it found a new enemy: environmentalists."[28] The institute's stated goal was to promote scientific literacy and inform policy. But the Marshall Institute had an agenda that was informed by more than just science. Its founders considered the institute an essential counterweight to the "left-wing activists" who "had taken over the mainstream of American science."[29] By the late 1980s, the Marshall Institute and its leaders already had a track record of aligning themselves with positions that ran counter to the scientific mainstream, including questioning the science behind the depletion of the ozone hole, acid rain, and the health consequences of smoking. In 1990, they added global warming to that list.

That spring the Marshall Institute released a report titled *Global Warming: What Does the Science Tell Us?* The report emphasized the challenges of measuring global temperatures (which required interpolating and calibrating a wide range of data sources), the shortcomings of the existing climate models used to forecast future climate change (singling out Hansen's modeling work at NASA), and the uncertainties regarding the role of the oceans, solar variability, and clouds. The report projected modest twenty-first century warming of 0.4 degrees to 1.8 degrees Celsius—well below Hansen's or the IPCC's projections. Numerous climate scientists sharply critiqued the Marshall report for unfairly representing Hansen's work by ignoring aspects of his research and omitting confounding factors, such as sulfate aerosols. But with authors including Robert Jastrow, the founding director of NASA's Goddard Institute for Space Studies, William Nierenberg, chief author of the 1983 National Academy of Sciences report on climate change, and Frederick Seitz, a past president of the National Academy of Sciences, the Bush administration took the contrarian report seriously. Ultimately, the authors did not deny climate change. Instead, they called for more research, arguing that rapid advances in climate science could be anticipated within five years, during which time they projected the climate might warm an additional 0.1 degrees Celsius. Such a small increase in temperature, they argued, would be a "small penalty" to pay for getting reliable information before adopting policies that would restructure the United States economy.[30] But the newspaper coverage was not nearly so nuanced. Soon headlines in the *Washington Post,* the *New York Times,* and *Investor's Business Daily* read: "'Greenhouse Effect' Seems Benign So Far"; "Scientists Confront Renewed Backlash on Global Warming"; and "Global Warming or Hot Air?"[31]

Focusing on these events alone, however, risks overemphasizing the role of science—and debates over climate science—in determining the nation's approach to global warming. Notably, the United States engaged in a robust discussion of national energy policy between 1989 and 1992 that culminated in the Energy Policy Act of 1992. But climate change hardly figured in the debate. Instead, the debate was dominated by other issues: the fate of the Arctic National Wildlife Refuge and fuel efficiency standards for vehicles. Much of the subsequent debate focused on improving the nation's energy security, especially after Saddam Hussein's Iraqi regime invaded Kuwait in 1990, setting in motion what would become the Persian Gulf War. The price of oil doubled within six months, making clear the cost to the United States of continued reliance on imported oil. On the supply side, the Bush administration—with the strong support of the petroleum industry—argued that expanding domestic energy production in places like the Arctic Refuge was an imperative, especially as domestic oil production slowed and imports increased. On the demand side, environmentalists countered that the United States could never solve its energy problems by expanding production. Although the Arctic Refuge was described as "by far the most outstanding frontier oil and gas area left in the United States," it was projected to supply less than 3 percent of the nation's annual petroleum needs. Environmental groups were united in their opposition to drilling in the Arctic Refuge, not least of all because a massive oil spill resulted when the tanker *Exxon Valdez* ran aground in Alaska's Prince William Sound in 1989, demonstrating the hollowness of the oil industry's assertion that the environment would be safe if oil drilling were expanded.

Environmentalists put their collective muscle behind a legislative proposal advanced by Senator Richard Bryan (D-Nevada) to curb demand for petroleum by increasing the nation's fuel economy standards for new vehicles by 40 percent by 2001. As they argued, it was a proposal that would save consumers money over the life of a car, reduce greenhouse gas emissions, and improve the nation's energy security by lessening demand for gasoline.[32] But there was no grand bargain on energy policy in the 1990s. As Keith Bradsher reported in his book on the rise of the sports utility vehicle (SUV), *High and Mighty,* a furious and coordinated lobbying campaign that included automakers, auto dealers, and citizens proved pivotal in blocking Bryan's proposal in the early 1990s, as it edged toward passage after the Iraqi invasion. Their lobbyists warned such policies would be a catastrophe for American automakers and their employees, would drive up the price of cars for consumers, and force Americans to drive unsafe, lightweight subcompact cars. (In truth, as Bradsher explained, rollover-prone SUVs offered little safety advantage over other cars.) The auto industry bankrolled a citizen group named the Coalition for Vehicle Choice that brought together farmers, law enforcement officials, and volunteers transporting the disabled to argue for the necessity of big vehicles. As Bradsher recounted, one Nebraska farmer asked, "Can you imagine pulling a livestock trailer or hauling grain and feed with a Honda Civic?" For conservatives, that not only seemed impossible, but downright un-American. When environmentalists refused to make the Arctic Refuge a bargaining chip in negotiations, the Bush administration made it clear it would veto any bill that omitted the refuge or included higher fuel economy standards.[33]

In the end, the Energy Policy Act of 1992 was a significant piece of energy legislation, but not for advancing environmental reforms or tackling greenhouse gas emissions. It expanded domestic energy production with new support for natural gas production and $1 billion in tax relief for oil and gas producers. It paved the way toward a deregulated electric utility industry. It also streamlined permitting for hydroelectric dams and nuclear power plants. But the bill included only modest incentives for renewable energy technology, support for alternative vehicle fuels (such as ethanol), and more extensive funds for energy- and climate-related research. The signature program of the 1992 energy act was the voluntary Energy Star labeling program. Thus, at a moment when the world began to focus its attention on global warming, the nation's dependency on imported oil entangled the United States in the Persian Gulf War, and Alaska mopped up the aftermath of the 1989 *Exxon Valdez* oil spill, the United States could only manage baby steps toward domestic policy that would promote efficiency and sustainability in the face of strong and well-organized interests invested in the status quo.[34] To the extent that U.S. leadership on international environmental policy was built on domestic policy, it seemed the nation was far from ready to lead on climate change.[35]

The surprising denouement of the Cold War in 1991 only further heightened the Bush administration's and conservative Republicans' wariness of international action on climate change. Since the 1960s, conservative Republicans had become increasingly frustrated with U.S. foreign aid policy and, in particular, support for United Nations programs if they were not clearly connected to national security interests. During the Cold War, such criticism was muted, on account of U.S. interest in maintaining U.S. leadership abroad as a bulwark against the Soviet Union and communism. The Bush administration was also concerned that tensions between the "global North" and the "global South" were growing, as developing countries saw less urgency in aligning their positions with those of the United States or other developed countries in a post–Cold War world. Some conservative commentators even warned that the international furor over global warming was a Trojan horse: alarmist claims of global warming are a "cynical attempt to restructure the world economy away from industrial capitalism and republican forms of government" that favored "Third World" countries.[36] Thus, at the very moment that developing countries began to press for more aid and concessions from developed countries, the Bush administration found itself facing growing opposition domestically—in part because of the end of the Cold War, but also due to the early 1990s economic recession—to any international environmental agreements that might increase U.S. foreign aid commitments. As the historian Joshua Howe has argued, "the fall of the Soviet Union had removed an important geopolitical incentive [for the Bush administration] to make a strong showing in Rio."[37]

The United Nations Conference on Environment and Development in Rio de Janeiro in June 1992 marked a turning point in U.S. and international environmental politics that would last until the Obama administration in 2008: the United States ceded its leadership role on global climate change to the Europeans. That spring, Europeans pressed for an ambitious international commitment, modeled on the Montreal Protocol, to address global warming. Following the recommendation of climate scientists, they argued for reducing greenhouse gas emissions to 1990 levels by 2000 and increasing foreign aid from developed countries to support sustainable development. Even if Bush signed such a treaty, he knew it would never be approved by the necessary two-thirds of the U.S. Senate. With American voters still shaking off the 1990–1991 recession, leaving public concern for the environment on the ebb, mindful of the disinterest in the United States in curbing energy consumption—evident in the debates over fuel economy standards—and under pressure from fossil fuel companies and conservative interest groups like the Marshall Institute, the Bush administration determined there was little support for taking significant steps to tackle a global, abstract, and seemingly distant issue such as global warming.

The United Nations Framework Convention on Climate Change (UNFCCC) that emerged from Rio in 1992 aimed to "prevent dangerous anthropogenic interference with the climate system." It stated the need for developed countries to take the lead on addressing climate change (since they were responsible for the bulk of historic greenhouse emissions). But the Bush administration maintained its opposition to including meaningful commitments to actually reduce greenhouse gas emissions, despite much pressure from environmentalists, some Democrats, and leading European countries such as Germany and Britain. Instead, the UNFCCC established a framework for monitoring emissions, sharing research, and negotiating such reduction commitments in the future. With little fanfare, the U.S. Senate ratified the treaty in October 1992, committing the United States to a framework for future negotiations on reining in greenhouse gas emissions that would capture international attention during meetings in Kyoto, Copenhagen, and Paris in the years to come.[38]

Clinton and the Energy Tax

Global warming was not a deeply partisan issue in the early 1990s. But the contours of partisan positioning on climate change were starting to become apparent in the presidential election campaign that pitted George H. W. Bush against Arkansas governor Bill Clinton. In its 1992 party platform, the Republican Party described global warming as "the common concern of mankind," but the party praised President Bush for "confronting the international bureaucrats at the Rio Conference" and refusing demands for "income redistribution" and "arbitrary targets" for emissions reductions that were "hostile to U.S. growth and workers." At a time when the average American family already paid $1,000 per year for environmental protection, according to the Republicans, they urged a more sound, careful approach to regulation; not using "junk science to foster hysteria instead of reason, demanding rigid controls, more taxes, and less resource production." They compared their vision, which saw people as the solution, to that of the "liberal Democrats," who viewed people as the "problem."[39]

On the campaign trail, Bill Clinton described President Bush as "reactive, rudderless, and expedient" on environmental issues and trapped in a way of thinking that pit environmental protection against economic growth. Such rhetoric ignored Bush's leadership on clean air and blocking offshore oil drilling outside the Gulf of Mexico. Where Clinton's critique was more accurate was on matters of international leadership. In the post–Cold War era, Clinton described the environment as a rising global challenge that demanded American leadership. Climate change and ozone depletion were "threats to our very survival." "We've seen eight of the hottest years in the history of our planet in the last decade," he warned. In April 1992, Clinton laid out an ambitious environmental agenda, much of which he credited to Al Gore, who would soon become his running mate. Clinton supported a United States commitment to reducing greenhouse gas emissions to 1990 levels by 2000, increasing national energy efficiency by 20 percent, expanding support for renewable energy, and increasing fuel economy standards for new vehicles to 40 miles per gallon by 2000. Although the 1992 presidential election that put Clinton in the White House turned largely on economic issues (including the lingering recession, Bush's tax increase following his solemn pledge to levy "no new taxes," and the growing national debt), Clinton positioned himself as a leader who saw advancing energy efficiency and sustainability as essential to ensuring the competitive position of the United States globally.[40]

Clinton moved aggressively on climate change and energy policy at the very start of his administration. As he put it bluntly, "we cannot lead the fight for environmental progress abroad unless we also do more here at home, all of us."[41] The centerpiece of Clinton's domestic policy agenda, introduced before a joint session of Congress in February 1993, was an economic plan that aimed to reduce government expenditures, encourage private investment, and increase government revenue. One of the key provisions of the proposal was a broad-based energy tax levied on coal, petroleum, natural gas, hydroelectricity, and nuclear power. It was a modest tax, raising the price of a gallon of gasoline about 6 cents and electricity bills an average of 3 percent. For an average family with a $40,000 per year income, the projected cost was $204 a year. Clinton argued it would not only lower the deficit, but reduce pollution, promote energy efficiency, and strengthen the nation's economy and energy independence. Clinton, with Gore's advice, had strategically opted for a broad-based energy tax based not on the source of the energy but on the amount, measured in British thermal units (BTUs). The Clinton administration carefully tailored the approach to avoid the downfalls of other, more targeted, policy strategies, such as a gas tax (which would hit rural states hard), an oil import tax (which would disadvantage farmers and heating oil-dependent New England), or a carbon tax (which would hit coal and, by extension, Appalachia hard). The biggest supporters of the proposal were environmental leaders, who had been pushing for a carbon tax since the late 1980s. It was the first and, at least as of 2017, the last time such a far-reaching energy tax was seriously considered by Congress.

Energy policy was a deeply political issue that fractured along regional lines and economic interests as much as it did along party lines. Conservative Republicans were quick to challenge the proposal, arguing it was not aimed at raising revenue, but at serving "the environmental agenda." As Senator Malcolm Wallop (R-Wyoming) argued, "What we are being asked to do is tax the working people of America to satisfy, in my judgment, a wrong-headed environmental crusade."[42] Legislators, Democrat and Republican alike, worried the proposal put their states at a disadvantage, despite the Clinton administration's efforts to distribute the burden equally. Legislators from the Pacific Northwest asked why hydroelectricity was being taxed, when it was a source of renewable energy. Legislators from farm states complained that corn-based ethanol was taxed, even though it was a renewable source of fuel. Those concerned about global warming asked why the proposed tax rates were similar for natural gas and coal, even though coal was twice as polluting. (They knew the answer: it was meant to placate Senator Robert Byrd of West Virginia, since he chaired the Senate Appropriations Committee.) And, even if the direct costs to consumers were modest, skeptics warned that the impact on energy-intensive industries would "dramatically echo throughout the economy."[43]

What most surprised opponents of the energy tax was just how easy it proved to defeat. The National Association of Manufacturers and a lesser-known lobby, Citizens for a Sound Economy, joined forces in 1993 to coordinate the opposition, mobilizing energy interests, the agricultural lobby, and concerned citizens, such as local farmers and miners, in common cause. With a $2 million public relations campaign, opponents used direct mail, newspaper ads, talk radio segments, and rallies to stir up a storm of opposition. They hammered home the message that an energy tax would cost the nation jobs, hurt farmers and families, and place the American economy at a competitive disadvantage.[44] Truckers warned it would eat up 50 percent of their profits. The American Farm Bureau Federation warned of the disproportionate impact on rural Americans, who relied on energy for farming inputs like fertilizer, fueling farm implements, traveling longer distances, and getting their goods to market. They projected $1 billion per year in additional costs, little of which could be passed on to consumers. The American Petroleum Institute opposed the tax on grounds that it distorted energy markets, hitting petroleum-based fuels hardest. It cited data indicating that the tax would result in a loss to the gross domestic product of nearly $34 billion and 400,000 jobs.[45]

As opposition began to mount in the spring of 1993, the Clinton administration was quick to compromise—it lowered the proposed tax on coal yet further, exempted ethanol and diesel from taxation, and shifted the tax downstream from industry and onto consumers. Then the Clinton administration started to back away from the tax entirely. Clinton made no mention of the proposed energy tax that April, when he spoke about the urgency of climate change on Earth Day.[46] As compromises and exemptions mounted, environmentalists saw few benefits in an energy tax driven by political expediency rather than environmental goals. The compromises were enough to keep House Democrats in line, and the Clinton administration prevailed on them to pass the budget bill, including the energy tax, in May 1993.[47] Dave McCurdy, a Democratic representative from Oklahoma, described it as being asked to "walk the plank."[48] Not a single Republican voted for the bill. Many Democrats who did saw their vote go on to be a campaign issue in the 1994 midterm elections: Fifty-four House Democrats lost their seats, as Republicans regained control of Congress. In McCurdy's case, he lost his campaign for an open Senate seat to James Inhofe (R-Oklahoma), who would go on to make his name nationally as the Senate's foremost skeptic of global warming. While other issues (failed health care reform, successful gun control legislation, and a halting effort to permit gays and lesbians to serve openly in the military) contributed to the electoral success of the Republicans in 1994, to this day, Washington insiders refer to getting "BTU'd" as what happens when House leadership forces a difficult vote on an issue that is never taken up in the Senate.[49]

Ultimately, the only thing the Clinton administration salvaged from the energy tax was an increased gasoline tax—even if it was modest (4.3 cents per gallon), the increase was precisely what Clinton had disavowed on the campaign trail. Yet, getting the Clinton administration's budget bill—which reduced federal spending, increased marginal taxes on the wealthy, and included the gas tax—through Congress, required Vice President Al Gore to cast a tie-breaking vote in the Senate. Although the policy helped rein in the federal deficit, what Republicans recalled during the 2000 presidential campaign was that Gore had cast the deciding vote for a 30 percent increase in the federal gasoline tax. No doubt, David and Charles Koch liked this turn of events. The Koch brothers, whose empire of energy and agricultural companies stood to lose greatly if the energy tax had passed, had both founded and bankrolled much of Citizens for a Sound Economy. The journalist Jane Mayer described the organization as a "prototype for the kind of corporate-backed opposition campaigns" that later proliferated during the Obama era, especially with the rise of the Tea Party.[50] The Koch brothers' political action committee also played an important role in the 1994 midterm election, making sizable contributions to conservative, energy-friendly candidates, including James Inhofe.[51]

Even with Democratic control of the White House and Congress, the Clinton administration had learned the hard way what George H. W. Bush already knew: the United States had little appetite for even modest steps toward the kind of deliberate, systemic energy reforms necessary to lay a domestic foundation for addressing climate change. A concerted campaign by opponents had whipped up a froth of opposition: public polling showed Americans opposed the proposed energy tax by a margin of nearly two to one. And economists estimated that Clinton's energy tax needed to be at least four times higher if the goal was to stabilize greenhouse gas emissions at 1990 levels by 2000.[52] With the energy tax dead, Clinton laid out a Climate Change Action Plan in October 1993 that set forth a laundry list of existing and new governmental programs aimed at improving energy efficiency and reducing emissions from government, residential, commercial, industrial, and transportation sectors. It was Clinton's version of an incremental policy strategy that optimistically promised to put the United States on a trajectory to realize its climate change reduction goals. But without the increases in fuel economy standards proposed during the Bush administration or energy taxes pushed half-heartedly by the Clinton administration, the ability of the United States to keep to its goal of holding emissions at 1990 levels by 2000 proved overly optimistic. Indeed, Clinton's plan was a far cry from the more muscular climate action plan Barack Obama would pursue starting in 2013, during his second term.

Despite the Clinton administration's inability to advance domestic energy policy, the administration was obliged by the terms of the UNFCCC to press ahead with international climate negotiations. In December 1995, the Intergovernmental Panel on Climate Change (IPCC) released its second assessment report, which, while acknowledging numerous uncertainties, also indicated that "the balance of evidence suggests that there is a discernible human influence on global climate." The next summer, the United States positioned itself at the helm of international climate negotiations. Former senator Timothy Wirth of Colorado, who joined the Clinton administration as the undersecretary for global affairs, set the agenda for climate negotiations at meetings in Berlin and

Geneva in 1995 and 1996 respectively. Emphasizing the IPCC's scientific assessment—and breaking with the Bush administration's policy—he stated in 1996 that the United States was now willing to commit to a "realistic, verifiable, and binding medium-term emission target."[53] The negotiators agreed to draft binding targets with a goal of adopting them in Kyoto in 1997. As the negotiations proceeded, the Clinton administration pressed for provisions that would give developed countries flexibility in meeting such commitments. The United States was the chief proponent of an emissions trading program between countries (similar to the Acid Rain Program in the Clean Air Act of 1990). And the United States supported giving credit for clean energy programs in other industrialized countries (such as transition economies in Eastern Europe and the former Soviet bloc) or developing countries.[54] But, as would turn out to be most problematic, the Clinton administration also maintained its support for what was known as the Berlin mandate. At the 1995 Berlin meeting, the United States had agreed that a binding climate agreement would "not introduce any new commitments" for developing countries, such as China, India, and Brazil beyond those included in the original UNFCCC. As Senator Robert Byrd later put it, that meant developing countries got a "free pass."[55]

The Clinton administration tried to keep climate negotiations on the "fast track" in 1997.[56] The administration scrambled to assess the domestic implications of a binding commitment, shore up domestic political support, and maintain its international leadership. Although numerous issues were on the table, the position of the United States and the fate of the Kyoto Protocol came to hinge on what commitments the treaty would require of developing countries. By the start of 1997, the Clinton administration saw that, in addition to binding commitments for developed countries, it was necessary for developing countries to make some commitments as part of an expanded climate agreement. The Clinton administration argued for additional language strengthening the commitments developing countries had already made in the original UNFCCC, such as adopting voluntary measures to reduce emissions and submitting annual reporting of their greenhouse emissions.[57] But the Clinton administration soon found itself in an impossible negotiating position. The European Union considered such commitments for developing countries premature.[58] China, India, and members of the Organization of the Petroleum Exporting Countries all stridently objected to making any such commitments—which they viewed as "new" commitments that broke with the Berlin mandate—until the United States and other developed countries lived up to their commitments to take the lead in addressing global warming that were made in the UNFCCC.[59]

In July 1997, the Republican-led Senate denounced any climate treaty that did not impose limits on both developed and developing countries. It passed the so-called Byrd-Hagel resolution, a bipartisan resolution introduced by Senate minority leader Robert Byrd (D-West Virginia) and Chuck Hagel (R-Nebraska) by a vote of 95 to 0. Although the resolution drew support from climate champions, such as John Kerry (D-Massachusetts) and John Chafee (R-Rhode Island), and skeptics, such as James Inhofe (R-Oklahoma) and Larry Craig (R-Idaho), the debate that preceded the vote revealed deepening fissures in climate politics. What every senator agreed upon was that a climate change treaty was a far-reaching commitment with the potential to restructure the nation's economy—it was precisely the kind of treaty that demanded the active advice and consent of the United States Senate. Hagel described the Senate resolution as a "bipartisan wake-up call" for the Clinton administration.[60] Many Republicans, following the lead of Senator Jesse Helms (R-North Carolina), were already resistant to any expansion of the State Department's activities, especially programs that channeled U.S. funds to support sustainable development abroad. Proponents of action in Kyoto, such as John Kerry, tried to frame the resolution as a referendum on the administration's negotiating position: he supported reconsidering the Berlin Mandate, as the only way to address global warming was to ensure that developing countries made some commitment now, not in the future.[61] Byrd put the point sharply: the Berlin mandate was a "fundamental blunder."[62] Much of the concern centered on the economic implications of a treaty that could put U.S. industry at a competitive disadvantage if the United States acted and developing countries, particularly China, did not. Senators cited studies warning of a 3 percent drop in economic growth, $110 billion in increased consumer costs, and 2 million lost jobs—concerns the Clinton administration also increasingly shared.[63] Hagel summed up the underlying concern, warning that the treaty "would have a devastating effect on American consumers, workers, farmers, and businesses."[64]

Although the text of the Byrd-Hagel resolution itself had nothing to say about the science of climate change, almost every Senator who spoke about the resolution did. Proponents of action, including Chafee and Kerry, argued that the scientific consensus articulated by the IPCC and affirmed by scientific bodies like the National Academy of Sciences demanded action. But many Republicans borrowed language, concerns, and arguments from an increasingly effective disinformation campaign which was specifically aimed at raising skeptical views and amplifying uncertainties to slow action on climate change policy. The strategy had gotten its start in the run-up to the Rio conference with the Marshall Institute in the lead and it had expanded in the 1990s with the support of the Marshall Institute and a new organization, the Global Climate Coalition, which was supported by fossil fuel companies such as Texaco, Exxon, Shell, and British Petroleum.[65] Senator Inhofe spoke for many Republicans: "The science is not there."[66] It was a point Senator Hagel echoed: "the scientific community has not even come close to definitively concluding that we have a problem."[67] Indeed, numerous scientists supported by conservative think tanks and industry interests had been invited to Congress to testify in the preceding year. Drawing on that testimony, Republicans enumerated a long list of concerns during the debate: they questioned the accuracy of climate models, discrepancies between temperature records, and whether the planet was warming at all. The nonpartisan National Academy of Sciences stood by its 1992 assessment, that "global warming poses a potential threat sufficient to merit prompt responses."[68] What Republicans signaled in the debate over Byrd-Hagel was a particular willingness to dismiss the overarching conclusions of the scientific research community, while entertaining the arguments of a small group of industry-supported, and increasingly vocal and well-coordinated, climate skeptics.

The Byrd-Hagel resolution was the legislative equivalent of a karate chop, splitting the Clinton administration's climate strategy in two—there was no chance of reconciling the Senate's demands with the expectations of the global community. Undersecretary Wirth tried to argue that the resolution "strengthens our hand," but the United States leadership and negotiating power waned in 1997 in the run-up to Kyoto as Europeans continued to push for more stringent reductions, country-by-country reduction goals, and the provisions of the Berlin mandate. The Clinton administration labored mightily to piece together a successful agreement, both before and once in Kyoto. But a two-step compromise in which developing countries would commit at a specified, but later, date never gained any traction.[69] With the Europeans pushing for a 15 percent cut in greenhouse gas emissions in developed countries by 2010, the best the United States could do was lessen the target to an average 5 percent reduction by 2010—which it thought more "realistic"— in exchange for more flexibility in meeting the goals, which had been a core U.S. negotiating principle from the start. That slight victory was credited to Vice President Gore, whose appearance two days before the negotiations concluded helped oil the gears of compromise.[70] The final agreement committed signatories to reducing greenhouse gas emissions an average of 5 percent below 1990 levels by 2008–2012 (the United States' specific commitment was 7 percent), and it allowed for both emissions trading and joint implementation to accomplish those goals. But it included no binding agreements for developing countries. Despite the shortcomings, the Natural Resources Defense Council (NRDC) described it as a "historic success" and the first step on a long road ahead.[71]

As expected, the Kyoto Protocol was dead on arrival in the United States. The NRDC may have hoped public outcry would overturn the "flat-earth viewpoint" in the Republican-led Senate, but that was not to be. Since the summer, the Clinton administration had lamented that environmentalists had failed to make a "clear and cogent" case for action.[72] Groups like the Environmental Defense Fund and NRDC struggled to mobilize environmentalists in support of the agreement. Although there was grassroots outreach, educational town meetings, and efforts to make the potential impacts of climate change more immediate with regional projections of how climate change might affect specific places like California, New England, or Washington, D.C., the efforts to build a political constituency for action had not yet matured. (By contrast, in 2007, an activist conference, Power Shift, drew 6,000 people and in 2014 and 2017, climate marches drew hundreds of thousands of participants.) Evangelical Christians and mainline Protestants joined together to form an interfaith movement to push for adoption of the Kyoto Protocol. One leader hopefully predicted, "When evangelical Christians take a position on the environment, it is noticed."[73] That had seemed to be the case in 1995 when Christian activists played an important role in blocking Republican efforts to weaken the Endangered Species Act. But evangelicals aligned with Creation Care or the Evangelical Environmental Network had less success in mobilizing activists on the issue of global warming. Instead, it was the opponents who beat the drums the loudest after the treaty was approved by UN negotiators in Kyoto. The Competitive Enterprise Institute continued to describe the policy as a back-door BTU tax that would add 40 cents to the cost of a gallon of gasoline and double electricity prices.[74] The Heritage Foundation warned the treaty would "result in lower economic growth in every state and nearly every sector of the economy." And conservatives mobilized the alliance of unions, industry trade groups, and lobbyists that had so effectively sunk Clinton's energy tax in 1993.[75] The best the environmental community could do in response was to lament the $13 million misinformation campaign sponsored by the fossil fuel companies and urge the president to "do what he knows is right" for the planet and future generations.[76]

With conservative Republicans in the lead, the U.S. Senate thumbed its nose at global efforts to address climate change in the late 1990s. Although the Clinton administration signed the Kyoto Protocol in November 1998, it never submitted it to the Senate. The issue was not simply questions about the science or projections of long-term economic losses. For many who opposed it, Senator Trent Lott (R-Mississippi) captured the crux of the issue: "The treaty is essentially an attack on America's life style."[77] Indeed, in the 1990s, Americans eagerly replaced four-door sedans with inefficient SUVs. As a result, instead of fuel economy increasing as the Bryan bill (which fell three votes short of passage in the U.S. Senate) had proposed in 1991, the average fuel economy of new vehicles sold in the United States actually declined in the 1990s. During the decade, Americans also continued to migrate to the suburbs, where they purchased homes that were an average of 7 percent larger in 2000 than in 1990. All of these changes drove up greenhouse gas emissions. In

1991, George H. W. Bush's senior advisers had confidently predicted, "as a result of efforts already in place, in the year 2000 the United States will have an aggregate level of greenhouse gas emissions equal to or below the 1987 level."[78] In fact, the opposite happened. By the year 2000, U.S. greenhouse gas emissions were 15 percent higher than the 1990 level. Yet, ironically, it was the Republicans who increasingly questioned the ability of climate scientists to make meaningful predictions about the future.

How George W. Bush Helped Start the War on Coal

For those concerned about global warming, the 2000 election campaign was surprising, even before the election was decided by the Supreme Court. During the campaign, both Texas governor and Republican nominee George W. Bush and his Democratic opponent, Vice President Al Gore, made statements on climate change at odds with their previous positions. On the campaign trail, Bush, leery of being depicted as an anti-environmental Texas oil driller, supported mandatory caps on pollution from power plants, including sulfur dioxide, nitrogen oxides, mercury, and carbon dioxide.[79] Bush was right to be concerned about his position on environmental issues: polls indicated strong public concern for the environment in 2000, with concern about global warming reaching a historic high that year—a point Bush was, no doubt, sensitive to. Despite the growing disinformation campaign, 72 percent of Americans indicated they were concerned about global warming "a great deal" or "a fair amount."[80] During the campaign, Bush assured voters that global warming was a "very serious issue."[81] In contrast, Gore, who had done more than almost any other politician to speak for the urgency of addressing climate change, only called for voluntary, incentive-based domestic programs to address emissions for fear of being painted as an overzealous environmentalist.

The true differences between the two candidates emerged on issues of energy development and international, rather than domestic, actions on climate change. On October 13, Bush outlined an agenda promoting national energy security: he called for opening up the Arctic National

Wildlife Refuge for oil exploration, expanding domestic drilling elsewhere, expanding renewable energy, and supporting energy conservation. In doing so, Bush omitted any mention of global warming, and
drew a distinction between himself and Gore on two points. Where Gore
saw regulation as necessary to rein in energy consumption, much like
Carter did in the late 1970s, Bush believed the solution was more production and innovation, much as Reagan had. He reminded his audience that it was Gore who cast the tie-breaking vote for a higher gas tax
in 1993. Where Gore supported the Kyoto Protocol—and its stipulation
that the United States reduce greenhouse gas emissions 7 percent from
1990 levels—Bush promised to oppose a treaty "that punishes" American industry and "treats America unfairly." In contrast, he saw American automakers and an abundance of energy as central to American
living standards. "That's freedom and opportunity and mobility," he explained. "That's America."[82] Although Bush did not speak of his religi-
osity often, his career in the oil industry and his policy positions aligned
with a conservative Christian tradition in the Sunbelt that saw in
the Bible an imperative to develop the nation's God-given natural
resources.[83]

Once in office, the direction of Bush's environmental agenda was unclear at first. Early on, environmentalists found themselves in the "unexpected role of offering guarded praise for an administration they
fought hard to defeat," observed the *New York Times*.[84] Several key appointees, including EPA administrator Christine Todd Whitman and
Secretary of the Treasury Paul O'Neill, urged the president to address
global warming through domestic energy policy at home and strong international leadership abroad. Speaking on CNN in February, shortly
after being confirmed, Whitman beat back questions about the president's commitment to addressing global warming. He was "very clear,"
she explained, on the scientific basis for taking action and the need to
regulate carbon dioxide.[85] Speaking to fellow environmental ministers
in Italy at a meeting of the Group of Eight industrialized countries in
March, Whitman's first point of her first international speech as EPA administrator was that "the United States considers global climate change
to be one of the greatest environmental challenges we face."[86] Indeed,
there was growing support within the business community for a plan

to address climate change, along with other air pollution issues, that could cut through the litigation and provide regulatory certainty with respect to the Clean Air Act. Some major petroleum companies, such as BP and Shell, and manufacturers, such as DuPont and Ford, had pulled their support from the Global Climate Coalition—the industry front group which had played an important role in advancing the misinformation campaign about climate science in the 1990s. Shell announced that "the oil industry must be part of the solution to emissions, not part of the problem."[87]

But in March 2001, President George W. Bush broke with his campaign promise and did an about-face on carbon dioxide regulations—spurred to action by pressure from the public interest right, led by the Competitive Enterprise Institute, and other energy interests, such as ExxonMobil (the two oil behemoths had agreed to merge in 1998). Responding to a formal query (orchestrated by the energy lobbyists) from Senator Chuck Hagel and other Republican senators, Bush signaled his continued support for reforming the Clean Air Act and taking global warming "very seriously," but he withdrew his support for regulating carbon dioxide under the Clean Air Act. To justify this decision, he cited a recently released Department of Energy report warning that such regulations would lead to "significantly higher electricity prices," which he deemed untenable at a time when utility prices were on the rise nationally and California was in the throes of an energy crisis. (No matter that the energy crisis would later turn out to be a product of market manipulation spearheaded by the Bush-allied Enron Corporation.) Bush maintained his avowed opposition to the Kyoto Protocol and made clear he had no plans to regulate carbon dioxide in the near future, considering the "incomplete state of scientific knowledge of the causes of, and solutions to, global climate change."[88] At the Competitive Enterprise Institute, its climate and energy policy lobbyist, Myron Ebell, could scarcely contain his glee. The next day, in an email to his allies in the Cooler Heads Coalition, a network of like-minded groups on the public interest right, he described Bush's public reversal as a "famous victory." He also warned that with people like Whitman and O'Neill in the administration, they still "have a lot of work to do."[89] The reversal was the product of an intensive lobbying campaign spearheaded by the Com-

Figure 4-1   George W. Bush's unwillingness to support efforts to address global warming raised questions about the influence of the energy industry. *Source:* Seppo Leinonen, "Reliable source for climate science," © 2005 Seppo Leinonen. Reprinted by permission of Graafinen Oy Maanpiiri.

petitive Enterprise Institute—which enjoyed strong support from the fossil fuel companies, notably ExxonMobil—and actively supported by Vice President Dick Cheney.[90] Insiders credited the Competitive Enterprise Institute, which helped initiate the Department of Energy's report, with giving the president the political cover he needed to reverse his campaign pledge.[91]

Publicly, the Bush administration doubled down on the largely voluntary approach to climate policy that his father had pursued, while emphasizing the need for more scientific research and diversified energy production. In 2002, Bush committed the United States to reducing its greenhouse gas intensity—the greenhouse gas emissions per unit of economic activity—by 18 percent by 2012.[92] That approach linked the nation's emissions target to economic growth, meaning if the economy grew rapidly, overall emissions could increase even as greenhouse gas intensity fell. Not only did that approach avoid a fixed cap on emissions, it also was in line with business as usual. Between 1992 and 2002, total U.S. emissions had grown, even as greenhouse gas intensity fell

20 percent, driven by a decline in manufacturing and growth in the service sector.[93] The administration's higher priority was developing a national energy plan, which was Vice President Cheney's pet project. When that plan was released in May 2001, Bush praised it for its balanced approach, emphasizing reducing the demand for energy, increasing supplies, and improving distribution.[94] But environmentalists criticized the plan for its minimal commitment to energy efficiency and conservation, inattention to climate change, efforts to weaken the Clean Air Act, and an overemphasis on expanding production of fossil fuels and nuclear power, including opening up the Arctic Refuge. The plan's tilt toward traditional energy interests came as little surprise. As the Natural Resources Defense Council put it, "The oil, coal, and auto industries . . . shoveled millions of dollars into Bush campaign coffers."[95] Indeed, in the 2000 election, the energy and natural resources sector had donated nearly ten times as much money to Bush's campaign as it did to Gore's campaign.[96] Now they were reaping the benefits.

Taking its cues from companies such as ExxonMobil and groups like the Cooler Heads Coalition, the Bush administration made climate change a leading front in its war on science.[97] In 2003, the administration launched the Climate Change Science Program meant to support and coordinate climate-related work across thirteen federal agencies.[98] In the name of the administration's commitment to "sound science," it was part of a "strategic plan to address some of the most complex questions and problems dealing with long-term global climate variability and change."[99] But for the Bush administration and its conservative allies and fossil fuel supporters, the policy implication of mainstream climate science posed a grave threat: in their view, it would expand government regulation, threaten profits, and put limits on American consumption. In 1998, in the aftermath of the debates over the Kyoto Protocol, the American Petroleum Institute warned it would be difficult for the United States to continue to avoid action on climate change "solely on economic grounds." That approach appeared to put American interests above the "greater concerns of mankind." Instead, API and its allies on the public interest right called for shifting debate back to the state of climate science. They outlined a campaign to "inject credible science and scientific accountability into the global climate debate, thereby raising questions

Figure 4-2   George W. Bush's administration adopted public lands policies that prioritized resource extraction, similar to those of James Watt and the Reagan administration. *Source:* Steve Greenberg, "James Watt days, encore," *Marin Independent Journal*, April 4, 2001. Reprinted by permission of the cartoonist.

about and undercutting the 'prevailing scientific wisdom.'"[100] It was an elaborate strategy aimed at the media, legislators, and the public. It was hardly a new idea for conservatives, but API and its allies pursued it with new vigor during the Bush administration. And, unlike the Marshall Institute's early 1990s lobbying campaign, which had argued for more research, the strategy outlined in the late 1990s focused on amplifying uncertainty, elevating dissenting points of view, and sowing doubt—not advancing more research. The strategy worked, in no small part because API's former chief climate lobbyist Phil Cooney served as chief of staff in Bush's Council on Environmental Quality from 2001 to 2005, where he coordinated the Bush administration's climate program.[101]

With an industry appointee at the helm, the Bush administration managed climate change–related activities with an iron fist, keeping scientists, the Environmental Protection Agency, and other administration appointees "on message." Cooney was at the center of the action.

Cooney vetted all major climate-related reports, such as the *Climate Action Report,* the *Report on the Environment,* and the *Strategic Plan for the Climate Change Science Program,* editing them to emphasize uncertainties and diminish urgency. Cooney funneled skeptical scientific studies to the administration. The most interesting such studies went all the way up to the vice president and president. Media requests to speak with government scientists were carefully reviewed, with Cooney's staff weighing in on whether the scientists would be "on message." Most troubling, investigative journalists revealed that Cooney's editing of government reports on climate extended past vetting to making substantive changes to scientific conclusions to cast doubt on the role of greenhouse gas emissions in contributing to climate change. When those activities came to light in 2005 they led to Cooney's resignation two days later.[102] Recalling her time in the administration for *Rolling Stone,* Christine Todd Whitman remembered going toe to toe with Cooney. She explained, "What disturbed me most was the administration's record of taking the most extreme of the science—what I call the 'political science'—and giving it the same weight as the real science."[103] In 2006, the House Oversight and Government Reform Committee initiated a bipartisan investigation into the Bush administration's oversight of climate science. In 2007, after collecting over 27,000 pages of internal documents and holding two hearings, the committee summed up its assessment: "The Bush Administration has engaged in a systematic effort to manipulate climate change science and mislead policymakers and the public about the dangers of global warming." But that effort was hardly a product of the Bush administration alone; instead, it represented the machinations of conservative interests which had long dismissed climate science and opposed any regulatory action. In a sign of the success of those efforts among conservatives, every Republican on the committee dissented.[104]

Although the Bush administration's production-first energy policy and disregard for climate change may have pleased many conservatives, the energy lobby, and the public interest right, it did not sit well with all Republicans, or even some of their likely supporters. In 1995, moderate Republicans, alarmed by the environmental agenda of the 104th Congress led by Gingrich, had joined together to found a group named Republicans for Environmental Protection with the goal of returning the

Republican Party to its conservation roots. It was a goal that almost always put the group at odds with the Bush administration and its appointees in the 2000s. The group made a name for itself by playing a key role in rallying Republican legislators to oppose the Bush administration's ultimately unsuccessful efforts to open the Arctic Refuge for oil exploration. Similarly, since 1998, the Evangelical Environmental Network had been mobilizing evangelical Christians in support of the Kyoto Protocol under the banner of creation care. In the early 2000s, the organization began to draw more attention when it launched a media campaign with the tag line: "What would Jesus drive?" It urged Christians to think about the moral consequences of driving fuel inefficient vehicles such as SUVs. "We have confessed Christ to be our savior and Lord, and for us, that includes our transportation choices," explained Reverend Jim Ball.[105] Evangelical environmental leaders expanded on this campaign in 2006, launching the Evangelical Climate Initiative. "As Christians, our faith in Jesus Christ compels us to love our neighbors and to be stewards of God's creation. The good news is that with God's help, we can stop global warming, for our kids, our world, and for the Lord."[106] Although the Republicans who championed Republicans for Environmental Protection or the evangelicals associated with the Evangelical Environmental Network each may have hoped to weave their vision into the mainstream of the Republican Party and American evangelical life, in the 2000s they increasingly found themselves on the outside of the conservative establishment looking in.

Efforts to address climate change were largely nonstarters in the early 2000s. Indeed, in the years after the September 11, 2001 terrorist attacks, public concern for global warming plummeted to a new low after peaking in 2000, as concerns about national security and terrorism ascended.[107] When Congress did take up energy legislation in 2005, it was driven largely by concerns over escalating energy costs: between 2001 and 2005, the price of gasoline, natural gas, and heating oil had all doubled. The Energy Policy Act of 2005—the first national energy bill since George H. W. Bush's administration—was a sprawling piece of legislation, but one that largely omitted command-and-control policies that would have shifted the nation away from fossil fuels, such as increasing fuel efficiency standards for vehicles, establishing targets for reducing oil consumption, or adopting a minimum target of 10 percent renewable energy production in 2020 (a modest provision which the Republican-led Senate approved 52 to 48, but which was opposed by the House and Bush administration).[108] The only strict command-and-control provision was one that appeased the farm lobby: a renewable fuel standard that required petroleum companies to blend more corn-based ethanol into gasoline. Much of the Energy Policy Act centered on providing tax breaks, regulatory relief, and incentives to support domestic energy production. It provided ample support for existing energy industries, including exempting or expediting oil and gas exploration from environmental laws, such as the National Environmental Policy Act, Clean Air Act, and Clean Water Act. For instance, the law included a provision that exempted fluids used in hydraulic fracturing for oil and gas ("fracking") from regulation under the Safe Drinking Water Act—an exemption now known as the Halliburton loophole—which has become a serious environmental problem.[109] The law also included $8.6 billion in tax credits aimed at the oil, gas, coal, and nuclear industries. Summing up the bill, the League of Conservation Voters complained that despite nominal commitments to efficiency and renewables, it "helps line the pockets of the oil and gas industry, which is already making record profits."[110]

But the Energy Policy Act of 2005 stands out for another reason: this was the first salvo in the twenty-first-century "war on coal." It was not meant to be. The law included $2 billion in funding to research and pilot "clean coal" technology that could siphon off carbon dioxide from power plants' exhaust and store it underground, thereby negating its impact on the climate. But, overall, the law sharply tilted the energy landscape away from coal and toward natural gas and, to a lesser extent, renewables. Although the origins of this policy shift dated back to the late 1970s, when Carter deregulated the natural gas industry, provisions of the Energy Policy Act of 2005, including the Halliburton loophole, tax breaks, and provisions expediting energy exploration, paved the way for an unexpectedly large surge of domestic natural gas and oil production. Between 2005 and 2015, natural gas production increased by 43 percent and oil production nearly doubled, with fracking accounting for 67 percent and 51 percent of production respectively. Starting in 2015, natural gas accounted for more electricity generation than coal, for the first time in American history (see Figure 4-3).[111] The law also helped lay the groundwork for large-scale deployments of renewable energy, such as solar and wind installations. It included $4 billion in research funds targeting renewable energy development and an additional $4.5 billion in tax credits to incentivize deployment.[112] Some arcane provisions of the law, such as language supporting net metering (a billing strategy crucial to the deployment of solar arrays), also proved essential to enabling the rapid growth of solar installations in states such as California, Arizona, and New Jersey and the growth of companies such as SolarCity and Sunrun.[113] Although the 2009 American Recovery and Reinvestment Act—pushed by President Obama and Democrats in response to the 2008 fiscal crisis—would expand these commitments, the 2005 law helped jumpstart a seventy-five-fold increase in solar and ten-fold increase in wind capacity by 2015. Amidst

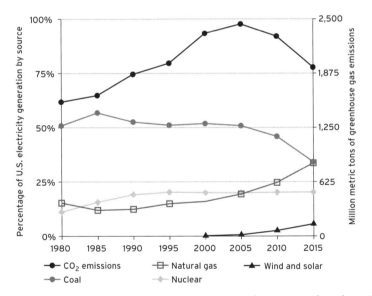

Figure 4-3   The percentage of U.S. electricity generation by source and resulting CO_2 emissions. The chart shows the dramatic shift in the U.S. electricity sector starting in 2005 as natural gas use and renewable energy deployments increased at the expense of coal. Note, in 2015, greenhouse gas emissions from the electricity sector had fallen to nearly the same level as in 1990. *Data source:* U.S. Energy Information Administration / EIA.gov.

all of this growth, there was one clear loser: coal. Production fell 20 percent during the same time period.[114] In short, the Energy Policy Act of 2005, by tweaking regulations to open the market for natural gas, solar, and other alternatives to coal, played a key supporting role in what became known as the "war on coal." Yet it was not just environmentalists or Democrats who shouldered the responsibility. Republicans, though unintentionally, did too.

Incremental Progress, Despite George W. Bush's Administration

When Hurricane Katrina barreled through New Orleans in August 2005, the massive storm flooded the city, killed 1,833 people, and caused $108 billion in damage. Although global warming did not directly cause the storm, it did leave many Americans newly concerned about the potential havoc of a warming world. The next summer Al Gore released *An Inconvenient Truth,* which had a tagline reading "the scariest movie you'll ever see" and a poster featuring a menacing hurricane spewing out of a smokestack. In one hundred minutes, Gore's narrated slideshow explained the basics of climate science and drew on it to raise the specter of intensifying storms, spreading disease, and climate refugees. In the same way that Rachel Carson's *Silent Spring* propelled concern about DDT into the limelight in 1962, *An Inconvenient Truth* accomplished much the same for global warming by synthesizing complex science for a public audience. In 2006, environmentally minded evangelical leaders launched their climate care initiative. In 2007, environmental groups including the Environmental Defense Fund and the Natural Resources Defense Council joined with major corporations including DuPont, General Electric, Lehman Brothers, Dow Chemical, PepsiCo, Shell, and Ford Motor Company to form the United States Climate Action Partnership in support of "prompt action to establish a coordinated, economy-wide, market-driven approach to climate protection."[115] And, finally, in September 2007, the Intergovernmental Panel on Climate Change released its fourth assessment report, which deemed global warming "unequivocal" and increased temperatures as "very likely due to the observed increase in anthropogenic GHG concentrations."[116] By 2008, global warming began to shift from being an abstract, distant, scientific concern to the most pressing environmental issue facing the United States and the world.

With public concern over climate change mounting, the Bush administration's intransigence could not stifle environmentalists' efforts to address climate change in the early 2000s. Instead, it energized efforts to pursue policy strategies that would run around, rather than through, the White House. As the political scientist Barry Rabe has argued, states became a focal point of climate change activism in the late 1990s and that trend accelerated during Bush's tenure.[117] For example, renewable energy portfolios became common in the early 2000s. These policies require utilities to source a minimum percentage of electricity from renewable sources, thus creating a larger and more stable market for renewable energy suppliers and decarbonizing the electricity supply. Along with the Energy Policy Act of 2005, such state-level policies played a key role in accelerating the adoption of renewable energy nationwide. Between 2004 and 2007 alone, more than thirty states adopted or revised their renewable portfolio standards. For instance, Hawaii, Colorado, New Mexico, and Delaware adopted goals of 20 percent renewable energy by 2020 at the latest.[118] And, while the Bush administration ignored the Kyoto Protocol, numerous states committed to comparable state-level greenhouse gas reduction targets. In September 2006, California became the first state to make a binding commitment to an overall cap on greenhouse gas emissions—setting a goal of returning to 1990 levels by 2020. Massachusetts followed in 2008, setting an even more ambitious target of returning to 25 percent below 1990 levels by 2020. (As of 2017, both states were largely on track to hit their targets.)

Environmentalists and their allies also turned to the courts to force the Bush administration's hand. In 1998, the Clinton administration concluded that the EPA had the authority to regulate carbon dioxide under the existing provisions of the Clean Air Act. But in 2003, the Bush administration concluded differently, arguing that carbon dioxide did not meet the definition of an "air pollutant" as defined by the Clean Air Act and, therefore, the agency was not specifically authorized to address global climate change. A coalition of states and environmental groups, with Massachusetts and the Environmental Defense Fund in the lead, sued the Environmental Protection Agency, pursuing the case until it was heard by the Supreme Court in November 2006. The case hinged on the potential of sea level rise to diminish the state of Massachusetts's sovereign territory. Before the court, Bush's EPA attorneys argued that Congress had not authorized the agency to "address global climate change" and, even if it had, "substantial scientific uncertainty" justified the agency's inaction.[119] While opponents of addressing climate change had proven their effectiveness in the political arena—where well-funded campaigns, exaggerations, and half-truths helped sway elections—those strategies proved less effective in the court of law. The Court's 5–4 decision dropped like a bombshell in April 2007. The Court affirmed the "existence of a causal connection between man-made greenhouse gas emissions and global warming," concluding that "greenhouse gases fit well within the Act's capacious definition of 'air pollutant,'" and finding that climate change posed an "actual" and "imminent" threat to the state of Massachusetts.[120] As one TV network summed up the decision, the "Supreme Court rejects Bush in global warming debate."[121] The decision threw open the door for the EPA to take action to regulate carbon dioxide emissions—a strategy the Obama administration would later pursue with the Clean Power Plan.

A congressional push for action on climate change also began to gain momentum over the objections of the Bush White House. With Senator John McCain (R-Arizona) and Joe Lieberman (D-Connecticut) in the lead, a small group of senators began to build support for a market-based, cap-and-trade approach to curbing greenhouse gas emissions in 2003. McCain and Lieberman borrowed a page from George H. W. Bush's playbook, modeling their proposal on the cap-and-trade provisions of the Acid Rain Program, which had broken the decade-long stalemate over regulating sulfur dioxide emissions in 1990. They hoped that strategy might work again, especially given the George W. Bush administration's interest in using cap-and-trade more broadly to reform the Clean Air Act. But the votes on such legislation in 2003 and 2005 fell short. The votes generally followed party lines, with some moderate Republicans such as John McCain and Olympia Snowe (R-Maine) voting in favor, and Democrats from coal and manufacturing states such as West Virginia and Michigan voting in opposition.[122] Yet, after the Supreme Court ruling in *Massachusetts v. EPA* in 2007, some form of greenhouse gas regulation—either by way of administrative action under the existing provisions of the Clean Air Act or preemptive legislative action by Congress—seemed increasingly likely. In 2008, Nancy Pelosi, the Democratic Speaker of the House, and Newt Gingrich, former Republican Speaker and leader of the Contract with America, even filmed a TV ad for Gore's climate campaign. In the thirty-second spot, Gingrich's big line was "We do agree our country must take action to address climate change."[123] And during the 2008 presidential campaign, such action seemed almost inevitable, with Senators John McCain and Barack Obama (D-Illinois) running for the presidency. Each politician had a track record of affirming the scientific consensus and supporting regulatory action on climate change. After eight years of stubborn opposition during the Bush administration, policy action seemed to be at hand, no matter which party won the White House. Hopes for bipartisan action on climate change were flickering to life.

The Slow Rise and Rapid Fall of Cap and Trade

In the summer of 2009, a red hot air balloon floated above farm fields and county fairgrounds from Wichita, Kansas, to Spartanburg, South Carolina, to Broomfield, Colorado. It advertised a seemingly cryptic message: "Cap and Trade Means: Lost Jobs, Higher Taxes, Less Freedom." Conservative activists who rallied beneath the balloon knew exactly what that meant. Cap and trade was the centerpiece of Democrats' strategy for addressing climate change during Obama's first term. At events in rural communities across the nation, dozens to hundreds of concerned citizens and their families turned out to hear organizers from Americans for Prosperity, a D.C.-based conservative outreach organization funded by David and Charles Koch. The group's national Hot Air Tour raised the alarm about proposed cap-and-trade legislation to lower greenhouse gas emissions and address global warming that was under consideration in Congress. This marked an important turning point in conservative opposition to climate change. As action on climate change was propelled to the forefront of American political debate at the start of the Obama administration, climate change opposition was swept up in the conservative, populist uprising that came to be known as the Tea Party.[124]

Indeed, when Obama arrived in the White House, his administration's forceful approach to climate change policy set toes tapping in anticipation at groups like the Environmental Defense Fund and the Natural Resources Defense Council, which pressed for action both domestically and internationally, and worry beads rattling within the energy industry. Speaking before Congress in February 2009, Obama said: "I ask this Congress to send me legislation that places a market-based cap on carbon pollution and drives the production of more renewable energy in America."[125] Obama framed the push for domestic action on climate change as a strategy to create jobs, improve energy security, and create a new foundation for economic growth. Action came swiftly, with solid Democratic majorities in the House and Senate (where Democrats allied with independents for a 60-vote filibuster-proof majority). In February 2009, Democrats delivered the American Recovery and Reinvestment Act, which was meant to help pull the nation out of the 2008 recession. The $787 billion stimulus package provided over $90 billion to fund research, support investments, and incentivize deployment of renewable energy and energy efficiency technologies, ranging from electric cars to advanced battery technology to weatherizing low-income homes.[126]

In June 2009, the House took the next step, narrowly passing the American Clean Energy and Security Act, which proposed a cap-and-trade system to reduce greenhouse gas emissions 17 percent below 2005 levels by 2020 and, far more ambitiously, 83 percent below by 2050. It was the first time either chamber of Congress had approved a greenhouse gas reduction target.[127] But like other votes in the 111th Congress, including the stimulus act, financial reform, and health care, Democrats moved the legislation with vanishingly little Republican support. In the case of the climate bill, 44 of 263 Democrats opposed it, suggesting that, if anything, it was the opposition to, rather than support for, climate policy that was bipartisan. Outside Congress, Obama signaled his administration's commitment to advance the United Nations Framework Convention on Climate Change. Since 2007, the international community had looked to the Copenhagen climate negotiations in December 2009, the first summit after Bush left office, to negotiate a commitment to succeed the Kyoto Protocol. With developing countries such as China and India publicly indicating a willingness to make commitments, and Obama staking his administration's reputation on forging a deal, expectations for a renewed global effort to address climate change soared.

But neither 2009, 2010, nor the years to follow were breakthrough years for climate policy. In the United States, the forces that had propelled climate change to the forefront of public discussion since 2006 had only served to antagonize conservatives, who increasingly viewed climate change as a Democratic fancy—championed by political elites such as Gore and Obama—that put global interests before American interests based on faulty science and wishful economic projections for green jobs. The Competitive Enterprise Institute railed against the American Clean Energy and Security Act, describing it as a form of "energy rationing" that would represent the "biggest tax increase in the history of the world and the biggest government intervention in people's lives since the Second World War."[128] The *Wall Street Journal*'s editorial page faulted the nonpartisan Congressional Budget Office's economic analysis of the bill as woefully optimistic. The newspaper dismissed projections that it would add only $175 to the annual expenses of the average family in 2020, siding instead with the Heritage Foundation, which argued that their more comprehensive economic analysis projected an additional burden of $1,870 per family in 2025 and $6,800 by 2035. The *Wall Street Journal* did not describe it as a major tax hike, but simply as "the biggest tax in American history."[129]

That November, as the cap-and-trade bill stalled in the Senate and eyes turned toward Copenhagen, an unidentified source leaked to a Russian website thousands of emails and computer files from a major British climate change research center in what quickly became known as "climategate." The emails included language that suggested to the skeptical reader that key climate data had been cooked. Although the involved scientists were later exonerated of any wrongdoing, the cries of scandal found an eager audience, especially in the United States.[130] Climate skeptics seized on the release in the weeks leading up to

Copenhagen to say, as the Competitive Enterprise Institute's chief anti-climate lobbyist Chris Horner put it: "Told you so."[131] On *Fox News,* Senator Inhofe explained, "Everything I said back then," about misconduct among climate scientists, "it appears they are saying now in these hacked emails."[132] The next month, in congressional hearings, Republican representatives decried the climategate emails as evidence of "scientific fascism."[133] Operatives on the public interest right continued to stoke the fires of the scientific misinformation campaign, which was now led by the Heartland Institute, a Chicago-based think tank with ties to the fossil fuel industry. It convened its annual International Conference on Climate Change with the goal of providing a venue for fringe scientists and others skeptical that humans were driving global warming. All of these factors helped sow doubt about the reality of climate change. The percentage of Americans who described themselves as unconcerned about global warming reached a record high in 2010 (see Figure 4-4).[134]

But the debate over climate science was not just in Congress or on the news. At a stop on the Hot Air Tour in Rapid City, South Dakota, Tim Phillips, president of Americans for Prosperity, spoke to members of Citizens for Liberty, one of the hundreds of local Tea Party organizations that sprouted nationwide after Obama's election. Sparing no hyperbole, Phillips attacked the economic implications of the cap-and-trade bill. He described a future of rationed energy with 35 to 60 percent increases in utility bills, $6 to $7 a gallon gasoline, and the loss of 1 million jobs. He described it as an anti-coal proposal pushed by liberals in San Francisco and New York.[135] Phillips would have liked Senator Joe Manchin's campaign ad the next fall: in it, the West Virginia Democrat literally shot a hole in the cap-and-trade bill with a rifle, "because it's bad for West Virginia."[136] The Hot Air Tour, later renamed the Regulation Reality Tour, ran in 2009 and 2010. It was an outgrowth of the organizing strategy that conservatives, with the support of the likes of the Koch brothers, had pioneered back in 1993 during the debates over the Clinton energy tax.

On the tour, Phillips saved his most powerful point for last. He described the cap-and-trade bill as "a loss of our freedoms" in the name of the government's "ideology on the environment." To make his point, he

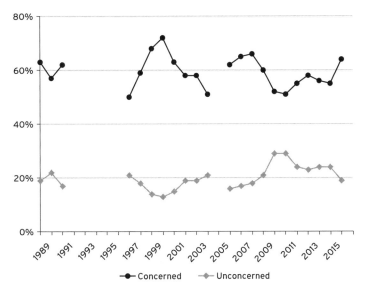

Figure 4-4   The percentage of survey respondents indicating they were either concerned or unconcerned about climate change, drawn from Gallup polling data. The number of respondents indicating they were unconcerned about climate change rose sharply from 2008–2010, during which time conservative interests intensified their campaign to discredit climate science. *Data source:* Gallup, Inc. / Gallup.com.

warned that the bill included a last-minute amendment that would require each and every owner of a home, ranch, or farm to "certify to a federal agency . . . that your [property] meets the new energy efficiency standards before you can sell it. This is your private property!"[137] Although the legislation did raise energy efficiency standards for new and renovated homes and buildings, it included no such requirements for existing properties at the time of sale (or any other time). But when local groups like Citizens for Liberty and national groups like Americans for Prosperity were fanning the flames of the Tea Party nationwide, such falsehoods, like false claims about "death panels" in the health care law, were just more fuel for the fire. In the November 2010 midterm election, the Tea Partiers showed they were not just a shallow movement seeded by conservative think tanks and funded by conservative plutocrats, but frustrated citizens ready to push an agenda focused on reducing taxes, slashing public spending, policing immigrants, and protecting gun rights

Figure 4-5   David and Charles Koch drew public attention for their efforts to block reforms aimed at addressing climate change. *Source:* Steve Greenberg, "The water boy," *VCReporter*, July 2011. Reprinted by permission of the cartoonist.

and family values.[138] Their success tipped the balance of power in Congress even more dramatically than during the midterm elections in 1994 when Republicans seized control under the banner of Newt Gingrich's Contract with America. Democrats lost sixty-three House seats and six Senate seats, with Republicans taking a majority in the House. That signaled not just a new era of partisan combat in Washington, D.C., but a rising tide of conservative populism that pushed Donald Trump into the White House in 2017.

The fusion of Tea Party politics fed off of frustrations with the health care bill, the economy, and immigration, among other issues. Under its broad banner, it seemed every conservative could find a reason to oppose government action on climate change, including libertarians, fiscal conservatives, frustrated workers, and, increasingly, Christian evangelicals. It was the repositioning and mobilization of this last group that was particularly noticeable in the first decade of the 2000s, for it signaled the extent to which climate had been transformed from an environmental or economic issue into a new front in the culture wars of the twenty-first century. Although there is a long and complicated history of Christian evangelical support for environmental protection, such efforts had also provoked intense backlash in the evangelical community. In 2007, the Southern Baptist Convention passed a resolution dismissing climate change. In 2008, the most prominent evangelical environmental leader, Richard Cizik, was dismissed from the National Association of Evangelicals. And since 2006, a faction of evangelical leaders began to harness climate skepticism to dominion theology in a coordinated public outreach campaign they launched at the Heritage Foundation. They posited that Christians "were put on this Earth as creatures of God to have dominion over the Earth." They considered organized environmentalism a "Green Dragon" that had to be slain.[139] They described Earth's climate as a self-regulating system that was the product of God's "infinitely wise design." As Senator James Inhofe remarked on the Voice of Christian Youth radio program in 2012, "my point is, God's still up there. The arrogance of people to think that we, human beings, would be able to change what He is doing in the climate is to me outrageous." From that perspective, it was easy to dismiss climate science as indicative of the kind of elitist, secular humanism that challenged a faith in God and ate away at the nation's moral fiber. Like-minded evangelicals believed there was no shortage of resources on God's Earth. To countenance limits on "abundant, affordable, reliable fossil fuels" was unconscionable in a world where billions of impoverished citizens of developing countries needed them to rise from poverty and disease.[140]

Many of these evangelical leaders dismissed the threat of global warming as they were mindful of the anticipated second coming of Christ, which was a core tenet of evangelical belief. In 2008, dominion theologists asked, "Did you notice that what Jesus warned would occur in the last days are almost identical to what some global warming theorists are saying is going to happen?" That suggestion cast stronger storms, rising seas, and fire-prone forests in new light. They reminded their fellow believers that it was at this moment, what they deemed "the two-minute drill," that efforts at "spiritual deception" such as those purveyed by "global warming alarmists" would be most tempting.[141] Although environmentalists may dismiss the significance of such statements, such beliefs have traction among both evangelicals and Republicans. The political scientists David Barker and David Bearce have found that 75 percent of Republicans profess a belief in the Second Coming. Their research shows that believers in Christian end-times theology are "significantly more resistant to government action aimed at curbing global warming."[142] Empirical studies of how religious belief figures in environmental attitudes more broadly reveal that evangelical Protestant denominations tend to be least concerned with environmental issues.[143] Not coincidentally, some 40 percent of Tea Partiers identified as evangelicals.[144] It seemed for many of these conservative Tea Party Republicans, climate change had joined abortion rights and same-sex marriage as a key litmus test in conservative American politics.

The Republicans' Tea Party-led takeover of the House in 2010 dashed any hopes for congressional action on a cap-and-trade bill, or any other form of climate legislation, in the 111th Congress. Just as disappointing, the Copenhagen climate negotiations ended in 2009 without decisive action, hampered, in no small part, by uncertainty abroad as to whether the Obama administration could back up its international climate pledges with domestic policy. Despite these setbacks, the Obama administration did set in motion the process by which the EPA could begin to regulate greenhouse gases under the existing provisions of the Clean Air Act, as authorized by the Supreme Court in *Massachusetts v. EPA*. In 2009, the agency issued its "endangerment finding," which determined that greenhouse gases constitute a form of "air pollution" that threatens both public health and welfare.[145] In 2012, the D.C. Circuit Court of Appeals rejected efforts to overturn the EPA's endangerment finding, and the Supreme Court refused to take up the case, much to the frustration of climate skeptics and conservative Republicans. World events in these years, increasingly attributed to global warming, affirmed the prudence of those judgments. A withering multiyear drought in Syria helped precipitate the start of civil war in that country in 2011.[146] Flooding caused damages in Australia in 2011 that amounted to 3.2 percent of its gross domestic product. A record drought in the United States, Europe, and Asia drove up food prices in 2012 by 10 percent. And Hurricane Sandy rolled up the eastern seaboard in October 2012, forming the most powerful and largest Atlantic hurricane in recorded history and pushing a storm surge that crippled coastal communities in New Jersey and New

York. To scientists the question was not when climate change would happen, but to what extent it was already exacerbating these climatic events.

By the 2012 presidential election, the partisan dividing line on climate change had split wide open. That year, Myron Ebell, the Competitive Enterprise Institute's chief climate lobbyist and an architect of the disinformation campaign, assessed the campaign's effectiveness: "There are holdouts among the urban bicoastal elite, but I think we've won the debate with the American people in the heartland, the people who get their hands dirty, people who dig up stuff, grow stuff and make stuff for a living, people who have a closer relationship to tangible reality, to stuff."[147] That was an overstatement, but it was clear that to be a contender for the Republican presidential nomination in 2012, dismissing global warming had become an imperative—a sharp reversal from just four years before. Newt Gingrich disavowed his 2008 advertisement with Nancy Pelosi in an interview with the *Washington Post,* describing it as "really stupid."[148] Mitt Romney, the eventual Republican nominee, had supported pioneering state-level climate policy as governor of Massachusetts. Indeed, among his chief advisors on climate issues at the time was Gina McCarthy, who would lead the EPA during Obama's second term, spearheading the administration's climate agenda.[149] But during the 2012 campaign, Romney reversed course, questioning climate science and the need for action. Even President Obama downplayed his climate agenda during the reelection campaign. Incidentally, his administration's rapid response to Hurricane Sandy, a week before the election, helped consolidate his support as he secured victory over Romney on November 6, 2012. When Obama started his second term, he was forthright about his intentions. During the State of the Union address the following February, he warned, "if Congress won't act soon to protect future generations" from climate change, "I will."[150] For those on the right, who had already helped organize to defeat the cap-and-trade bill in Congress, such promises of executive action only fanned the flames of populist anger and frustration.

The kickoff came that June, as Obama spoke on a sweltering summer day in Washington, D.C., sweat pouring from his brow, as he outlined his Climate Action Plan. With it, the administration launched a concerted effort to enforce the nation's existing environmental laws to protect public health, reduce greenhouse gas emissions, and reaffirm U.S. leadership on global warming. Major initiatives included implementing rules approved in 2012 to raise fuel economy standards for new cars to 54.5 miles per gallon by 2025, rules to protect streams from being polluted by mountaintop mining removal, a halt on new coal leases on public lands (including the Powder River Basin), and expediting renewable energy development on public lands, among other administrative initiatives. The centerpiece of this administrative push was the Clean Power Plan, which the EPA developed under the Clean Air Act (as legitimated by the Supreme Court's *Massachusetts v. EPA* decision) to regulate greenhouse gas emissions from the power sector. It required states to develop their own plans to reduce emissions an average of 30 percent below 2005 levels by 2030 through fuel switching, renewable energy deployment, and energy efficiency.[151] Underlying all of the administrative actions the Obama administration undertook was economic analysis that pegged the ill effects of greenhouse gas emissions, or the "social cost of carbon," at $36 per ton of pollution. Based on those avoided costs and other benefits, the administration estimated the Clean Power Plan would return from $6 to $12 in benefits for every dollar in costs in 2030.[152]

To opponents, the Clean Power Plan represented the height of Obama's "war on coal"—a rallying cry that got its start in Appalachia in response to the Democrats' cap-and-trade bill in 2010, but which drew national attention when Mitt Romney embraced it on the campaign trail in 2012. Although employment in the coal industry had been in decline since the expansion of mountaintop removal, and losses accelerated with the natural gas boom kicked off by fracking in the early 2000s, environmentalists and bureaucrats in Washington, D.C. made for an easy target. From that perspective, the Clean Power Plan seemed purposefully fashioned to seal the industry's fate. In July 2014, thousands of coal miners marched in protest in Pittsburgh, Pennsylvania, holding signs that read, "Our kids matter too" and chanting, "Hey, Hey EPA, Don't Take Our Jobs Away."[153] In Alabama, public officials turned to religion to decry a regulation that was "an assault on our way of life." "Who has the right to take what God's given a state?" asked the president of the Alabama Public Service Commission. "I hope all the citizens of Alabama will be in prayer that the right thing will be done."[154] At hearings in Atlanta that summer, an Alabama miner, Walter Parker, made clear that no matter the debates over the science or the cost-benefit analyses, for these workers, their families, and communities, coal was their lifeblood. As he testified, "I've never asked for handouts from the people around me or from the government. I want to pay my own way. I want to work. I feel pride in my work. I want to be able to continue my profession to produce coal to power this nation. And I'm sorry that I get emotional, but I can't help it. In the end, I don't see the agency's proposed policy as a real solution. We will lose what we have worked for all of our lives and our communities. We will struggle in poverty. How can the EPA call this a success story?"[155] Understandably, he would likely have taken little consolation in the fact that jobs in solar and wind had grown by more than 80 percent since 2010 and outnumbered coal miners more than six to one in 2016.[156]

The Clean Power Plan would never be a success for coal miners, but it could make a measurable contribution to efforts to advance clean energy and to address global warming in the United States and abroad. Building on its domestic agenda, the Obama administration laid the groundwork for an international commitment to address climate change that included both developed and developing countries. In November 2014, Obama and President Xi Jinping of China announced a "historic agreement," with the United States building on its domestic strategy, and China, for the first time, agreeing to reach peak greenhouse gas emissions by 2030 and increase clean energy to 20 percent of its primary energy consumption by 2030.[157] Those commitments paved the way for the most consequential climate agreement since the United Nations Framework Convention on Climate Change was adopted in 1992. The Paris climate accord, which was agreed upon in December 2015 and went into force in October 2016, included commitments from almost all the world's nations to greenhouse gas reductions, even as it put the greatest burden on developed countries to take the lead, since they had done the most, historically, to contribute to climate change. The agreement aimed to push the world onto a path that could hold the increase in global average temperatures to 2 degrees Celsius above preindustrial levels. If fully implemented, Obama suggested, "history may well judge it as a turning point for our planet."[158] Yet, Republicans were quick to point out, if the agreement was of such magnitude and import, then surely it represented a treaty requiring Senate approval. But, from start to finish, the Obama administration had guided international negotiations such that the final agreement was a nonbinding extension of provisions already agreed to by the United States when the Senate ratified the United Nations Framework Convention on Climate Change in 1992. That strategy meant the agreement did not need to go to the Senate for consent, but it also meant the commitment of the United States to the Paris climate accord was only as strong as that of president of the United States. As promised, within months of taking office in 2017, President Trump and EPA administrator Scott Pruitt initiated processes to scrap the Clean Power Plan and to withdraw the United States from the Paris climate accord, marking a wholesale retreat of American leadership in the international environmental arena.

Conclusion

The historian Michael Bess once described the rise of modern environmentalism as the advent of the "light-green society." In his words, when faced with the choice between environmental protection and economic growth, modern societies hedged their bets and chose both.[159] That uneasy bargain held in the United States: core environmental laws, such as the Clean Air Act, Clean Water Act, and the National Environmental Policy Act, had largely been implemented in ways that substantially improved the nation's public health and environment, but without posing a fundamental threat to economic growth or consumer choice. And when the United States had committed to international governance, it did so largely on its terms when global environmental protections built on well-established national interests.[160] But without strong domestic policy on energy conservation or greenhouse gas emissions, the U.S. commitment to addressing climate change was weak and uneven. It might be easy to pin the blame for policy inaction on the climate disinformation campaign and the well-financed, fossil fuel-led lobbying campaign—as many environmentalists did—but the real challenge is more fundamental. Addressing global warming meant not just reshaping the nation's energy economy, but challenging an American culture that celebrates independence, abundance, and exceptionalism. Even modest efforts to rein in the nation's energy consumption had run up hard against the limits of the light-green society—whether in the late 1970s, when President Carter first countenanced energy conservation, in the early 1990s, when President Clinton proposed an energy tax, or the 2010s, when President Obama championed a transition away from fossil fuels.

From this perspective, what was at issue in debates over an energy tax, cap and trade, or the Paris climate accord was never fundamentally about the science of climate change or the reach of Obama's executive powers. No matter how certain predictions were of increased temperatures, likelihood of droughts, or increases in storm surges—those predictions could not match more immediate realities: taking action to regulate greenhouse gas emissions would reshape the nation's economy in ways, large and small, that would reorder winners and losers in the near term. Farmers, coal miners, factory workers, and rural Americans—not to mention the executives who profited from their work—all knew such changes put their interests at risk. For increasing numbers of evangelical Christians, it was illogical that using a natural, God-given resource could destabilize God's creation. And other conservatives resisted what they perceived as liberal experts who seemed determined to subvert American interests in favor of global environmentalism. It was these people who gravitated to the kinds of arguments that Alex Epstein made in his 2014 book, *The Moral Case for Fossil Fuels*. "I think it's good that we use a lot of fossil fuels," wrote Epstein. Dismissing the concerns of climate scientists and environmentalists, Epstein explains: "I think the world would be a much better place if people used a lot more."[161] Compared to the complexities and uncertainties of climate science and the potential social impacts, Epstein's simplistic and intuitive energy equation resonated powerfully with conservative Americans' beliefs in the nation's providential destiny: abundant and cheap fossil fuels meant more economic growth, more security, and more individual freedom, especially at a time when the United States was, literally, awash in natural gas and petroleum as a result of the boom in fracking.

Despite these challenges, many times since the early 1990s, the nation had stood at the edge of a metaphorical chasm, rooted in the status quo, but peering across the void to a more sustainable future powered by renewable energy and more efficient technologies. In 1991 the Senate nearly passed Bryan's fuel economy bill; in 2009 the House passed the American Clean Energy and Security Act; and in 2016 Obama's EPA finalized the Clean Power Plan. For some Americans, this leap looked like the next iteration of the light-green society, where technologies such as wind turbines, solar panels, and electric cars could become a new engine for economic growth that promised abundant energy and a safer, healthier planet. But adopting policies that would hasten that transition required a collective leap of faith (even if in practice the transition away from fossil fuels would be gradual). Why make the leap, if you were the ones least likely to make it to the other side? Indeed, the prospect of that decision—or, far more troubling, having that decision made for you by liberal Democrats, climate scientists, and elites such as Al Gore or Barack Obama—left those most vulnerable to change scared, angry, and ready to defend themselves. Since the start of the Reagan administration, conservative Republicans had succeeded in turning such fears to their political advantage, as they advanced the Republican reversal. Indeed, these conservative Americans, many of whom lived in rural areas and struggling manufacturing zones of states such as Michigan, Wisconsin, and Pennsylvania, helped tip the Electoral College in Donald Trump's favor in November 2016. Trump turned this unease and angst to his "America First" vision; his goal was not energy independence, but American "energy dominance." That required "unleash[ing] America's $50 trillion in untapped shale, oil, and natural gas reserves, plus hundreds of years in clean coal reserves." Without even a nod to the potential environmental repercussions, he pronounced: "It's all upside: more jobs, more revenues, more wealth, higher wages, and lower energy prices."[162]

Trump's brusque and coarse political style bears little resemblance to the practiced folksiness of Ronald Reagan, yet in Trump's evocation of the abundance of American fossil fuel reserves, his faith in innovation (it is rarely just coal but usually "clean coal" for him), and his imagining of the prosperity that will result from exploiting fossil fuels, it is hard not to hear the echoes of Reagan's dismissal of environmentalists as crabbed "doom-cryers" and his celebration of American exceptionalism. It has been nearly forty years since the Republican reversal began, and in that time disdaining the warnings of environmentalists and exalting the economic blessings of cheap energy from the political stump (and, increasingly, from the pulpit) have become commonplace on the right. It has become hard to remember that when Reagan first campaigned for the White House, many in his party supported environmental protections, and indeed in its second term, the Reagan administration heeded the warnings of atmospheric scientists and supported the Montreal Protocol to protect the ozone layer. Conservatives now have little incentive to support initiatives to reduce carbon dioxide and other heat-trapping gases: neither their corporate donors nor evangelicals nor the struggling Rust Belt workers who voted for Trump in 2016 see any advantage to it. With conservatism seemingly on the rise, the prospect for effective reforms to stem climate change would seem bleak. But it is well to remember that conservatism was on the rise in the 1960s and 1970s, too, when the environmental movement first took the political scene by storm. Environmentalism helped blunt the rise of conservatism then; it remains to be seen whether Republicans will heed environmentalists again.

Conclusion

IN THE FIRST YEARS of George W. Bush's presidency, the Republican pollster and wordsmith Frank Luntz was at the apex of his influence. For a decade, Luntz had honed his talent for sensing the mood of voters and finding the right phrases to appeal to them. In 1992, Luntz's polling had helped fuel Patrick Buchanan's insurgent campaign for the Republican nomination. He later worked closely with Newt Gingrich in crafting the language of the Contract with America. During the 2000 campaign, Republicans struck a chord with voters by heeding Luntz's advice to substitute the term "death tax" for "estate tax" or "inheritance tax."[1] Later, in 2009, Luntz advised Republicans to cast President Obama's proposals to revamp the health care system as a "government takeover"—a description that stuck, even after the proposal was pared back. Among environmentalists, however, Luntz remains best known for his 2002 briefing book, issued to Republican congressional candidates, which included instructions on how to talk about Republican environmental policies with voters.

At the time, Luntz's recommendations were meant to help congressional Republicans weather the potential fallout from the Bush administration's environmental agenda—which had included efforts to block action on climate change, weaken the Clean Air Act, and open up the

Arctic National Wildlife Refuge for oil exploration—as the 2002 mid-term elections approached. In retrospect, his ideas signaled an important evolution in the Republican reversal. Luntz urged Republicans to talk about environmental issues not in terms of science or economics, but in terms of core conservative values. Luntz believed that approach could allay the concerns of mainstream voters who might otherwise be alarmed about the Republicans' environmental agenda. By the time conservatives voted Donald Trump into office, however, Luntz's strategy had taken on new significance. By harnessing anti-environmentalism to core conservative values—resource abundance, free market innovation, and American exceptionalism—Donald Trump turned opposition to environmental reform, especially action on climate change, from a potential liability into a potent rallying cry for his most ardent supporters.

In 2002, Luntz's work with focus groups had showed him that, as he put it, "the environment is probably the single issue on which Republicans in general—and President Bush in particular—are most vulnerable." Democrats had successfully created a narrative in which Republicans were "the bad guys," who did the bidding of "sinister companies drooling at the prospect of strip mining every picturesque mountain range, drilling for oil on every white sand beach, and clear cutting every green forest." In this narrative, "Republicans are depicted as cold, uncaring, ruthless, even downright anti-social." As Luntz put it, "No one wants polluted air and water, yet that's what a majority of Americans think Republicans stand for."[2] Indeed, in a series of polls taken in 2002, no more than 31 percent of Americans believed that the Republican Party did a good job of protecting the environment; in contrast, roughly 60 percent of voters ranked Democrats as doing a good job of protecting the environment.[3]

Luntz counseled Republicans to play down their longstanding, cherished argument that environmental regulations led to job losses, higher taxes, and slower economic growth. "Absolutely do not raise economic arguments first," Luntz advised. "It is the least effective approach among the people you most want to reach—average Americans."[4] Luntz recognized that most voters were more or less where they had been at the time of the first Earth Day in 1970: they believed that environmental quality was a manifest problem, and they were willing to sacrifice economic growth in the interest of protecting the environment. Indeed, at the time Luntz wrote his briefing book, the number of Republican voters who agreed with the statement that "the country should do whatever it takes to protect the environment" hovered at just under 70 percent.[5]

Because economic arguments generally failed to persuade voters on environmental issues, Luntz advised Republican candidates to refrain from economic claims and focus instead on values. "As Republicans," he wrote, "we have the moral and rhetorical high ground when we talk about values, like freedom, responsibility, and accountability." Rather than criticize laws that safeguard the environment, he urged Republicans to emphasize a faith in American technological progress to meet, for instance, the challenges of excessive carbon dioxide in the atmosphere. Candidates could circle back to economics by reminding voters that only a free market on its own could develop those technological innovations; "bureaucratic or international intervention and regulation" would stifle them. Democrats, he alleged, "are simply attempting to involve bureaucrats in areas in which the private sector is already making tremendous progress." Appealing to progress, the future, and the innovative potential of unfettered American industry allowed Republicans to "show the public that we are for something positive, not just against existing environmental regulations."

The environmental issue that most concerned voters in 2002, Luntz recognized, was global warming—as it was generally called at the time. In the first instance, to try to soothe voters' fears, Luntz proposed a change of vocabulary. He advised that "it's time for us to start talking about 'climate change' instead of global warming" because "'climate change' is less frightening." As one of the participants in a Luntz focus group put it, "climate change 'sounds like you're going from Pittsburgh to Fort Lauderdale.'" More importantly, Luntz advised Republicans to contest the science on which environmental regulations were based. "The scientific debate is closing [against us] but not yet closed," Luntz wrote. "There is still a window of opportunity to challenge the science." Luntz's work with focus groups led him to conclude in 2002 that voters were not yet sure that the planet was warming as a result of carbon dioxide in the atmosphere. "Should the public come to believe that the scientific issues are settled," he warned that "their views about global warming will change accordingly. Therefore, you need to continue to make the lack of scientific certainty a primary issue in the debate." In short, Luntz advised Republicans to tell a narrative about climate change that asserted that the science was inconclusive and the cost of action high. Luntz was unbothered by whether that narrative was true. He wrote, "A compelling story, even if factually inaccurate, can be more emotionally compelling than a dry recitation of the truth."[6]

By 2015, as a crowded field of Republicans began jockeying for the party's nomination for the presidency, virtually all Republicans had embraced Luntz's talking points on the environment—except Donald Trump. Of course, like the other candidates for the nomination, Trump expressed his disdain for climate science. Like the other candidates, Trump argued that environmental protection was best accomplished not through government regulation but private innovation. Like the other Republicans, he claimed that the United States was a nation built not on scarcity and restraint but abundance and growth. Yet while Luntz had advised Republicans to resort to expressions of these values out of a wariness of voters' support for environmental protection, Trump offered them in a spirit of defiance. More importantly, Trump often seemed to flout Luntz's advice to downplay claims that environmental protection cost jobs. Instead, Trump railed against the EPA, the Clean Air Act and Clean Water Act, and efforts to address climate change as bad not only for jobs but for U.S. economic competitiveness. Infusing his opposition to environmental laws with the "America First" populism that animated his campaign, Trump made the jobs-versus-the environment question one of us-versus-them: Did the United States want to protect the environment abroad or did it want clean air and water at home? Should the president act in the interest of people living in Pittsburgh or Paris? Did the United States want to protect American jobs or ship them overseas to countries where environmental regulations were lax? While Luntz had been concerned that the Republican opposition to environmental reform would be a political liability for conservatives in the early 2000s, Trump wrapped longstanding anti-environmental policy positions in a positive assertion of core conservative values to make a populist, conservative critique of climate change activism, federal environmental regulations, and the Obama administration one of the most powerful planks of his "America First" political agenda.

This strategy was on full display when Trump took the podium in the Rose Garden on June 1, 2017, to formally announce his intention to withdraw the United States from the Paris climate accord. "The bottom line is that the Paris Accord is very unfair, at the highest level, to the United States," he claimed. It would force the United States to put "under lock and key" the nation's abundant energy resources. It would undermine the nation's economy, lowering gross domestic product by $3 trillion and thwarting the creation of 6.5 million industrial jobs by 2040. And, it would oblige the United States to pay billions of dollars into the Green Climate Fund under the United Nations Framework Convention on Climate Change to support sustainable development and emission reductions in developing countries. In Trump's view, the restrictions and commitments the treaty placed on the United States added up to a "massive redistribution of United States wealth to other countries." And, despite the onerous terms, he argued that it yielded little benefit to the global climate. Trump cited research indicating that even if fully implemented, the Paris accord would reduce global temperatures only by 0.2 degrees Celsius by 2100: in Trump's words, a "Tiny, tiny amount." He explained that the terms of the Paris climate accord left him no other choice. "My job as President is to do everything within my power to give America a level playing field and to create the economic, regulatory, and tax structures that make America the most prosperous and productive country on Earth, and with the highest standard of living and the highest standard of environmental protection."[7]

Not surprisingly, when Trump withdrew from the Paris climate accord, the announcement drew ample praise from conservative interests. Murray Energy Corporation, whose chief executive, Robert Murray, had enthusiastically supported Trump during the campaign, praised the president for following through on his campaign promise and "supporting America's uncompromising values, saving coal jobs, and promoting low-cost, reliable electricity for Americans and the rest of the world."[8] When he justified his decision, Trump relied on research financed by the U.S. Chamber of Commerce (and questioned by other economists and scholars) that warned of severe economic impacts and job losses. This was the research "the Obama administration should have done in the first place," argued the chamber's representative.[9] Myron Ebell, the energy czar at the Competitive Enterprise Institute, described the agreement as enormously costly while yielding "zero benefits." It was the product of a "25-year misadventure in global governance."[10] The Heartland Institute echoed that point, describing Trump as the only world leader "willing to call a spade a spade." The Paris agreement was "less about saving the planet" than it was "about transferring wealth and ceding governing control from the U.S. to other nations of the world."[11] One prominent Christian evangelical leader, tapping into the belief that God-given fossil fuels were meant to lift the world out of poverty, praised the president for giving hope to the billions of people worldwide who otherwise would have been "trapped" in poverty and giving them the chance to enjoy "a clean, healthful, beautiful environment."[12]

In large part, Trump's environmental strategy followed the playbook of the Republican reversal that had begun with Ronald Reagan—it dismissed the urgency of environmental issues, disregarded scientific expertise, and downplayed the need for government regulation to protect public health and the environment. While the Reagan administration's anti-regulatory, pro-energy agenda marked the advent of the Republican reversal, considering the first year of the Trump administration highlights important ways that the Republican reversal and environmental politics have evolved since the 1980s. First, as Luntz recommended in the early 2000s, conservatives had succeeded in transforming the debate over environmental politics from one largely driven by science and expert information into a debate over culture and values. Second, in a way that Luntz, who viewed climate change as an issue on which Republicans were vulnerable, did not imagine, conservatives capitalized on the specter of global warming—and the regulations it might entail—as a unifying issue around which to organize Republican opposition, thereby obscuring fissures in conservative concerns about other environmental issues. Third, conservatives cultivated their administrative capabilities, wielding the powers and privileges of the executive branch to challenge the gains of environmentalists and their allies to an unprecedented degree. These changes have given conservative opposition to the nation's environmental laws and policy new consequence in the twenty-first century.

Before considering these ways in which the Republican reversal has evolved since the early 1980s, however, it is worth first remembering that the Trump administration's environmental agenda, even the decision to withdraw from the Paris climate accord, represented a departure from a longer history of Republican leadership on the environment. In the 1960s, 1970s, and, in some instances, into the 1980s, Republicans approached environmental issues with a sense of urgency, put faith in scientific research and scientific expertise, and embraced the necessary role of government in regulating business and industry to safeguard the environment and public health. In the mid-1980s, even the conservative Reagan administration, despite its opposition to environmental regulations generally, assumed global leadership on addressing the stratospheric ozone hole.

All of those qualities were absent when Trump announced his intent to withdraw the United States from the Paris climate accord. Despite the urgent need for action on global warming, his announcement entirely omitted the potential consequences of climate change—such as changing weather patterns, more intense storms, and sea level rise, all of which disproportionately disadvantage developing countries—focusing instead only on the near-term economic impacts in the United States. The announcement dismissed scientific expertise, not only by ignoring the voluminous research on the consequences of climate change, but by misrepresenting the one scientific study used to justify the decision. After Trump's announcement, researchers at the Massachusetts Institute of Technology, whose work Trump had misconstrued, issued a press release correcting the White House. Their analysis indicated that the Paris climate accord would reduce global temperatures by 0.2 degrees Celsius relative to the 2008 Copenhagen climate agreement, but would result in a full 1 degree Celsius reduction relative to no climate agreement. They considered the Paris agreement "an unprecedented and vital effort" in response "to the urgent threat of global climate change."[13] And, lastly, the announcement reflected Republicans' unwavering faith in the free market and opposition to government regulation. EPA Administrator Scott Pruitt praised Trump's decision, explaining that the United States already had a strong record of greenhouse gas reductions (largely as a result of the natural gas fracking boom that had displaced coal over the previous decade). Pruitt maintained that "this was accomplished largely by American innovation and technology from the private sector rather than government mandate."[14]

As Pruitt's praise suggests, one of the ways in which the Republican reversal has changed the most since the early 1980s is the success with which conservatives have reframed environmental debates to elevate conservative values at the expense of the role of science and expertise in environmental decision making. To understand how the politics of values changes policies, it is useful to think about what the political scientist Roger A. Pielke Jr. calls "tornado politics." In a thought exercise, Pielke posited a town meeting of fifty or so people interrupted by someone who bursts into the town hall and declares that a tornado is quickly approaching. In Pielke's telling, the assembled townspeople do what any group of rational people would do under such circumstances: they quickly seek information by turning on a radio to hear a meteorologist's report, and, if so advised, agree to take cover.[15] The environmental reforms passed just before and after the first Earth Day were an example of tornado politics: pollution of the air and water and the threat of species extinction had reached the point of crisis; politicians heeded the advice of scientists and took immediate and effective action. In the 1960s and 1970s, environmentalists experienced great success practicing tornado politics. They relied on scientists such as Rachel Carson, Barry Commoner, and Paul Ehrlich to raise the alarm about environmental quality—often in the wake of environmental catastrophes—and a host of landmark environmental laws quickly resulted.

Conservatives have become increasingly adept at practicing another form of politics, which Pielke describes as "abortion politics." Imagine, Pielke wrote, if someone had burst into that town meeting not to warn the townspeople of an oncoming tornado, but to ask the community to decide whether abortion should be legalized in the town. In such a circumstance, few people—no matter what their position on the issue— would expect either deference to experts or an immediate consensus. A debate over abortion—or, for that matter, the separation of church and state, the death penalty, or whether the government should provide universal health care—is primarily a debate over values. The views of experts are not excluded from such a debate. However, the view of an expert that, for instance, a fetus is not viable outside of the womb, or that there are inherent racial and class biases in the application of the death penalty, are not necessarily determinative to a person who believes that life begins at conception or that the death penalty is an appropriate punishment for a murder. In what Pielke calls "abortion politics," such expert information does not command the same kind of authority as that of a meteorologist during a storm. Instead, on such topics, for many people "science is just politics by another name."[16] And, in the tug-of-war of "abortion politics," scientific expertise has often been misrepresented or manipulated to align with particular values.

Conservatives have succeeded in transforming environmental politics from a process that was once largely driven by science and expert information into one that has become, increasingly, a messy and lengthy debate over values. Their success in doing so was evident in the aftermath of Trump's announcement on the Paris climate accord. Every time EPA Administrator Pruitt was asked about the science of climate change, he avoided the question, instead focusing on other values that justified Trump's decision. Of course, since the Trump administration had publicly questioned the basics of climate science, dissolved the EPA's scientific advisory boards, proposed funding cuts for climate science programs, and pulled scientific research on global warming from the EPA's website, those questions seemed to go right to the heart of the matter. But Trump withdrew from the Paris climate accord because it conflicted with what he considered to be fundamental American values: economic growth, energy abundance, and international "fairness."[17] Some in the Trump administration's highest ranks openly acknowledged the gravity of global warming, and the administration itself approved the release of a scientific report affirming the threat in November 2017. Nor did the Trump administration entirely close the door on future negotiations, provided the terms of a future climate agreement were more favorable to the United States. But for the Trump administration, the threat posed by global warming paled in comparison to more immediate concerns for American jobs, industry, and the economy. For Pruitt, prioritizing such values did not mean forgoing efforts to protect the environment. "We have nothing to be apologetic about as a country," he explained. U.S. greenhouse gas emissions had fallen to levels of the early 1990s, a result of innovation and technology, not commitments like Kyoto, Copenhagen, or Paris. In Pruitt's view, a United States that honored conservative values—the free market, innovation, and democracy—would ultimately lead with "action and not words."[18]

Shifting the political discourse from science to values is a critical component of the Republican reversal. In the first place, conservative Republicans such as Pruitt benefit simply by not discussing science—and thus not having to be confronted by scientific facts, such as rising global temperatures and sea levels and melting glaciers, that contradict their beliefs. Secondly, conservatives have managed to tie their environmental policy ideas to a set of values that many conservative Americans hold dear: a distrust of government, science, and secular intellectuals; and a faith in the market, technological innovation, and perhaps above all in a God who has provided a cornucopia of resources for human use. Such values are, by their very nature, difficult to challenge. Instead of advancing outright opposition to environmental regulations, Trump's appointees consistently emphasized the importance of conservative values in advancing their agency's core missions. Pruitt described his as a "back-to-basics" agenda for the Environmental Protection Agency that focused on air and water pollution and hazardous waste, as it had when Richard Nixon created it; Pruitt implied that Obama's EPA, overly concerned with global climate change, had ignored those issues. Ryan Zinke, Trump's secretary of the Interior, reached even further back into the past for his model of a Republican protector of the environment: he described himself as a conservationist in the mold of Teddy Roosevelt. Both emphasized that the "rule of law," which they believed had been disregarded by activist appointees in the Obama administration, would guide their work. They also highlighted the importance of paying greater attention to the "local voice"—whether it was farmers affected by the Clean Water Act or the ranchers affected by national monument designations—rather than assuming that Washington, D.C. knows best. And both argued that harnessing America's exceptional resources, both natural and entrepreneurial, was the best way to protect the environment at home and abroad.[19] "We as a nation do it better than anyone in the world in striking the balance between growing jobs and our economy—while also being a good steward of our environment," argued Pruitt.[20]

The disproportionate attention the Trump administration gave to issues of climate change and energy policy points to the second way that the Republican reversal has evolved since the 1980s: opposing action on climate change has become a galvanizing force for conservative activists. Indeed, during the 2016 campaign, Trump intuited that a pro-energy strategy that dismissed the risks climate change posed had particular power to draw a wide-range of conservative interests, including the fossil fuel industry, farmers, blue-collar workers, libertarians, and anti-globalists to his "America First" agenda. When it came to other environmental issues, such as toxic waste, air pollution, or biodiversity, Trump had vanishingly little to say either on the campaign trail or once in office. What Luntz worried would be a political liability for Republicans, Trump turned to his advantage. He invigorated a strand of evangelical opposition to climate change which sees belief in climate change as the province of secular leftists who disregard the beauty and divinity of God's creation. He engaged farmers, blue-collar workers, and rural voters—and the often Republican elected officials who represent them—who see in restrictions on greenhouse gas emissions and international agreements like the Paris climate accord policies that raise the cost of gasoline, destroy American jobs, and put the interests of other countries before those of the United States. He appealed to conservative isolationists who see in international agreements such as the Paris climate accord a plot to subject the United States to global governance under the auspices of the United Nations. And he appealed to free market optimists who believe that an unfettered market that encourages private investment and innovation is the most realistic and efficient way to solve even the largest-scale global problems.

Despite the breadth of environmental actions the Obama administration pursued, from the creation of national monuments to reforms of the Clean Water Act's implementation, what inflamed the conservatives most consistently was Obama's approach to energy policy and climate change. In their view, the administration's climate agenda was predicated on biased scientific and economic analyses that downplayed the economic costs and exaggerated the environmental benefits of climate action. The success of the Paris climate accord rested, in no small part, on the Obama administration's effort to develop the Clean Power Plan through administrative rulemaking—a strategy that conservatives believed was contrary to the Clean Air Act (an argument that gained credence when the Supreme Court stayed the rule in March 2016). Most fundamentally, the Obama administration had flagrantly ignored the United States Constitution by committing to an international agreement—especially one with such far-reaching implications for the nation's economy and its standing in the world—without submitting it for consent and ratification in the Senate.[21] In short, they believed, the Obama administration had repeatedly flouted the rule of law to advance an unpatriotic, anti-capitalist, job-killing regulatory boondoggle, all premised on the dubious notion that human activities were driving global warming.[22]

The Obama administration's aggressive campaign to pursue its environmental agenda through executive action points to a third way in which the Republican reversal has evolved since the 1980s: to focus on administrative action. More so than at earlier moments of Republican power, the Trump administration and its allies have focused their reform agenda almost entirely on administrative strategies to roll back existing environmental regulations. This is notable, considering that Republicans held majorities in both the House and Senate in the 115th Congress, offering a rare opportunity to advance major reforms of the nation's core environmental statutes, such as the National Environmental Policy Act, Endangered Species Act, and Clean Air Act without the threat of a presidential veto. But such legislative initiatives would have tested the strength and unity of the Republican Party's commitment to an anti-environmental agenda. Instead, the Trump administration invested its energy in working through "alternative policymaking pathways" to weaken the implementation of existing environmental laws. As scholars have argued, such strategies had gained importance since the 1990s, as environmental reform was stymied by legislative gridlock in Congress—a trend exemplified by the Obama administration's efforts to protect the public lands using the Antiquities

Act of 1906 or develop limits on greenhouse gas emissions using the Clean Air Act of 1970. Although conservatives have pursued such strategies too, their efforts have more often been blocked in the courts. Thus, on balance, such alternative policymaking pathways have often worked to the advantage of environmentalists, resulting in a slow process of regulatory reform that has often aligned with environmentalists' goals. This trend is what the political scientists Christopher Klyza and David Sousa describe as "green drift."[23] But such administrative gains largely share the same vulnerability: although such reversals must follow the rule of law and due process, they are far more vulnerable to reversal by future administrations than congressional action. This reality was on full display at the start of the Trump administration. Although Trump may have rallied conservative support by focusing on climate change, he challenged the nation's environmental and public health policies on all fronts.

For example, although Pruitt described his agenda for the EPA as "back to basics," the first law he took a swipe at was the Clean Water Act. Clean water regulations had become bogged down in uncertainty, due to conflicting agency rules and legal decisions, that left farmers, developers, and state regulators confused as to the scope of the Clean Water Act's regulations. Was a seasonal wetland subject to regulation? What about an irrigation ditch? What about a small tributary distant from a navigable waterway? To resolve such uncertainties, the Obama administration undertook a two-year rulemaking process that resulted in the Waters of the United States rule in 2015, which provided new guidance for which waters fell under the jurisdiction of the Clean Water Act. Even though the rule grandfathered in many agricultural activities—a significant loophole that hampered the efforts to address nonpoint source pollution—the American Farm Bureau and its allies organized in protest.[24] In their view, the rule provided "No clarity, no certainty, no limits on agency power."[25] Critics argued the EPA had used trumped-up scientific analysis and technical assessments to ignore the plain meaning of the Clean Water Act and local concerns. And then the agency went further, engaging in what a government auditor described as illegal "covert propaganda" when it launched a social media campaign to draw attention to the proposed rule—an effort the auditors determined went beyond government outreach to political advocacy.[26]

Shortly after the Waters of the United States rule went into effect, it was stayed by a federal court in October 2015 in response to suits filed by states (including one filed by Oklahoma when Scott Pruitt served the state as attorney general), agricultural interests, and other stakeholders. In February 2017, Trump issued an executive order directing the EPA to rewrite the rule. After the signing ceremony, Pruitt proceeded directly to an advocacy meeting of the American Farm Bureau Federation, where news of the executive order drew rousing applause from the group that had rallied most effectively in opposition to the rule, using the hashtag #ditchtherule.[27] Upon the decision, Breitbart News headlined that the decision "frees 247 million acres of farmland" from unnecessary regulatory oversight.[28] Kansas governor Sam Brownback praised the decision, arguing that the Obama "Clean Water Rule was another example of bureaucrats in Washington, D.C. trying to run Kansas farms and ranches."[29] In its decision, the Trump administration sidestepped the scientific analysis underlying the 2015 rule, recommending instead that the EPA reinstate a Reagan-era regulation developed in 1986.[30]

Meanwhile, Trump's Department of the Interior signaled the administration's intent to put energy development before endangered species and ecosystem protection. A significant threat to oil and gas development in the American West was the possibility that the sage grouse—a chicken-like bird that inhabited the western sagebrush—might be placed on the endangered species list.[31] If it were so designated, the consequences could rival that of the listing of the spotted owl, which vastly expanded protection of Pacific Northwest forests in the 1990s, but also curbed the region's logging industry. Like the spotted owl, the sage grouse is an important indicator species, signaling the ecological health of large expanses of western land. The threat of listing the species, however, brought western states, oil and gas companies, ranchers, scientists, conservationists, and others to the negotiating table in hopes that already existing programs and future plans could strike a balance between resource extraction and ecosystem protection that could avert an endangered species listing. That collaborative process led to a decision by the Obama administration that the sage grouse did not warrant listing, in light of the collaborative land-use planning and restoration efforts underway at the local and state level, as codified in sage grouse conservation plans, which were approved in 2015. Over the objections of western governors, both Republican and Democrat, Interior Secretary Ryan Zinke signaled his intent to review those plans in June 2017. Zinke made clear that as the Department of the Interior explored "possible plan modifications, it will also consider local economic growth and job creation."[32] That approach should have come as little surprise. In 2016, before joining the Trump administration, Zinke described "false tears for the sage grouse" as a way to "arbitrarily restrict energy exploration activities." In his view, the federal government was more interested in how much land they could control, not the number of birds they could protect.[33] Based on a preliminary review, Zinke decided to withdraw the 2015 plans in October 2017 and to rewrite them, giving states more say. The group that reacted most enthusiastically was the mining industry. The National Mining Association praised the Department of the Interior for reversing "a damaging and unnecessary ban" that would have "barred mining on 10 million acres of mineral-rich lands, further increasing our import dependence."[34]

Trump appointees drawn from industries and their trade groups oversaw many such rollbacks. A coal lobbyist with strong ties to Murray Energy Corporation, a key Trump supporter, became the EPA's deputy administrator. Another coal consultant was appointed to direct the Office of Surface Mining Reclamation and Enforcement. An executive with the chemical industry's trade group, the American Chemistry Council, was appointed to a key post overseeing chemical safety at the EPA. That latter decision raised eyebrows within the public health community because the appointee, Nancy Beck, had a long history of challenging federal environmental regulatory policy, starting her work in the White House regulatory oversight office during George W. Bush's administration, before working at the American Chemistry Council. She earned a reputation as a skeptic by questioning scientific studies and risk assessments that underpinned regulations for lead paint exposure, safe drinking water, and chemicals used in semiconductor manufacturing and dry cleaning. As the *New York Times* reported, Beck, who had earned a doctorate in environmental health, "comes from a camp—firmly backed by the chemical industry—that says the government too often directs burdensome rules at what she has called 'phantom risks.'"[35] She had arrived at a pivotal moment in 2017, as the EPA finalized rules drafted by the Obama administration to implement the Chemical Safety for the Twenty-First Century Act of 2016. That law, a much-needed update to the Toxic Substances Control Act of 1976, gave the agency new powers to oversee common chemicals used in products such as paint, flame retardants, and nonstick coatings on cookware. But in a key move, the EPA included language in the final rule that permitted the agency to "exclude certain activities that EPA has determined to be conditions of use," thereby giving the agency the discretion to ignore some exposure pathways for risky chemicals—for instance, those that were not consistent with manufacturer guidelines.[36] The change closely followed the recommendations of the chemical industry, which worried the agency would go on "fishing" expeditions for unlikely uses.[37] That the agency sided with industry was no surprise, since Beck personally oversaw the final revisions of the rule.

The Trump administration's anti-environmental agenda marked the culmination of a Republican reversal that began in the early 1980s. As the historian Christopher Sellers has observed of Pruitt's EPA, "in its overt hostility and in the pressures it has brought to bear, this assault has surpassed" even that of the start of the Reagan administration, "long recognized as the darkest years in the [EPA's] history."[38] Much the same could be said of the Department of the Interior, where Secretary Zinke prioritized expanding access to the nation's public lands for oil and gas development, including in the Arctic, in the sagebrush country of the American West, and in much of the nation's coastal waters. Although Zinke has championed his embrace of Theodore Roosevelt's conservative ethic, his leadership more often aligned with Trump's vision for American energy dominance. It was on his recommendation that Trump dramatically reduced the national monuments that Presidents Obama and Clinton had established in Utah, shrinking Bears Ears by 85 percent and Grand Staircase-Escalante by nearly 50 percent. "Some people think that the natural resources of Utah should be controlled by a small handful of very distant bureaucrats located in Washington," President Trump trumpeted at the Utah state capitol as he announced his decision. "And guess what? They're wrong." That statement ignored the 2.8

million public comments the Department of the Interior received in 2017, which the administration itself described as "overwhelmingly in favor of maintaining existing monuments."[39] It was also emblematic of the administration's disregard for matters of environmental justice: local Native Americans had urged the president to maintain the monuments, which protected land and artifacts sacred to local tribes.[40] What had seemed to concern the administration most in its deliberations was re-drawing the boundaries to exclude potential oil and gas, coal, or ura-nium resources.[41]

The consequences of this most recent manifestation of the Republican reversal for American environmental policy are by turns immediate, un-certain, and unsurprising. In some respects, the consequences are im-mediate, such as the United States abdication of its leadership role in global efforts to address climate change, the expanded availability of public lands open for energy development, the weakening of the EPA's environmental justice program, and the loss of career staffers and civil servants at the EPA and Department of the Interior. Indeed, the morale in both agencies plummeted in 2017, as longtime staffers saw their ad-vice and guidance ignored, budgets cut, and their jobs placed in jeop-ardy. As one EPA staffer explained in May 2017, "I think there's a gen-eral consensus among the career people that at bottom," Pruitt and the Trump administration are, "basically trying to destroy the place."[42] In August 2017, Zinke questioned the loyalty of 30 percent of the Depart-ment of the Interior's staff.[43]

But, in other respects, the consequences of the Trump administra-tion's agenda were highly uncertain. As was the case with earlier mo-ments of Republican reversal, the Trump administration's environ-mental reform agenda faces sharp opposition, among environmentalists, Democrats, and even some Republicans. Indeed, one of the most impor-tant bulwarks against the Republican reversal historically has been moderate Republicans. Although the ranks of moderates have dwindled, Republican concern for environmental programs has not disappeared entirely, as was evident during debates over the Trump administration's proposed budgets for the Environmental Protection Agency and the De-partment of the Interior.[44] The Trump administration proposed slashing the Environmental Protection Agency's budget by 31 percent and laying off 3,500 employees, providing the agency with only the resources it needed to "focus on its core statutory work and the appropriate federal role in protecting human health and the environment."[45] It proposed reducing the Interior Department's budget by 13 percent, while shifting some funding from environmental protection programs toward energy production. Yet, during hearings on the proposed budgets, the most surprising objections came from Republicans. Although Republicans raised few concerns with the administration's approach to climate change or energy policy, they raised numerous concerns about cuts to programs that safeguarded clean air, water, and environmental cleanup and restoration: an Ohio Republican defended the Great Lakes Restoration Initiative, an Idaho Republican defended funding for the Office of Pesticide Programs, a California Republican championed a grant program for communities fighting smog, a New Jersey Republican defended the agency's Superfund program. Ultimately, Congress passed a budget that maintained basic EPA funding at the same level as 2017, but included increases for specific programs such as clean water infrastructure and toxic waste site cleanup, and increased overall Interior funding by 6 percent.[46] While Republicans have largely been united in their disregard for climate change and support for expanding domestic energy production (another budget bill paved the way for opening the Arctic Refuge for drilling), the debate over the 2018 budget makes clear that unity about reforming or cutting programs that protect public health and environmental quality cannot be taken for granted, even among Republicans.

As a reporter from *Wired Magazine* astutely observed, while the Trump administration may have rolled into Washington, D.C., expecting to advance a "blitzkrieg on environmental regulations" during his first year, what he got was "trench warfare."[47] That portended yet more uncertainty for Trump's agenda. Environmental organizations and the states quickly signaled their intention to follow suit and challenge the Trump administration's environmental regulatory initiatives using every legal tool at their disposal, including the procedural steps required by laws such as the Administrative Procedures Act and substantive requirements required by federal environmental laws. In June, environmentalists, led by the Natural Resources Defense Council, forced the EPA to reinstate an Obama-era regulation aimed at reducing mercury pollution that the EPA had withdrawn in January. The story was much the same with the EPA's efforts to hold up implementation of an Obama-era rule to restrict methane emissions from new oil and gas wells—the EPA was overturned in July and again, after an appeal, in August. Other rules, such as the administration's weakening of the chemical safety regulations, and executive actions, such as modifying national monuments, were also subject to immediate legal challenge. As Jonathan Adler, a law professor at Case Western Reserve University School of Law, told the *New York Times,* "If I were in this administration, this should be seen as a warning sign. The message is clear: Guys, we have a problem here. We are trying to do stuff that is hard and we are not [dotting our] i's and crossing our t's."[48] Some of the uncertainty also stemmed from within the Trump administration itself. Just how far would it go to advance its agenda? Would it revisit the EPA's 2009 endangerment finding that underpinned federal regulation of greenhouse gas emissions? Would it seek legislative reforms to explicitly bar regulating carbon dioxide under the Clean Air Act? Would it withdraw the United States from the 1992 United Nations Framework Convention on Climate Change—a far more aggressive stance than just withdrawing from the Paris climate accord? Some on the conservative right saw in the Trump administration's first year small steps toward more far-reaching and aggressive policy reversals.[49]

In one troubling respect, however, the Trump administration and the Republican-controlled 115th Congress ushered in little change at all. It seems highly unlikely that there will be any progressive legislation to reform existing environmental laws or pass new laws to address the array of environmental challenges the United States and the world face in the coming years. As Judith Layzer argues in *Open for Business,* her analysis of conservative opposition to environmental reform, this is the most troublesome consequence of what we describe as the Republican reversal. Even if the Trump administration is but an interlude in a broader trend toward "green drift," as was largely the case with previous moments of Republican power such as the Contract with America in the mid-1990s or George W. Bush's administration in the early 2000s, that remains a cause for concern. For, no matter how strong the current of green drift is, no amount of administrative rulemakings, executive actions, state initiatives, or favorable judicial rulings can keep pace with the nation's environmental challenges—indeed, they have not to date. That is to say, the golden era environmental laws of the 1970s cannot be expected to serve as the foundation for an effective response to the scope and scale of the nation's mounting environmental challenges. At a moment when such legislative action is most needed—to address climate change by taxing carbon, to reform the consumer products industry by requiring product stewardship, or to ensure environmental equity by mandating that environmental justice be a primary consideration in the nation's core environmental laws—they are almost politically unimaginable.

Yet such action is what many Americans want. Support for environmental protection remains strong. Since 1994, Pew reports that the number of respondents who agree with the statement that "the country should do whatever it takes to protect the environment" has never been lower than 71 percent.[50] Yet while Americans support environmental action, they disagree about what actions to take. The picture is a bit more muddled if Americans are asked to prioritize environmental quality and economic growth. The Gallup polling organization has asked that question since the mid-1980s. Those who put the environment first has fallen from a high of 71 percent in the early 1990s to 56 percent in 2017, but importantly, at only one point in the last thirty years—in the aftermath of the 2008 economic collapse—did more Americans prioritize economic growth. As political scientists have long observed, however, Americans rarely put environmental issues at the top of their list of concerns when they cast their ballots. But there have been moments in American political history when environmental concerns have loomed large at the polls. One such moment was the early 1970s, when in the aftermath of Earth Day, environmental concerns seized national attention. Another such moment was 1996, when voters responded with alarm to the Republican reversal during Newt Gingrich's Contract with America. And, at the end of Donald Trump's first year in office, it is evident that his administration's environmental agenda puts him at odds with the vast majority of the American people. In a September 2017 poll that included a battery of policy issues, such as health care, race relations, North Korea, immigration, the economy, and the environment and global warming, only 24 percent of respondents approved of Trump's handling of the environment and climate change—the lowest approval rating the administration received in any category.[51] An October 2017 poll reported that seven in ten Americans believed that global warming was happening. Even Frank Luntz, the pollster who once advised Republicans to spin climate science irrespective of the truth, had a change of heart on the issue of global warming. Not only did he come to believe the scientists, he recognized that most Americans believed them, too.[52] In 2010, Luntz, joined by Fred Krupp, the president of the Environmental Defense Fund, released a poll showing that "A clear majority of Americans believe climate change is happening." Luntz said: "People are much more interested in seeing solutions than watching yet another partisan political argument."[53] That statement is as true now as it was then. One can only hope that conservative Republicans will once again heed Luntz's advice.

NOTES

ACKNOWLEDGMENTS

INDEX

Notes

Introduction

1. For the transcript of the interview, see "Donald Trump Talks Taxes, Trade, 9 / 11 and Why He Takes Personal Shots at Political Rivals," *Fox News,* October 18, 2015, http://www.foxnews.com/transcript/2015/10/18/donald -trump-talks-taxes-trade-11-and-why-takes-personal-shots-at-political.html.
2. Oliver Milman, "Republican Candidates' Calls to Scrap EPA Met with Skepticism by Experts," *The Guardian,* February 26, 2016.
3. Louis Jacobson, "Yes, Donald Trump Did Call Climate Change a Chinese Hoax," *PolitiFact,* June 3, 2016, http://www.politifact.com/truth-o-meter /statements/2016/jun/03/hillary-clinton/yes-donald-trump-did-call-climate -change-chinese-h/.
4. "No Climate Tax Pledge," accessed November 7, 2017, NoClimateTax.com.
5. Lee Fang, "Member of Congressional Science Committee: Global Warming a 'Fraud' to 'Create Global Government,'" *The Nation,* August 10, 2013.
6. Jessica Bryce Young, "Florida Congressman Matt Gaetz Files Bill to 'Perma- nently Abolish' the EPA," *Orlando Weekly,* February 1, 2017, http://www .orlandoweekly.com/Blogs/archives/2017/02/01/florida-congressman-matt -gaetz-files-suit-to-permanently-abolish-the-epa; Justin Worland, "No, President Trump Isn't Going to Eliminate the EPA. But He Might Do This," *Time,* February 16, 2017.
7. "Pruitt v. EPA: 14 Challenges of EPA Rules by the Oklahoma Attorney General," *New York Times,* January 14, 2017, sec. U.S., https://www.nytimes .com/interactive/2017/01/14/us/politics/document-Pruitt-v-EPA-a -Compilation-of-Oklahoma-14.html.

8. Andrew Miller, Southern Company, as quoted in "War on the EPA," PBS Frontline, October 11, 2017, https://www.pbs.org/wgbh/frontline/film/war-on -the-epa/transcript/.

9. See League of Conservation Voters, "National Environmental Scorecard," http://scorecard.lcv.org/moc/ryan-zinke.

10. "Press Briefing by Secretary of Interior Ryan Zinke on the Executive Order to Review the Designations under the Antiquities Act," The White House, April 25, 2017, https://www.whitehouse.gov/briefings-statements/press -briefing-secretary-interior-ryan-zinke-executive-order-review-designations -antiquities-act-042517/.

11. Bill Johnson, "Bill Johnson Leads House Effort to Protect Coal Jobs by Overturning Ill-Advised 'Stream Protection Rule,'" January 30, 2017, https://billjohnson.house.gov/news/documentsingle.aspx?DocumentID =399135.

12. "Remarks by President Trump at Signing of Executive Order to Create Energy Independence," The White House, March 28, 2017, https://www.whitehouse .gov/the-press-office/2017/03/28/remarks-president-trump-signing-executive -order-create-energy.

13. "Statement by President Trump on the Paris Climate Accord," The White House, June 1, 2017, https://www.whitehouse.gov/the-press-office/2017/06/01 /statement-president-trump-paris-climate-accord.

14. Christina Wolbrecht, *The Politics of Women's Rights: Parties, Positions, and Change* (Princeton, NJ: Princeton University Press, 2000), 3.

15. "Republican Party Platform of 1972," August 21, 1972, The American Presidency Project, http://www.presidency.ucsb.edu/ws/?pid=25842.

16. Committee on Arrangements for the 2016 Republican National Convention, "Republican Platform 2016," http://www.presidency.ucsb.edu/papers_pdf /117718.pdf.

17. Studies that investigate the relationship between Republicans and the environment include J. Brooks Flippen, *Nixon and the Environment* (Albuquerque: University of New Mexico Press, 2000); J. Brooks Flippen, *Conservative Conservationist: Russell E. Train and the Emergence of American Environmentalism* (Baton Rouge: Louisiana State University Press, 2006); Thomas G. Smith, *Green Republican: John Saylor and the Preservation of America's Wilderness* (Pittsburgh: University of Pittsburgh Press, 2006); Judith Layzer, *Open for Business: Conservatives' Opposition to Environmental Regulation* (Cambridge, MA: MIT Press, 2012); Brian Drake, *Loving Nature, Fearing the State: Environmentalism and Antigovernment Politics before Reagan* (Seattle: University of Washington Press, 2013); Paul Sabin, *The Bet: Paul Ehrlich, Julian Simon, and Our Gamble over Earth's Future* (New Haven, CT: Yale University Press, 2013). Excellent studies of conservatism include Lisa McGirr, *Suburban Warriors: The Origins of the New American Right* (Princeton, NJ: Princeton University Press, 2001);

Donald T. Critchlow, *The Conservative Ascendancy: How the GOP Right Made Political History* (Cambridge, MA: Harvard University Press, 2007); David Farber, *The Rise and Fall of Modern American Conservatism: A Short History* (Princeton, NJ: Princeton University Press, 2010); Kim Phillips-Fein, *Invisible Hands: The Businessmen's Crusade against the New Deal* (New York: Norton, 2010); Darren Dochuk, *From Bible Belt to Sunbelt: Plain-Folk Religion, Grassroots Politics, and the Rise of Evangelical Conservatism* (New York: Norton, 2011); Kevin M. Kruse, *One Nation under God: How Corporate America Invented Christian America* (New York: Basic Books, 2016).

18. See, for instance, Thomas Dunlap, *DDT: Scientists, Citizens, and Public Policy* (Princeton, NJ: Princeton University Press, 1981); Thomas Dunlap, *Saving America's Wildlife: Ecology and the American Mind, 1850–1990*, 3rd ed. (Princeton, NJ: Princeton University Press, 1988); Kirkpatrick Sale, *The Green Revolution: The American Environmental Movement, 1962–1992* (New York: Hill & Wang, 1993); Mark W. T. Harvey, *A Symbol of Wilderness: Echo Park and the American Conservation Movement* (Seattle: University of Washington Press, 1994); Mark Hamilton Lytle, *The Gentle Subversive: Rachel Carson,* Silent Spring, *and the Rise of the Environmental Movement* (New York: Oxford University Press, 2007); Thomas Robertson, *The Malthusian Moment: Global Population Growth and the Birth of American Environmentalism* (New Brunswick, NJ: Rutgers University Press, 2012); Christopher Sellers, *Crabgrass Crucible: Suburban Nature and the Rise of Environmentalism in Twentieth-Century America* (Chapel Hill: University of North Carolina Press, 2012); Adam Rome, *The Genius of Earth Day: How a 1970 Teach-In Unexpectedly Made the First Green Generation* (New York: Hill & Wang, 2013).

19. Roger A. Pielke Jr., "Forests, Tornadoes, and Abortion: Thinking about Science. Politics, and Policy," in *Forest Futures: Science, Politics, and Policy for the Next Century,* ed. Karen A. Arabas and Joe Bowersox (Lanham, MD: Rowman & Littlefield, 2004), 145. See also Roger A. Pielke Jr., *The Honest Broker: Making Sense of Science in Policy and Politics* (Cambridge: Cambridge University Press, 2007), 40–41.

20. On the Republican cornucopian vision, see Sabin, *The Bet.*

21. Helene von Damm, *Sincerely, Ronald Reagan* (Ottawa, IL: Green Hill, 1976), 156–158.

22. Critchlow, *The Conservative Ascendancy.*

23. Naomi Oreskes and Erik M. Conway, *Merchants of Doubt: How a Handful of Scientists Obscured the Truth on Issues from Tobacco Smoke to Global Warming* (New York: Bloomsbury, 2010).

24. Kim Phillips-Fein and Julian E. Zelizer, "Introduction," in *What's Good for Business: Business and American Politics since World War II* (New York: Oxford University Press, 2012), 9.

25. Jefferson Decker, *The Other Rights Revolution: Conservative Lawyers and the Remaking of American Government* (New York: Oxford University Press, 2016).

26. Phillips-Fein, *Invisible Hands*, 205.

27. On the "public interest right," see Decker, *The Other Rights Revolution*.

28. James Morton Turner, *The Promise of Wilderness: American Environmental Politics since 1964* (Seattle: University of Washington Press, 2012); Jane Mayer, *Dark Money: The Hidden History of the Billionaires behind the Rise of the Radical Right* (New York: Anchor, 2016).

29. Dochuk, "Moving Mountains, 72–90. See also Laurel Kearns, "Noah's Ark Goes to Washington: A Profile of Evangelical Environmentalism," *Social Compass* 44, no. 3 (September 1997): 349–366; Katharine K. Wilkinson, *Between God and Green: How Evangelicals Are Cultivating a Middle Ground on Climate Change* (New York: Oxford University Press, 2012); Joseph D. Witt, *Religion and Resistance in Appalachia: Faith and the Fight against Mountaintop Removal Coal Mining* (Lexington: University Press of Kentucky, 2016).

30. Sale, *The Green Revolution*, 49; Rome, *The Genius of Earth Day*.

31. U.S. Environmental Protection Agency, "Benefits and Costs of the Clean Air Act 1990–2020, the Second Prospective Study," updated April 2011, https://www.epa.gov/clean-air-act-overview/benefits-and-costs-clean-air-act -1990-2020-second-prospective-study?; David A. Keiser and Joseph S. Shapiro, "Consequences of the Clean Water Act and the Demand for Water Quality" (working paper, Yale University, June 2016), http://www.econ.yale .edu/~js2755/CleanWaterAct_KeiserShapiro.pdf.

32. Peter Huber, *Hard Green: Saving the Environment from the Environmentalists: A Conservative Manifesto* (New York: Basic Books, 2000).

33. One of the few recent exceptions to this state of legislative gridlock is the passage of the Chemical Safety Act of 2016, which updated the Toxic Substances Control Act of 1976.

34. Christopher McGrory Klyza and David J. Sousa, *American Environmental Policy: Beyond Gridlock,* rev. ed. (Cambridge, MA: MIT Press, 2013).

1. Conservatives before and after Earth Day

1. Mark Harvey, *A Symbol of Wilderness: Echo Park and the American Conservation Movement* (Seattle: University of Washington Press, 2000). Hal K. Rothman, *The Greening of a Nation? Environmentalism in the United States since 1945* (Fort Worth, TX: Harcourt Brace, 1998), is a critical assessment of environmentalism in which Rothman argues that Echo Park was an important early moment in defining the movement.

2. Rachel Carson, *Silent Spring* (Boston: Houghton Mifflin, 1962). For Carson, see Linda Lear, *Rachel Carson: Witness for Nature* (New York: Henry Holt, 1997); Mark Lytle, *The Gentle Subversive: Rachel Carson, Silent Spring, and the Rise of*

Environmentalism (New York: Oxford University Press, 2007). Kirkpatrick Sale, *The Green Revolution: The American Environmental Movement, 1962–1992* (New York: Hill & Wang, 1993), begins his account with *Silent Spring*.

3. For Earth Day, see Adam Rome, *The Genius of Earth Day: How a 1970 Teach-In Unexpectedly Made the First Green Generation* (New York: Hill & Wang, 2014).

4. Arthur F. McEvoy, "Environmental Law and the Collapse of New Deal Constitutionalism," *Akron Law Review* 46 (2013): 881–908.

5. James Morton Turner, *The Promise of Wilderness: American Environmental Politics since 1964* (Seattle: University of Washington Press, 2012), 17–42.

6. Andrew C. Isenberg, *Mining California: An Ecological History* (New York: Hill & Wang, 2005), 13–15.

7. Roderick Nash, *Wilderness and the American Mind,* 4th ed. (New Haven: Yale University Press, 2001), 106–110, 133; Samuel P. Hays, *Conservation and the Gospel of Efficiency: The Progressive Conservation Movement, 1890–1920* (Cambridge, MA: Harvard University Press, 1959). George W. Bush approached Roosevelt's record and Barack Obama exceeded it if the protection of the Papahanaumokuakea Marine National Monument is included.

8. Andrew Needham, *Power Lines: Phoenix and the Making of the Modern Southwest* (Princeton, NJ: Princeton University Press, 2016), 99–102.

9. "Goldwater's 1964 Acceptance Speech," *Washington Post* online, 1998, http://www.washingtonpost.com/wp-srv/politics/daily/may98 /goldwaterspeech.htm.

10. See, for instance, John C. Skipper, *The 1964 Republican Convention: Barry Goldwater and the Beginning of the Conservative Movement* (Jefferson, NC: McFarland, 2016). John A. Andrew III, *The Other Side of the Sixties: Young Americans for Freedom and the Rise of Conservative Politics* (New Brunswick, NJ: Rutgers University Press, 1997), argues that Goldwater's 1964 campaign reinvigorated what had been a struggling and marginalized conservative movement.

11. William E. Leuchtenberg, *Franklin D. Roosevelt and the New Deal, 1932–1940* (New York: Harper & Row, 1963), 89, 93; Otis L. Graham Jr., "The Broker State," *Wilson Quarterly* 8 (Winter 1984): 86–97; Anthony J. Badger, *The New Deal: The Depression Years, 1933–1940* (New York: Hill & Wang, 1989), 2–4.

12. *The Papers of Robert A. Taft,* vol. 1, *1889–1938,* ed. Clarence E. Wunderlin Jr. (Kent, OH: Kent State University Press, 1997), 554; quoted in David Farber, *The Rise and Fall of Modern American Conservatism* (Princeton, NJ: Princeton University Press, 2010), 16.

13. William M. Emmons III, "Franklin D. Roosevelt, Electric Utilities, and the Power of Concentration," *Journal of Economic History* 53 (December 1993): 880–907. For the history of one electric company in the West, see Needham, *Power Lines.*

14. Kim Phillips-Fein, *Invisible Hands: The Businessmen's Crusade against the New Deal* (New York: Norton, 2009), 3–25.

15. For the influence of European ideas on American conservatism, see Donald T. Critchlow, *The Conservative Ascendancy: How the GOP Right Made Political History* (Cambridge, MA: Harvard University Press, 2007), 6–40.

16. Friedrich Hayek, *The Road to Serfdom,* ed. Bruce Caldwell (Chicago: University of Chicago Press, 2007), 124–133.

17. For an excellent analysis of Hayek, see Phillips-Fein, *Invisible Hands,* 32–52.

18. Phillips-Fein, *Invisible Hands,* 68–77.

19. Kevin M. Kruse, *One Nation under God: How Corporate America Invented Christian America* (New York: Basic Books, 2016), 3–11.

20. See Darren Dochuk, *From Bible Belt to Sun Belt: Plain-Folk Religion, Grassroots Politics, and the Rise of Evangelical Conservatism* (New York: Norton, 2011), 223–256.

21. Barry Goldwater, *The Conscience of a Conservative* (Shepherdsville, KY: Victor, 1960), 17, 21.

22. Farber, *The Rise and Fall of Modern American Conservatism,* 79.

23. Nicol C. Rae, "Class and Culture: American Political Cleavages in the Twentieth Century," *Western Political Quarterly* 45 (September 1992): 629–650; Gary Miller and Norman Schofield, "The Transformation of the Republican and Democratic Party Coalitions in the U.S.," *Perspectives on Politics* 6 (September 2008): 433–450.

24. John Kenneth Galbraith, *American Capitalism: The Concept of Countervailing Power* (Boston: Houghton Mifflin, 1952).

25. For the rise of Reagan see Farber *The Rise and Fall of Modern American Conservatism,* 159–172; Haynes Johnson, *Sleepwalking through History: America in the Reagan Years* (New York: Norton, 1991), 56–69; Thomas W. Evans, *The Education of Ronald Reagan: The General Electric Years and the Untold Story of His Conversion to Conservatism* (New York: Columbia University Press, 2006).

26. Ronald Reagan, "A Time for Choosing," in *A Time for Choosing: The Speeches of Ronald Reagan, 1961–1982,* ed. Alfred A. Balitzer and Gerald M. Bonetto (Chicago: Regnery, 1983), 41–57. See a video of the speech, posted by the Reagan Presidential Library, at https://www.youtube.com/watch?v=qXBswFfh6AY.

27. Hayek, *The Road to Serfdom,* 87.

28. Ronald Brownstein, "The Parties Invert," *The Atlantic,* May 23, 2016.

29. Thomas G. Smith, *Green Republican: John Saylor and the Preservation of American Wilderness* (Pittsburgh, PA: University of Pittsburgh Press, 2006), 4–5, 223; Steven C. Schulte, *Wayne Aspinall and the Shaping of the American West* (Boulder: University Press of Colorado, 2002); Stephen C. Sturgeon, *The Politics of Western Water: The Congressional Career of Wayne Aspinall* (Tucson: University of Arizona Press, 2002).

30. Peter Iverson, "'This Old Mountain Is Worth the Fight': Barry Goldwater and the Campaign to Save Camelback Mountain," *Journal of Arizona History* 38 (Spring 1997): 41–56.

31. Barry Goldwater, *The Conscience of a Majority* (Englewood Cliffs, NJ: Prentice Hall, 1970), 212, 217. For Goldwater, see Brian Allen Drake, "The Skeptical Environmentalist: Barry Goldwater and the Environmental Management State," *Environmental History* 15 (October 2010): 587–611.

32. McEvoy, "Environmental Law."

33. *Earth Day—The Beginning* (New York: Arno Press, 1970); David Stradling, ed., *The Environmental Moment: 1968–1972* (Seattle: University of Washington Press, 2012); Andrew Hurley, *Environmental Inequalities: Class, Race, and Industrial Pollution in Gary, Indiana, 1945–1980* (Chapel Hill: University of North Carolina Press, 1995); Chad Montrie, *The Myth of the Silent Spring: Rethinking the Origins of American Environmentalism* (Berkeley: University of California Press, 2018).

34. For suburbs and the rise of conservatism, see Matthew Lassiter, *The Silent Majority: Suburban Politics in the Sunbelt South* (Princeton, NJ: Princeton University Press, 2007); Kevin M. Kruse, *White Flight: Atlanta and the Making of Modern Conservatism* (Princeton, NJ: Princeton University Press, 2007).

35. See Christopher C. Sellers, *Crabgrass Crucible: Suburban Nature and the Rise of Environmentalism in Twentieth-Century America* (Chapel Hill: University of North Carolina Press, 2012). For environmentalism as a consumer movement, see Samuel Hays, *Beauty, Health, and Permanence: Environmental Politics in the United States, 1955–1985* (New York: Cambridge University Press, 1987). For consumerism in American politics and culture, see Lizabeth Cohen, *A Consumer's Republic: The Politics of Mass Consumption in Postwar America* (New York: Vintage, 2003). For the suburbs and environmentalism, see Adam Rome, *The Bulldozer in the Countryside: Suburban Sprawl and the Rise of American Environmentalism* (New York: Cambridge University Press, 2001).

36. Paul R. Ehrlich, *The Population Bomb* (New York: Sierra Club / Ballantine Books, 1968), xi, 1–2. See also Thomas Robertson, *The Malthusian Moment: Global Population Growth and the Birth of American Environmentalism* (New Brunswick, NJ: Rutgers University Press, 2012).

37. Paul Sabin, *The Bet: Paul Ehrlich, Julian Simon, and Our Gamble over Earth's Future* (New Haven, CT: Yale University Press, 2013), 42–43.

38. Arlene Alligood, "Two Big Political Issues of Election '70," *St. Petersburg Times,* October 29, 1970, 20-A.

39. Rome, *The Genius of Earth Day,* 211–213; Gladwin Hill, "Conservationists Count Successes: See Their Role as Vital in Many Election Contests," *New York Times,* November 5, 1970, 37.

40. National Commission on the BP Deepwater Horizon Oil Spill and Offshore Drilling, "The History of Offshore Oil and Gas in the United States (Long Version)" (Staff Working Paper No. 22), 1–13.

41. Richard Nixon, "Special Message to Congress Transmitting Reorganization Plan No. 3 of 1970," July 9, 1970, in *Public Papers of the Presidents of the United States: Richard Nixon, 1970* (Washington, DC: Government Printing Office, 1971), 578–586.

42. Edmund Muskie, "A Whole Society," in *Earth Day—The Beginning*, 90–92.

43. "Republican Party Platform of 1972," August 21, 1972, The American Presidency Project, http://www.presidency.ucsb.edu/ws/?pid=25842. For the Nixon administration and the environment, see J. Brooks Flippen, *Nixon and the Environment* (Albuquerque: University of New Mexico Press, 2000), 74; J. Brooks Flippen, *Conservative Conservationist: Russell E. Train and the Emergence of American Environmentalism* (Baton Rouge: Louisiana State University Press, 2006).

44. William L. Andreen, "Water Quality Today—Has the Clean Water Act Been a Success?" *Alabama Law Review* 55 (June 2004): 537–593.

45. Flippen, *Nixon and the Environment*, 155.

46. Richard Nixon, "Veto of the Federal Water Pollution Control Act Amendments of 1972," October 17, 1972, in *Public Papers of the Presidents of the United States: Richard Nixon, 1972* (Washington, DC: Government Printing Office, 1973).

47. *Federal Water Pollution Control Act Amendments of 1972: Veto Message*, U.S. Senate Debates, Congressional Record—Senate, 92nd Cong., 2d Sess., October 17, 1972 (Washington, DC: Government Printing Office, 1972), 36871–36875. Available at the Muskie Archives and Special Collection Archives, Bates College, http://abacus.bates.edu/muskie-archives/ajcr/1972/CWA%20Override.shtml.

48. Flippen, *Nixon and the Environment*, 129–138, 155–157; Flippen, *Conservative Conservationist*, 110.

49. Ronald Reagan, quoted in Geoffrey Kabaservice, *Rule and Ruin: The Downfall of Moderation and the Destruction of the Republican Party, from Eisenhower to the Tea Party* (New York: Oxford University Press, 2011), 169, 189.

50. "Ecology Corps Created for C.O.'s by Reagan," *New York Times*, May 2, 1971, 30.

51. George Skelton, "The Man in the White Hat Who Saved the Sierra," *Los Angeles Times*, June 28, 1997.

52. Jordan Rau, "A Seasoned Style, Green Record as Gov.," *Los Angeles Times*, June 7, 2004.

53. Lou Cannon, *Governor Reagan: His Rise to Power* (New York: Public Affairs, 2003), 309–313.

54. Tom Goff, "Environment Stressed in Reagan Water Plan," *Los Angeles Times*, November 15, 1969, B12.

55. John S. Saloma, "California's Reagan Tests Politics of the Environment," *Boston Globe*, February 8, 1970, A23.

56. Jerry Gillam, "Reagan Presents Clean Air Law to Legislature," *Los Angeles Times,* January 23, 1970, A1.

57. Cannon, *Governor Reagan,* 307.

58. Ralph Nader, *Unsafe at Any Speed: The Designed-In Dangers of the American Automobile* (New York: Grossman, 1965); Charles Reich, *The Greening of America* (New York: Bantam, 1970), 1, 5.

59. For the long tradition of anti-intellectualism, see Richard Hofstadter, *Anti-intellectualism in American Life* (New York: Knopf, 1964).

60. Lewis F. Powell Jr., "Attack of American Free Enterprise System," Confidential Memorandum to Mr. Eugene B. Sydnor Jr., August 23, 1971. https://www.pbs .org/wnet/supremecourt/personality/print/sources_document13.html.

61. Robert Moses, "Bomb Shelters, Arks and Ecology," *National Review,* September 8, 1970.

62. Phillips-Fein, *Invisible Hands,* 188.

63. Julian Simon, "And Now, the Good News: Life on Earth Is Improving," *Washington Post,* July 13, 1980, E1–E2. See also Julian Simon, "Will We Run Out of Energy?" *Dialogue* 56 (1982): 16–20. For Simon, see Sabin, *The Bet.*

64. Jacqueline Vaughan Switzer, *Green Backlash: The History and Politics of Environmental Opposition in the U.S.* (Boulder, CO: Lynne Rienner, 1997), 165.

65. Watt, quoted in Jefferson Decker, *The Other Rights Revolution: Conservative Lawyers and the Remaking of American Government* (New York: Oxford University Press, 2016), 80–81.

66. Gerald R. Ford, *A Time to Heal* (New York: Harper & Row, 1979), 272.

67. See David Frum, *How We Got Here: The 70s* (New York: Basic Books, 2000); Meg Jacobs, *Panic at the Pump: The Energy Crisis and the Transformation of American Politics in the 1970s* (New York: Hill & Wang, 2016).

68. Gerald R. Ford, "Address to the Nation on Energy Policy," May 27, 1975, in *Gerald R. Ford, 1913–: Chronology, Documents, Bibliographical Aids,* ed. George J. Lankevich (Dobbs Ferry, NY: Oceana, 1977), 138–139.

69. "Republican Party Platform of 1976," August 18, 1976, The American Presidency Project, http://www.presidency.ucsb.edu/ws/?pid=25843.

70. Jacobs, *Panic at the Pump,* 182ff.

71. Burton I. Kaufman, *The Presidency of James Earl Carter Jr.* (Lawrence: University Press of Kansas, 1993), 140–148; Otis L. Graham Jr., *Presidents and the American Environment* (Lawrence: University Press of Kansas, 2016), 252–271.

72. Frances Fitzgerald, *Cities on a Hill: A Journey through Contemporary American Culture* (New York: Simon & Schuster, 1986), 125.

73. See George Marsden, *Understanding Fundamentalism and Evangelicalism* (Grand Rapids, MI: William Eerdmans, 1991), 1–61.

74. Johnson, *Sleepwalking through History,* 196–203.

75. Robert McG. Thomas Jr., "Robert J. Billings Is Dead at 68; Helped Form the Moral Majority," *New York Times,* June 1, 1995.

76. Jerry Falwell, "Future-Word: An Agenda for the Eighties," in *The Fundamentalist Phenomenon: The Resurgence of Conservative Christianity,* ed. Jerry Falwell with Ed Dobson and Ed Hindson (Garden City, NY: Doubleday-Galilee, 1981), 186–223.

77. Loren Wilkinson, ed., *Earthkeeping: Christian Stewardship of Natural Resources* (Grand Rapids, MI: William Eerdmans, 1980), 3–5, 224.

78. Cannon, *Governor Reagan,* 177.

79. Susan Schrepfer, *The Fight to Save the Redwoods: A History of Environmental Reform, 1917–1978* (Madison: University of Wisconsin Press, 1979), 146.

80. William Endicott, "Reagan Unveils Environmental Protection Plan but Hits 'Doomcriers,'" *Los Angeles Times,* April 8, 1972, 10A. For Proposition 9, see Carl E. Lutrin and Allen K. Settle, "The Public and Ecology: The Role of Initiatives in California's Environmental Politics," *Western Political Quarterly* 28 (June 1975): 352–371.

81. Helene von Damm, *Sincerely, Ronald Reagan* (Ottawa, IL: Green Hill, 1976), 156.

82. David Kinkela, *DDT and the American Century: Global Health, Environmental Politics, and the Pesticide that Changed the World* (Chapel Hill: University of North Carolina Press, 2011).

83. Mark Green and Gail MacColl, *Reagan's Reign of Error* (New York: Pantheon, 1987), 98–102.

2. Visions of Abundance

1. "Is There a Twentieth-Century West?" the historian Michael McGerr asked in 1992, in *Under an Open Sky: Rethinking America's Western Past,* ed. William Cronon, George Miles, and Jay Gitlin (New York: Norton, 1992), 239–256. Historians have generally answered that question in the affirmative, yet have struggled over how, exactly, to define the region. In this chapter, the West is defined as states in which the federal government owns at least 25 percent of the land. This includes Alaska, Arizona, California, Colorado, Idaho, Montana, Nevada, Oregon, New Mexico, Utah, Washington, and Wyoming.

2. Ted Stevens, "Speech before the League for Advancements of States' Equal Rights," November 21, 1980, Sierra Club Member Papers, box 224, folder 11, Bancroft Library, University of California, Berkeley.

3. "Interview with James Watt," *Human Events: The National Conservative Weekly,* Autumn 1982.

4. U.S. Bureau of Land Management, *Managing the Nation's Public Lands* (Washington, DC: Department of the Interior, 1981), 1–6.

5. William Engdahl, "The Halbouty Report on Energy: Recommending a Growth Perspective," *Executive Intelligence Review* 7, no. 49 (December 16, 1980): 60–61.

6. See William Cronon, *Nature's Metropolis: Chicago and the Great West* (New York: Norton, 1991); Robert Bunting, *The Pacific Raincoast: Environment and Culture in an American Eden, 1778–1900* (Lawrence: University Press of Kansas, 1997); Andrew C. Isenberg, *The Destruction of the Bison: An Environmental History, 1750–1920* (New York: Cambridge University Press, 2000), 121–163; David Igler, "The Industrial Far West: Region and Nation in the Late Nineteenth Century," *Pacific Historical Review* 69 (May 2000): 159–192; David Igler, *Industrial Cowboys: Miller & Lux and the Transformation of the Far West* (Berkeley: University of California Press, 2001); Andrew C. Isenberg, *Mining California: An Ecological History* (New York: Hill & Wang, 2005).

7. Letter from James Wilson, Secretary of the U.S. Department of Agriculture to the Forest Service (March 3, 1905), https://foresthistory.org/wp-content /uploads/2017/02/Wilson_letter.pdf. The letter was written by Pinchot.

8. Karen R. Merrill, *Public Lands and Political Meaning: Ranchers, the Government, and the Property between Them* (Berkeley: University of California Press, 2002), 179–180; Donald Worster, *Dust Bowl: The Southern Plains in the 1930s* (New York: Oxford University Press, 1979).

9. Andrew Needham, *Power Lines: Phoenix and the Making of the Modern Southwest* (Princeton, NJ: Princeton University Press, 2014), 139–140.

10. *Sagebrush Rebellion: Impacts on Energy and Minerals, Oversight Hearing,* House of Representatives, 96th Cong. (November 22, 1980) (statement of James Santini).

11. "People versus the Feds," *Greybull Standard,* March 6, 1981.

12. An Act Relating to the Public Lands, Assembly Bill No. 413, Nevada State Legislature (June 2, 1979).

13. James R. Skillen, *The Nation's Largest Landlord: The Bureau of Land Management in the American West* (Lawrence: University Press of Kansas, 2009), 120–124; Jefferson Decker, *The Other Rights Revolution: Conservative Lawyers and the Remaking of American Government* (New York: Oxford University Press, 2016), 86–94.

14. Reagan, quoted in Robert Henry Nelson, *Public Lands and Private Rights: The Failure of Scientific Management* (Lanham, MD: Rowman & Littlefield, 1995), 176–177.

15. Mountain States Legal Foundation, "Second Annual Report, 1978–1979," 1979, James Watt Papers, box 7, folder 4, American Heritage Center, University of Wyoming.

16. Decker, *The Other Rights Revolution,* 82–86.

17. *James G. Watt Nomination: Hearings before the Committee on Energy and Natural Resources,* U.S. Senate, 97th Cong. 30 (1981) (testimony of James Watt).

18. As quoted in Richard Sandomir, "William Turnage, Who Reinvented the Wilderness Society, Is Dead at 74," *New York Times,* October 18, 2017.

19. Doug Scott, "Status of Major Conservation Campaigns," August 31, 1981, Sierra Club Records, box 224, folder 16.

20. See Michael Sherry, *In the Shadow of War: The United States since the 1930s* (New Haven, CT: Yale University Press, 1997). The philosopher William James coined the term "the moral equivalent of war" in 1906.

21. Jimmy Carter, "Address to the Nation on Energy," April 18, 1977, The American Presidency Project, http://www.presidency.ucsb.edu/ws/index.php ?pid=7369. On the central importance of abundance and scarcity in the history of modern American environmental politics, see Paul Sabin, *The Bet: Paul Ehrlich, Julian Simon, and Our Gamble over Earth's Future* (New Haven, CT: Yale, 2013).

22. Engdahl, "The Halbouty Report on Energy."

23. American Petroleum Institute, *Two Energy Futures: A National Choice for the 80s* (Washington, DC: American Petroleum Institute, 1980), iii.

24. James Watt, "Reducing America's Energy Independence," December 12, 1983, Wilderness Society Papers, series 5, box 36, folder 29, Conservation Collection, Denver Public Library.

25. "Petroleum Prayer Breakfast," November 11, 1996, C-SPAN, https://www.c -span.org/video/?76718-1/petroleum-prayer-breakfast&start=38.

26. James Watt, "Memo re: Monday Morning Group," September 12, 1983, James Watt Papers, box 7, folder 3.

27. "Strip Mining Control Bill Signed," in *CQ Almanac 1977,* 33rd ed. (Washington, DC: Congressional Quarterly, 1978), 617–626, https://library.cqpress.com /cqalmanac/document.php?id=cqal77-1203778.

28. As quoted in Joanne Omang, "Man with a Mission: Watt Targets Strip-Mine Law," *Washington Post,* March 9, 1981.

29. *Implementation of the Surface Mining Control and Reclamation Act of 1977: Hearing before the Subcommittee on Energy and Mineral Resources of the Committee on Energy and Natural Resources,* U.S. Senate, 97th Cong. 297 (1981) (testimony of James E. Baker).

30. Philip Shabecoff, "Pact Halts a Revamping of Rules on Strip Mining," *New York Times,* April 17, 1982.

31. Ben A. Franklin, "Settlement to Require U.S. to Enforce Strip-Mine Laws," *New York Times,* October 14, 1984.

32. Timothy J. Considine, "Powder River Basin Coal: Powering America," *Natural Resources* 4, no. 8 (2013): 514–533.

33. Bureau of Land Management, *The Federal Coal Management Program and the Department's Coal Leasing Policy* (Washington, DC: Department of the Interior, 1984), 95.

34. Philip Shabecoff, "U.S. Plans Biggest Land Shift since Frontier Times," *New York Times,* July 3, 1982; Skillen, *The Nation's Largest Landlord,* 129–30.

35. Comptroller General, *Analysis of the Powder River Basin Federal Coal Lease Sale: Economic Valuation Improvements and Legislative Changes Needed: Report to Congress* (Washington, DC: General Accounting Office, 1983).

36. A. Dan Tarlock, "The Making of Federal Coal Policy: Lessons for Public Lands Management from a Failed Program, an Essay and Review," *Natural Resources Journal* 25 (1985): 349–374.

37. Tom Sanzillo, "The Great Giveaway: An Analysis of the Costly Failure of Federal Coal Leasing in the Powder River Basin," Institute for Energy Economics and Financial Analysis, June 2012, http://www.ieefa.org/wp-content/uploads/2012/06/062512_IEEFA_PRB_coal_report_FINAL2.pdf.

38. James Surowiecki, "America's Incoherent Coal Policy," *New Yorker,* December 7, 2015.

39. *Coal as a Catalyst in America's Revitalization: Hearing before the Joint Economic Committee,* 97th Cong. 8384 (1982) (testimony of R. E. Samples, National Coal Association).

40. Considine, "Powder River Basin Coal."

41. Jimmy Jackson, Comments in *Excess Spoil Minimization—Stream Buffer Zones, Proposed Rule: Environmental Impact Statement* (Washington, DC: Office of Surface Mining, September 2008), 82.

42. U.S. General Accounting Office, *Mineral Resources: Federal Coal-Leasing Program Needs Strengthening* (Washington, DC: General Accounting Office, September 1994), 53.

43. Nidhi Thakar and Michael Madowitz, "Federal Coal Leasing in the Powder River Basin: A Bad Deal for Taxpayers," Center for American Progress, July 29, 2014, https://cdn.americanprogress.org/wp-content/uploads/2014/07/ThakarPowderRiver-brief.pdf.

44. James Surowiecki, "America's Incoherent Coal Policy," *New Yorker,* December 7, 2015.

45. Thakar and Madowitz, "Federal Coal Leasing in the Powder River Basin."

46. American Petroleum Institute, *Two Energy Futures.*

47. *Oversight Hearings before the Subcommittee on the Panama Canal / Outer Continental Shelf of the Committee on Merchant Marine and Fisheries,* U.S. House of Representatives, 97th Cong. (1981) (Charles DiBona, American Petroleum Institute).

48. National Commission on the BP Deepwater Horizon Oil Spill and Offshore Drilling, "The History of Offshore Oil and Gas in the United States (Long Version)" (Staff Working Paper No. 22, 2011), 15–21.

49. Mark E. Gaffigan, "Oil and Gas Royalties: Royalty Relief Will Likely Cost the Government Billions, but the Final Costs Have Yet to Be Determined," testimony before the Committee on Energy and Natural Resources, U.S. Senate (Washington, DC: Government Accountability Office, January 18, 2007).

50. "Crude Oil Production," accessed May 17, 2017, Energy Information Administration, https://www.eia.gov/dnav/pet/pet_crd_crpdn_adc_mbblpd_a.htm.

51. Steve Greenberg, "James Watt Days Are Here Again, Encore," *Marin Independent Journal,* April 4, 2001.

52. David Rosenbaum, "Senate Blocks Fuel Drilling in Alaska," *New York Times,* April 19, 2002; Mark Silva, "Bush Urges Offshore Oil Drilling," *Los Angeles Times,* June 19, 2008; Dan Eggen and Steven Mufson, "Bush Rescinds Father's Offshore Oil Ban," *Washington Post,* July 15, 2008.

53. Erik Rush, "Drill, Baby, Drill!," WorldNetDaily.com, August 28, 2008, http://www.wnd.com/2008/08/73559/#.

54. Newt Gingrich, *Drill Here, Drill Now, Pay Less: A Handbook for Slashing Gas Prices and Solving Our Energy Crisis* (Washington, DC: Regnery, 2008), 3.

55. Wayne A. Grudem, *Voting as a Christian: The Economic and Foreign Policy Issues* (Grand Rapids, MI: Zondervan, 2012).

56. Jennifer Steinhauer, "Republicans Cry Foul on Obama Catchphrase," *New York Times,* March 23, 2012.

57. The White House, Office of the Press Secretary, "Remarks by the President in a Discussion of Jobs and the Economy in Charlotte, North Carolina, April 2, 2010," cited in National Commission, "The History of Offshore Oil and Gas," 55.

58. Natural Resources Defense Council, "Summary of Information Concerning the Ecological and Economic Impacts of the Deepwater Horizon Oil Spill Disaster" (NRDC issue paper, June 2015), https://www.nrdc.org/file/4218 /download?token=M2Bxrq5m.

59. Donald J. Trump, "An America First Energy Plan," *Trump Pence 2016,* May 26, 2016, accessed December 13, 2016, archived at https://perma.cc /2MMZ-4K45.

60. "Trump proposal would allow oil and gas drilling along most of U.S. coastline," *Houston Chronicle,* January 5, 2018; Zachary T. Sampson, "Florida gets an exemption from Trump administration on oil drilling; other governors not happy," *Tampa Bay Times,* January 10, 2018.

61. Ronald Reagan, "Address before a Joint Session of the Congress on the Program for Economic Recovery," February 18, 1982, The American Presidency Project, http://www.presidency.ucsb.edu/ws/index.php?pid=43425.

62. "83 Federal Programs: A Profile of Reagan Targets," *New York Times,* February 20, 1981.

63. See Turner, *The Promise of Wilderness,* chap. 10; James R. Skillen, *The Nation's Largest Landlord: The Bureau of Land Management in the American West* (Lawrence: University Press of Kansas, 2009), 102–113.

64. Peter Emerson, Anthony T. Stout, and Deanne Klopfer, "The Feds Can't See Their Losses in the Trees," *Wall Street Journal,* November 14, 1984.

65. Christopher Klyza, *Who Controls Public Lands?* (Chapel Hill: University of North Carolina Press, 1996), 135.

66. Edward Abbey, "Free Speech: The Cowboy and His Cow," in *Welfare Ranching,* ed. George Wuerthner and Mollie Matteson (Washington, DC: Island Press, 2002), 57, originally published in 1985.

67. As quoted in "User Fees," editorial, *Washington Post,* February 3, 1986.

68. Alan K. Simpson, "Note re: Grazing Issues," December 20, 1985, Alan K. Simpson Papers, box 271, folder 15, American Heritage Center, University of Wyoming.

69. Simpson, "Note re: Grazing Issues."

70. Bruce Babbitt, "Remarks to the National Press Club," April 27, 1993, Wilderness Society Papers, box 5:10, folder 47.

71. Turner, *The Promise of Wilderness*, 335–337.

72. People for the West!, "Election '94 presents opportunities," 1993, Wilderness Society Papers, box 12:3, folder 7.

73. Western States Coalition, "Western Legislators Reveal 12-Point Program to Rejuvenate the West," June 12, 1995, Wilderness Society Papers, box 9:17, folder 15.

74. Turner, *The Promise of Wilderness*, 351–362.

75. "The Second Gore-Bush Presidential Debate," October 11, 2000, Commission on Presidential Debates, http://www.debates.org/?page=october-11-2000-debate-transcript.

76. Turner, *The Promise of Wilderness*, 368–370.

77. As quoted in Alex Breitler, "Back in the Beltway: Richard Pombo Returns to D.C., in More Ways than One," Recordnet.com, August 16, 2015, http://www.recordnet.com/article/20150816/NEWS/150819775.

78. *Endangered Species Act: Information on Species Protection on Nonfederal Lands* (Washington, DC: General Accounting Office, December 1994).

79. *Endangered Species Act—Riverside, CA: Oversight Hearing before the Task Force on Endangered Species Act of the Committee on Resources,* House of Representatives, 104th Cong. (1995).

80. *Endangered Species Act Reauthorization: Innovation, Habitat Recovery, and Private Property Rights, Hearing before Committee on Environment and Public Works,* U.S. Senate, 104th Cong. 756 (August 3, 1995) (testimony of Robert J. Smith).

81. Richard Nixon, "Statement on Signing the Endangered Species Act of 1973," December 28, 1973, The American Presidency Project, http://www.presidency.ucsb.edu/ws/index.php?pid=4090.

82. For an introduction to the Endangered Species Act, see Peter Alagona, *After the Grizzly: Endangered Species and the Politics of Place in California* (Berkeley: University of California Press, 2013); Dale Goble, J. Michael Scott, and Frank W. Davis, eds., *The Endangered Species Act at Thirty,* vol. 1, *Renewing the Conservation Promise* (Washington, DC: Island Press, 2006); Shannon Petersen, *Acting for Endangered Species: The Statutory Ark* (Lawrence: University Press of Kansas, 2002).

83. Alagona, *After the Grizzly,* 101.

84. James Watt, "Letter for Department of the Interior's Annual Report," October 1, 1981, James Watt Papers, box 8, folder 20.

85. Tennessee Valley Authority v. Hill, 437 U.S. 153 (1978).

86. *Endangered Species Act: Hearings before the Subcommittee on Fisheries and Wildlife Conservation and the Environment of the Committee on Merchant Marine and Fisheries,* House of Representatives, 97th Cong. (1982) (testimony of Russell Train, World Wildlife Fund; statement of Alan Simpson, Senator).

87. Daniel Nelson, *Nature's Burdens: Conservation and American Politics, the Reagan Era to the Present* (Logan: Utah State University Press, 2017), chap. 5.

88. *Nomination of James E. Cason: Hearing before the Committee on Agriculture, Nutrition, and Forestry,* U.S. Senate, 101st Cong. (1989).

89. *Northern Spotted Owl Preservation Act: Hearing before the Subcommittee on Environmental Protection of the Committee on Environment and Public Works,* U.S. Senate, 102nd Cong. 48 (1992) (testimony of Evelyn Badger).

90. Larry Tuttle, "Memo re: Post-Listing Blues," June 26, 1990, Wilderness Society Records, box 23:12, folder "Ancient Forests—Memos, 1991."

91. George H. W. Bush, "Remarks to Burrill Lumber Employees in Medford, Oregon," September 14, 1992, George Bush Presidential Library and Museum.

92. Turner, *The Promise of Wilderness,* 280–289.

93. E. Thomas Tuchmann et al., *Northwest Forest Plan: A Report to the President and Congress* (Portland, OR: U.S. Department of Agriculture, 1996).

94. Alagona, *After the Grizzly,* 103–106.

95. Laurel Kearns, "Noah's Ark Goes to Washington: A Profile of Evangelical Environmentalism," *Social Compass* 44, no. 3 (September 1997): 356–357.

96. Christopher McGrory Klyza and David J. Sousa, American Environmental Policy: Beyond *Gridlock, American Environmental Policy,* rev. ed. (Cambridge, MA: MIT Press, 2013), 184–186.

97. Sharon Levy, "Turbulence in the Klamath River Basin," *BioScience* 53, no. 4 (April 1, 2003): 315–320.

98. Chris Mooney, *The Republican War on Science* (New York: Basic Books, 2005), 142–144.

99. Kimberley A. Strassel, "Rural Cleansing," *Wall Street Journal,* July 26, 2001.

100. Eric Brazil, "Farmers Protest Loss of Water," SFGate, May 8, 2001, https://www.sfgate.com/news/article/Farmers-protest-loss-of-water-10-000 -protest-2924237.php.

101. On this approach, see Lynn Scarlett, Assistant Secretary, U.S. Department of the Interior, "Moving beyond Conflict: Private Stewardship and Conservation Partnerships," Heritage Foundation Lectures, no. 762 (September 27, 2002).

102. William M. Lewis Jr., National Research Council, *Scientific Evaluation of Biological Opinions on Endangered and Threatened Fishes in the Klamath River Basin: Interim Report* (Washington, DC: National Academy Press, 2002), 4.

103. Dennis D. Lynch and John C. Risley, *Klamath River Basin Hydrologic Conditions Prior to the September 2002 Die-Off of Salmon and Steelhead,* Report 03-4099 (Portland, OR: U.S. Geological Survey, 2003).

104. Mooney, *The Republican War on Science,* 156.

105. Deborah Reis, Marjorie Miller, and Selena Caldera, *Cost Estimate: HR 3824 Threatened and Endangered Species Act of 2005* (Washington, DC: Congressional Budget Office, September 25, 2005).

106. George W. Bush, "Statement of Administration Policy: HR3824—Threatened and Endangered Species Recovery Act of 2005," September 29, 2005, The American Presidency Project, http://www.presidency.ucsb.edu/ws/index.php?pid=24888.

107. Congressional Record, vol. 151, Part 16, September 29, 2005, 21779.

108. Jo Becker and Barton Gellman, "Leaving No Tracks," *Washington Post*, June 27, 2007; Tom Hamburger, "Oregon Water Saga Illuminates Rove's Methods with Agencies," *Wall Street Journal*, July 30, 2003.

109. "Salmon Experts Pressured to Change Findings," accessed May 15, 2017, Union of Concerned Scientists, http://www.ucsusa.org/our-work/center-science-and-democracy/promoting-scientific-integrity/klamath-river-salmon.html.

110. Inspector General, "Report of Investigation: Julie MacDonald" (U.S. Department of the Interior, March 2007).

111. John M. Broder, "U.S. Agency May Reverse 8 Decisions on Wildlife," *New York Times*, July 21, 2007.

112. Earl E. Devaney, Inspector General, Department of the Interior, "Letter to Secretary of the Interior D. Kempthorne," December 15, 2008, Department of the Interior, https://www.doioig.gov/sites/doioig.gov/files/EndangeredSpeciesFINAL.pdf.

113. *Oversight of the Endangered Species Act: Hearing before the Subcommittee on Fisheries, Wildlife, and Water of the Committee on Environment and Public Works*, U.S. Senate, 108th Cong. (2006).

114. Matt Kettman, "Why the Endangered Species Act Is Broken, and How to Fix It," *Smithsonian*, May 15, 2013.

115. Doc Hastings et al., *Endangered Species Act Congressional Working Group: Report, Findings, and Recommendations* (Washington, DC: U.S. House of Representatives, February 4, 2014).

116. Decker, *The Other Rights Revolution*, 137–138.

117. Turner, *The Promise of Wilderness*, 235–236.

118. "Election Overview," accessed November 6, 2017, OpenSecrets.org, www.opensecrets.org/overview/index.php.

119. Lori Weigel and Dave Metz, "The 2017 Conservation in the West Poll," Colorado College State of the Rockies Project, January 2017, https://www.coloradocollege.edu/other/stateoftherockies/conservationinthewest/2017/.

120. "Federal Lands in the West: Liability or Asset?" Headwaters Economics, February 2017, https://headwaterseconomics.org/public-lands/federal-lands-performance/.

121. Katherine Cramer, "How Rural Resentment Helps Explain the Surprising Victory of Donald Trump," *Washington Post*, November 13, 2016.

122. Jowei Chen and Jonathan Rodden, "Unintentional Gerrymandering: Political Geography and Electoral Bias in Legislatures," *Quarterly Journal of Political Science* 8, no. 3 (June 27, 2013): 239–269.

123. Lazaro Gamio, "Urban and Rural America Are Becoming Increasingly Polarized," *Washington Post,* November 17, 2016.

3. The Cost of Clean Air and Water

1. C. Jerry Simmons, "Documerica: Snapshots of Crisis and Cure in the 1970s," *Prologue* 41, no. 1 (2009), https://www.archives.gov/publications/prologue /2009/spring/documerica.html.

2. Richard Nixon, "Special Message to the Congress on Environmental Quality," February 10, 1970, The American Presidency Project, http://www.presidency .ucsb.edu/ws/?pid=2757.

3. Phil McCombs, "The Costs of Cleanup vs. Cost to Lives: Costs of Clean Air Act under Attack by Industry, Reagan Economists," *Washington Post,* July 5, 1981.

4. Jacqueline Dowd Hall, "The Long Civil Rights Movement and the Political Uses of the Past," *Journal of American History* 91 (March 2005): 1233–1263.

5. Bruce A. Ackerman and Richard B. Stewart, "Reforming Environmental Law: The Democratic Case for Market Incentives," *Columbia Journal of Environmental Law* 13, no. 2 (1988): 171–200.

6. As quoted in Joanne Omang, "Clean Air Act May Be Facing Drastic Overhaul: Administration Is Considering a Drastic Overhaul of Clean Air Act," *Washington Post,* May 26, 1981.

7. Anne Gorsuch, "Statement of Anne McGill Gorsuch before the U.S. Senate Committee on Environment and Public Works," May 1, 1981, National Service Center for Environmental Publications, https://nepis.epa.gov/Exe /ZyPURL.cgi?Dockey=200183SB.txt.

8. Benjamin C. Waterhouse, "Uncertain Victory: Big Business and the Politics of Regulatory Reform," in *Lobbying America: The Politics of Business from Nixon to NAFTA* (Princeton, NJ: Princeton University Press, 2013), 174–200.

9. Ronald Reagan, "Inaugural Address," January 20, 1981, The American Presidency Project, http://www.presidency.ucsb.edu/ws/?pid=43130.

10. Benjamin C. Waterhouse, *Lobbying America: The Politics of Business from Nixon to NAFTA* (Princeton, NJ: Princeton University Press, 2013), 198.

11. Christopher Sellers et al., *The EPA under Siege: Trump's Assault in History and Testimony* (Environmental Governance and Data Initiative, 2017), https:// 100days.envirodatagov.org/epa-under-siege.

12. As quoted in Steven Hoover, "'Depression at EPA,'" *Washington Post,* November 9, 1981.

13. As quoted in Jonathan Lash, "EPA: What Really Happened," *Washington Post,* July 29, 1984.

14. Richard A. Colignon, *Power Plays: Critical Events in the Institutionalization of the Tennessee Valley Authority* (Albany: State University of New York Press, 1997), 181–184.

15. Peter D. Junger, "The Inapplicability of Cost-Benefit Analysis to Environmental Policies," *Ekistics* 46, no. 276 (1979): 184–194.

16. McCombs, "The Costs of Cleanup vs. Cost to Lives."

17. UPI, "Clean Air Act Defended by Ranking GOP Lawmaker," *Los Angeles Times,* January 16, 1981; Bill Stall, "Bid to Weaken Clean Air Act Would Face Fight," *Los Angeles Times,* February 27, 1981.

18. *Possible Amendments to the Federal Water Pollution Control Act, before the Subcommittee on Water Resources of the Committee on Public Works and Transportation,* House of Representatives, 98th Cong. (1983) (statement of James Taylor Banks).

19. Jennings Randolph et al., "Letter to John W. Hernandez, Jr., Acting Director, EPA," in *Hearings before the Subcommittee on Environmental Pollution of the Committee on Environment and Public Works on S. 431 A Bill to Amend the Clean Water Act, As Amended, to Authorize Funds for Fiscal Years 1983, 1984, 1985, 1986, and 1987, and for other Purposes,* 98th Cong. (1983), 4–5.

20. Robert F. Durant, *The Administrative Presidency Revisited: Public Lands, the BLM, and the Reagan Revolution* (Albany: State University of New York Press, 1992).

21. Edward Strohbehn Jr., "Reasoned Decisionmaking in Regulatory Reform: The Third Circuit Reinstates EPA's Pretreatment Rules," *Environmental Law Reporter* 13, no. 1 (1983).

22. Environmental Law Reporter, "Tall Stacks versus Scrubbers: $3.5-Million Publicity Campaign Fails to Discredit Emission Reduction Technology," *Environmental Law Reporter* 5, no. 1 (January 1975).

23. Laurens H. Rhinelander, "The Proper Place for the Bubble Concept under the Clean Air Act," *Environmental Law Reporter* 13, no. 12 (1983): 10406–10417. Aspects of this strategy were initially advanced during the Carter administration.

24. Donald E. Elliott, "Chevron Matters: How the Chevron Doctrine Redefined the Roles of Congress, Courts and Agencies in Environmental Law," *Villanova Environmental Law Journal* 16 (2005): 1–18.

25. Eric Citron, "The Roots and Limits of Gorsuch's Views on *Chevron* Deference," SCOTUSblog, March 17, 2017, http://www.scotusblog.com/2017/03/roots-limits-gorsuchs-views-chevron-deference/.

26. Nolan E. Clark, "Why I'm No Longer at EPA," *Washington Post,* March 5, 1983.

27. Steven Hoover, "'Depression at EPA,'" *Washington Post,* November 9, 1981.

28. Andrew Szasz, "The Process and Significance of Political Scandals: A Comparison of Watergate and the 'Sewergate' Episode at the Environmental Protection Agency," *Social Problems* 33, no. 3 (1986): 202–217.

29. Philip Shabecoff, "Reagan and Environment: To Many, a Stalemate," *New York Times,* January 2, 1989.

30. Dale Russakoff, "Poll Finds Broad Support for Environmental Laws," *Washington Post,* November 11, 1982.

31. "William D. Ruckelshaus: Oral History Interview," EPA Web Archive, January 1993, https://archive.epa.gov/epa/aboutepa/william-d-ruckelshaus -oral-history-interview.html.

32. William D. Ruckelshaus, "Remarks of The Honorable William D Ruckelshaus, Administrator EPA, National Newspaper Association, Reno, Nevada." Presented at the Annual Meeting of the National Newspaper Association, September 27, 1984, National Service Center for Environmental Publications.

33. Michael Weisskopf, "'Tall Stacks' and Acid Rain," *Washington Post,* June 5, 1989.

34. Carolyn Curtis and Edison Electric Institute, *Before the Rainbow: What We Know about Acid Rain* (Washington, DC: Edison Electric Institute, 1980).

35. As quoted in Chris Mooney, *The Republican War on Science* (New York: Basic Books, 1995), 42.

36. Ronald Reagan, "President Reagan Assigns EPA Four Priority Tasks," *EPA Journal* 9, no. 1 (July 1983): 2.

37. Philip Shabecoff, "Panel of Scientists Bids U.S. Act Now to Curb Acid Rain," *New York Times,* June 28, 1983.

38. Congressional Budget Office, *Curbing Acid Rain: Allocating Sulfur Dioxide Control Costs under an Emissions Control Program* (Staff Working Paper, January 1984), 26.

39. Philip Shabecoff, "Utilities Say Move to Control Acid Rain Will Push Up Rates," *New York Times,* June 29, 1983.

40. Bill Neikirk, "Stockman's Imprint Will Be Slow to Fade," *Chicago Tribune,* July 14, 1985.

41. Mooney, *The Republican War on Science,* 40–43.

42. Michael Weisskopf, "Acid Rain Compromise Is Offered in Senate," *Washington Post,* July 14, 1988.

43. "Cool It: Cleaning Up the Old Act," *The Economist,* August 31, 1991.

44. Frederic D. Krupp, "New Environmentalism Factors in Economic Needs," *Wall Street Journal,* November 20, 1986.

45. As quoted in Philip Shabecoff, "Environmentalists Say Either Bush or Dukakis Will Be an Improvement," *New York Times,* September 1, 1988.

46. John Holusha, "Bush Pledges Efforts to Clean Up Air and Water," *New York Times,* September 1, 1988.

47. As quoted in Kathy McCauley, Bruce Barron, and Morton Coleman, *Crossing the Aisle to Cleaner Air: How the Bipartisan 'Project 88' Transformed Environmental Policy* (University of Pittsburgh Institute of Politics, 2008), 23, http:// d=scholarship.pitt.edu/28739/1/Crossing%20the%20Aisle%20to%20 Cleaner%20Air.pdf.

48. George H. W. Bush, "Remarks Announcing Proposed Legislation to Amend the Clean Air Act," June 12, 1989, George Bush Presidential Library and Museum, https://bush41library.tamu.edu/archives/public -papers/524.

49. Gabriel Chan, Robert N. Stavins, Robert C. Stowe, and Richard Sweeney, *The SO₂ Allowance Trading System and the Clean Air Act Amendments of 1990: Reflections on Twenty Years of Policy Innovation* (Harvard Environmental Economics Program, 2012), 14, https://heep.hks.harvard.edu/publications/so2 -allowance-trading-system-and-clean-air-act-amendments-1990-reflections -twenty.

50. George H. W. Bush, "Remarks Announcing Proposed Legislation to Amend the Clean Air Act," June 12, 1989, The American Presidency Project, http://www.presidency.ucsb.edu/ws/?pid=17134.

51. *Clean Air Act Reauthorization: Hearing before the Subcommittee on Energy and Power of the Committee on Energy and Commerce,* U.S. House of Representatives, 101st Cong. (1990) (testimony of William W. Berry).

52. *Clean Air Act Amendments of 1989, before the Subcommittee on Environmental Protection of the Committee on Environment and Public Works,* U.S. Senate, 101st Cong., vol. 5 (1989) (statements of Richard Lawson, National Coal Association, Richard Trumka, United Mine Workers, and G. M. Hidy, Electric Power Research Institute).

53. Barry Commoner, "Free Markets Can't Control Pollution," *New York Times,* April 15, 1990.

54. *Clean Air Act Amendments of 1989* (statement of Daniel J. Dudek, Environmental Defense Fund).

55. Rose Gutfeld, "Senate Votes Down Byrd Amendment for Clean Air Bill," *Wall Street Journal,* March 30, 1990; Philip Shabecoff, "Senate Rejects Plan on Aid to Miners," *New York Times,* March 30, 1990.

56. George H. W. Bush, "Remarks on Signing the Bill Amending the Clean Air Act," November 15, 1990, George Bush Presidential Library and Museum, https://bush41library.tamu.edu/archives/public-papers/2435.

57. Paul R. Portney, "Policy Watch: Economics and the Clean Air Act," *Journal of Economic Perspectives* 4, no. 4 (1990): 173–181.

58. Robert N. Stavins, "What Can We Learn from the Grand Policy Experiment? Lessons from SO₂ Allowance Trading," *Journal of Economic Perspectives* 12, no. 3 (September 1998): 69–88.

59. Daniel J. Weiss and Miranda Peterson, "Groundhog Days: Utilities Wrong Again about Pollution Safeguard Costs," March 19, 2014, Center for American Progress, https://www.americanprogress.org/issues/green/reports/2014/03/19 /85923/groundhog-days/.

60. Lauraine G. Chestnut and David M. Mills, "A Fresh Look at the Benefits and Costs of the US Acid Rain Program," *Journal of Environmental Management* 77, no. 3 (November 2005): 252–266.

61. Theodore L. Garrett, "Downwind Ozone: Clearing the Air," *Natural Resources & Environment* 18, no. 3 (2004): 10–15.

62. *Nomination of Christine Todd Whitman, before the Committee on Environment and Public Works,* U.S. Senate, 107th Cong. (January 17, 2001) (statement of Christine Todd Whitman), 30.

63. Bruce Barcott, "Changing All the Rules," *New York Times,* April 4, 2004.

64. *Clear Skies Act of 2003, before the Subcommittee on Clean Air, Climate Change, and Nuclear Safety of the Committee on Environment and Public Works,* U.S. Senate, 108th Cong. (2003) (statement of Jim Roger, Edison Electric Institute).

65. George W. Bush, "Remarks Announcing the Clear Skies and Global Climate Change Initiatives," February 14, 2002, The American Presidency Project, http://www.presidency.ucsb.edu/ws/index.php?pid=73200.

66. *Clear Skies Act of 2003* (statement of Christine Todd Whitman, Administrator of the EPA), https://archive.epa.gov/clearskies/web/html/testimony.html.

67. *Clear Skies Act of 2003* (statement of David Hawkins, Natural Resources Defense Council), https://archive.org/stream/gov.gpo.fdsys.CHRG-108shrg91748/CHRG-108shrg91748#page/n123/mode/2up/search/david+hawkins.

68. Leslie Valentine, *Clearing the Air on Clear Skies* (Environmental Defense Fund, July 15, 2002).

69. Michael Shore, "Out of Control and Close to Home: Mercury Pollution from Power Plants," Environmental Defense, 2003, www.edf.org/go/mercurypowerplants.

70. According to OpenSecrets.org, the energy and natural resources sector directed 55.3 percent of $22 million and 74.4 percent of $68 million to Republican congressional candidates in 1990 and 2000, respectively. Democratic candidates received the balance. "Election Overview," accessed November 6, 2017, OpenSecrets.org, https://www.opensecrets.org/overview/sectors.php?cycle=2000.

71. Barcott, "Changing All the Rules."

72. Edison Electric Institute, "Straight Talk about Electric Utilities and New Source Review," July 2001, www.eei.org/issuesandpolicy/environment/air/Documents/NSRST.pdf.

73. As quoted in Meg Jacobs, "Wreaking Havoc from Within: George W. Bush's Energy Policy in Historical Perspective," in *The Presidency of George W. Bush: A First Historical Assessment,* ed. Julian E. Zelizer (Princeton, NJ: Princeton University Press, 2010), 139–168.

74. As quoted in Barcott, "Changing All the Rules."

75. For a helpful treatment of New Source Review, see Christopher M. Klyza and David J. Sousa, *American Environmental Policy: Beyond Gridlock,* rev. ed. (Cambridge, MA: MIT Press, 2013), 123–135.

76. David Marshall, "Comments of Clean Air Task Force on Clean Air Interstate Rule" (Clean Air Task Force, July 26, 2004), EPA Docket ID OAR-2003-0053, https://www.regulations.gov.

77. Frank O'Donnell, "The Legal Equivalent of a Dirty Bomb," July 11, 2008, Clean Air Watch, http://www.cleanairwatch.org/2008_07_01_archive.html.

78. Environmental Protection Agency, "Air Pollutant Emissions Trends Data," accessed November 6, 2017, https://www.epa.gov/air-emissions-inventories /air-pollutant-emissions-trends-data.

79. *Water Pollution Control Legislation: Hearings before the Subcommittee on Air and Water Pollution of the Committee on Public Works,* U.S. Senate, 92nd Cong. 1764 (1971) (testimony of Don F. Magdanz, National Livestock Feeders Association).

80. Testimony of William Ruckelshaus, in Claudia Copeland, ed., *A Legislative History of the Water Quality Act of 1987,* vol. 3 (Washington, DC: Government Printing Office, 1988), 2001–2016.

81. *Possible Amendments to the Federal Water Pollution Control Act, before the Subcommittee on Water Resources of the Committee on Public Works and Transportation,* U.S. House of Representatives, 98th Cong, (1983) (statement of Natural Resources Defense Council).

82. Edward Walsh, "Reagan's First Hill Showdown Already Brewing: Pocket-Vetoed $20 Billion Clean-Water Bill Revived in House by Lopsided 406–8," *Washington Post,* January 9, 1987; Helen Dewar, "Reagan Faces First Challenge from New Congress: Senate Joins House in Overwhelming Approval of Vetoed '86 Water-Cleanup Measure," *Washington Post,* January 22, 1987.

83. Silvio Conte, in Congressional Record—House, February 3, 1987, H2510.

84. *Clean Water Act Amendments: Non-Point Source Management Program: Hearings before the Committee on Environment and Public Works,* U.S. Senate, 98th Cong. 60 (1983) (testimony of Jay Hair, National Wildlife Federation).

85. *Clean Water Act Amendments* (Earl W. Sears letter), 550.

86. Statement of Senator Alan Simpson in Claudia Copeland, ed., *A Legislative History of the Water Quality Act of 1987,* vol. 2 (Washington, DC: Government Printing Office, 1988), 498.

87. Robert K. Craig and Anna M. Roberts, "When Will Governments Regulate Nonpoint Source Pollution?" *Boston College Environmental Affairs Review* 41, no. 1 (2015): 1–64, at 12.

88. U.S. Environmental Protection Agency, "President Clinton's Clean Water Initiative" (February 1994), National Service Center for Environmental Publications.

89. *The Water Quality Act of 1994, and Issues Related to Clean Water Act Reauthorization, H.R. 3948, Hearing before the Subcommittee on Water Resources and Environment of the Committee on Public Works and Transportation,* U.S. House of Representatives, 103rd Cong. (1994) (statement of Christine Todd Whitman).

90. *The Water Quality Act of 1994, and Issues Related to Clean Water Act Reauthorization (H.R. 3948): Hearing before the Subcommittee on Water Resources and Environment of the Committee on Public Works and Transportation,* U.S. House of Representatives, 104th Cong. (1995).

91. Newt Gingrich, in Congressional Record—House, September 22, 1994, H9526.

92. Job Creation and Wage Enhancement Act of 1995, H.R. 9, 104th Cong. (1995).

93. Cindy Skrzycki, "In Regulatory Assault, GOP Has a Lot to Be Thankful For," *Washington Post,* December 2, 1994.

94. Mitchell Bernard, Natural Resources Defense Council, *Breach of Faith: How the Contract's Fine Print Undermines America's Environmental Success* (New York: Natural Resources Defense Council, 1995), 7.

95. For a more detailed explanation of these executive orders and legislative options considered, see Fred Anderson, Mary A. Chirba-Martin, E. Donald Elliott, and Cynthia Farina, "Regulatory Improvement Legislation: Risk Assessment, Cost-Benefit Analysis, and Judicial Review," *Duke Environmental Law & Policy Forum* 11 (2000): 89–138.

96. William J. Clinton, "Remarks on the 25th Observance of Earth Day in Havre de Grace, Maryland," April 21, 1995, The American Presidency Project, http://www.presidency.ucsb.edu/ws/index.php?pid=51253.

97. Alon Tal, "Environmental Policy Analysis, Peer Reviewed: Assessing the Environmental Movement's Attitudes Toward Risk Assessment," *Environmental Science & Technology* 31, no. 10 (1997): 470A–476A.

98. "Bud Shuster's Dirty Water Act," editorial, *New York Times,* April 2, 1995.

99. Claudia Copeland, "Clean Water: Summary of H.R. 961, as Passed" (Congress Research Service Report 95-427 ENR, May 30, 1995).

100. Bud Shuster and Jimmy Hayes, "Big Lie on Clean Water," *Washington Post,* May 16, 1995.

101. Kathleen Gildred, "SCCED Forum on the Clean Water Act Reauthorization Bill" (discussion, Southern California Council on Environment and Development, December 20, 1995), http://web.archive.org/web/20101129060827/http://www.scced.org/sccedinfo/cleanwa.html.

102. Gregory Wetstone, "Congressional Efforts to Eradicate Environmental Laws," *Pace Environmental Law Review* 14, no. 1 (1996): 123–127.

103. American Viewpoint National Monitor Survey, November 1996, Survey Question: USAMVW.96NOV6.R4, Roper Center for Public Opinion Research, iPOLL.

104. "Think Globally, Act Locally: A Pro-Active, Pro-Environment Agenda for House Republicans," August 17, 1995, Wilderness Society Records, box 9:17, folder 15.

105. Jessica Mathews, "Earth First at the Polls," *Washington Post,* November 11, 1996; Brad Knickerbocker, "In 1997, Expect Moderation in All Things Environmental," *Christian Science Monitor,* November 14, 1996.

106. John McCain, "Nature Is Not a Liberal Plot: Extreme Anti-Environmentalism Hurts the G.O.P.," *New York Times,* November 22, 1996.

107. Government Accountability Office, "Clean Water Act: Changes Needed If Key EPA Program Is to Help Fulfill the Nation's Water Quality Goals," December 2013, https://www.gao.gov/assets/660/659496.pdf.

108. Robert Meltz and Claudia Copeland, "The Wetlands Coverage of the Clean Water Act (CWA): *Rapanos* and Beyond" (Congressional Research Service, 2015).

109. Thomas E. Dahl and Craig E. Johnson, *Wetlands Status and Trends in the Conterminous United States, Mid-1970's to Mid-1980's: First Update of the National Wetlands Status Report* (Washington, DC: U.S. Department of the Interior, Fish and Wildlife Service, 1991).

110. *The Water Quality Act of 1994, and Issues Related to Clean Water Act Reauthorization (H.R. 3948): Hearings before the Subcommittee on Water Resources and Environment of the Committee on Public Works and Transportation,* U.S. House of Representatives, 103rd Cong. 532 (1994) (testimony of National Association of Home Builders).

111. Donald Trump, "Remarks by President Trump at Signing of Waters of the United States (WOTUS) Executive Order," February 28, 2017, The White House, https://www.whitehouse.gov/the-press-office/2017/02/28/remarks-president-trump-signing-waters-united-states-wotus-executive.

112. David J. Sousa and Christopher M. Klyza, "'Whither We Are Tending': Interrogating the Retrenchment Narrative in U.S. Environmental Policy," *Political Science Quarterly* 132, no. 3 (September 2017): 467–494.

113. "The Benefits and Costs of the Clean Air Act from 1990 to 2020: Summary Report" (U.S. Environmental Protection Agency, April 2011).

114. David A. Keiser and Joseph S. Shapiro, "Consequences of the Clean Water Act and the Demand for Water Quality" (working paper, Yale University, June 2016), http://www.econ.yale.edu/~js2755/CleanWaterAct_KeiserShapiro.pdf.

115. Jeff Inglis et al., "Waterways Restored: The Clean Water Act's Impact on 15 American Rivers, Lakes and Bays," Environment America Research and Policy Center, October 2014, https://environmentamerica.org/sites/environment/files/EA_waterways_scrn.pdf.

116. *Clean Power Act: Hearings before the Environment and Public Works Committee,* U.S. Senate, 107th Cong. (July 2001) (testimony of United Mine Workers).

117. Maryanne Vollers, "Razing Appalachia," *Mother Jones,* July 1999.

118. Michael Hendryx and Benjamin Holland, "Unintended Consequences of the Clean Air Act: Mortality Rates in Appalachian Coal Mining Communities," *Environmental Science & Policy* 63 (September 2016): 1–6.

119. Bill Chameides, "A Look at Environmental Justice in the United States Today," *Huffington Post,* January 20, 2014.

120. Timothy Cama, "EPA's Environmental Justice Head Resigns," March 9, 2017, The Hill, http://thehill.com/policy/energy-environment/323209-epas

-environmental-justice-head-resigns. For detailed analysis of the consequences of the Trump administration for environmental justice, see Britt S.
Paris et al., "Pursuing a Toxic Agenda: Environmental Injustice in the Early
Trump Administration," September 19, 2017, Environmental Data & Governance Initiative, https://envirodatagov.org/publication/pursuing-toxic
-agenda.

4. American Exceptionalism in a Warming World

1. Ronald Reagan, "Statement on Signing the Montreal Protocol on Ozone-
   Depleting Substances," April 5, 1988, The American Presidency Project,
   http://www.presidency.ucsb.edu/ws/?pid=35639.
2. Richard Elliot Benedick, *Ozone Diplomacy: New Directions in Safeguarding
   the Planet* (Cambridge, MA: Harvard University Press, 1998), 68.
3. Reagan, "Statement on Signing the Montreal Protocol on Ozone-Depleting
   Substances."
4. Mario J. Molina and F. S. Rowland, "Stratospheric Sink for Chlorofluoro-
   methanes: Chlorine Atomic-Catalysed Destruction of Ozone," *Nature* 249
   (June 1, 1974): 810–812.
5. J. C. Farman, B. G. Gardiner, and J. D. Shanklin, "Large Losses of Total
   Ozone in Antarctica Reveal Seasonal ClO_x / NO_x Interaction," *Nature* 315,
   no. 6016 (May 16, 1985): 207–210.
6. Susan Solomon as quoted in James Gleick, "Hole in Ozone over South Pole
   Worries Scientists," *New York Times,* July 29, 1986.
7. Bendick, *Ozone Diplomacy,* 64; Cass R. Sunstein, "Of Montreal and Kyoto: A
   Tale of Two Protocols," *Environmental Law Review: News and Analysis* 38
   (August 2008): 10567.
8. Clean Air Act Amendments of 1977, Pub. L. No. 95-95, 42 USC 7401, sec. 126
   (1977).
9. Benedick, *Ozone Diplomacy,* 62.
10. Kurkpatrick Dorsey, *The Dawn of Conservation Diplomacy: U.S.-Canadian
    Wildlife Protection Treaties in the Progressive Era* (Seattle: University of
    Washington Press, 1998); Kurkpatrick Dorsey, *Whales and Nations:
    Environmental Diplomacy on the High Seas* (Seattle: University of Wash-
    ington Press, 2013); Mark Cioc, *The Game of Conservation: International
    Treaties to Protect the World's Migratory Animals* (Athens: Ohio University
    Press, 2009).
11. Elizabeth R. DeSombre, *Domestic Sources of International Environmental
    Policy: Industry, Environmentalists, and U.S. Power* (Cambridge, MA: MIT
    Press, 2000).
12. Cathleen Decker and Larry Stammer, "Bush Asks Ban on CFC to Save Ozone:
    Urges End to Production by Year 2000 if Safe Alternatives Can Be Devel-
    oped," *Los Angeles Times,* March 4, 1989.

13. U.S. State Department, Bureau of Environment, Health, and Natural Resources, "Memo re: Environmental Issues," February 15, 1989, National Security Archive, George Washington University, Electronic Briefing Book, No. 536, Document 9.

14. As quoted in Naomi Oreskes and Erik M. Conway, *Merchants of Doubt: How a Handful of Scientists Obscured the Truth on Issues from Tobacco Smoke to Global Warming* (London: Bloomsbury, 2011), 185.

15. Tom Ross and Neal Lott, *A Climatology of 1980–2003 Extreme Weather and Climate Events,* Rep. No. 2003-01 (Washington, DC: National Oceanic and Atmospheric Administration, 2003), 6.

16. *The Greenhouse Effect: Impacts on Current Global Temperatures and Regional Heat Waves, before the Committee on Energy and Natural Resources,* U.S. Senate, 100th Cong. (1988) (statements of James Hansen, Michael Oppenheimer, and George Woodwell).

17. Shannon Hall, "Exxon Knew about Climate Change Almost 40 Years Ago," *Scientific American,* October 26, 2015.

18. Spencer R. Weart, *The Discovery of Global Warming* (Cambridge, MA; Harvard University Press, 2004); Joshua P. Howe, *Behind the Curve: Science and the Politics of Global Warming* (Seattle: University of Washington Press, 2016).

19. As quoted in Philip Shabecoff, "Haste on Global Warming Trend Is Opposed," *New York Times,* October 21, 1983, A1.

20. George M. Hidy, "Coping with Climate Change," *EPRI Journal* 13, no. 4 (June 1988): 4.

21. Mobil, "People Who Live in Greenhouses . . ." advertisement, *New York Times,* July 6, 1989, A21.

22. Maxwell T. Boykoff and Jules M. Boykoff, "Balance as Bias: Global Warming and the US Prestige Press," *Global Environmental Change* 14, no. 2 (July 2004): 125–136.

23. George H. W. Bush, "Remarks at the Opening Session of the White House Conference on Science and Economics Research Related to Global Change," April 17, 1990, The American Presidency Project, http://www.presidency.ucsb.edu/ws/index.php?pid=18366.

24. Intergovernmental Panel on Climate Change, *IPCC First Assessment Report* (Geneva: Intergovernmental Panel on Climate Change, 1990).

25. William Booth, "Action Urged against Global Warming," *Washington Post,* February 2, 1990.

26. Warren Washington, *Odyssey in Climate Modeling, Global Warming, and Advising Five Presidents* (Raleigh, NC: Lulu.com, 2007).

27. On controversy over the science of global warming and research funding in the early 1980s, see Howe, *Behind the Curve,* 125–130.

28. This quote is from Naomi Oreskes and Erik M. Conway, "Global Warming Deniers and Their Proven Strategy of Doubt," YaleEnvironment360, June 10, 2010, https://e360.yale.edu/features/global_warming_deniers_and_their

_proven_strategy_of_doubt. The argument is made fully in Oreskes and Conway, *Merchants of Doubt,* 186.

29. Oreskes and Conway, *Merchants of Doubt,* 62.

30. Robert Jastrow, William A. Nierenberg, and Frederick Seitz, *Global Warming: What Does the Science Tell Us?* (Washington, DC: George C. Marshall Institute, 1990).

31. Boyce Rensberger, "'Greenhouse Effect' Seems Benign So Far," *Washington Post,* June 1, 1993; William K. Stevens, "Scientists Confront Renewed Backlash on Global Warming," *New York Times,* September 14, 1993; Michael Fumento, "Global Warming or Hot Air," *Investors Business Daily,* June 2, 1992.

32. Richard D. Bryan, "Let's Get Serious about Gas Mileage," *Christian Science Monitor,* September 21, 1990.

33. Keith Bradsher, *High and Mighty: SUVs—The World's Most Dangerous Vehicles and How They Got That Way* (New York: Public Affairs, 2002), 62–68.

34. James Morton Turner, *The Promise of Wilderness: American Environmental Politics since 1964* (Seattle: University of Washington Press, 2012), 289–294.

35. DeSombre, *Domestic Sources of International Environmental Policy,* 2000.

36. Carol White and Rogelio Maduro, "'Greenhouse Effect' Hoaxsters Seek World Dictatorship," *Executive Intelligence Review,* January 6, 1989.

37. Howe, *Behind the Curve,* 180.

38. Howe, *Behind the Curve,* 180–185.

39. Republican Party, *The Vision Shared: The Republican Platform, Uniting Our Family, Our Country, Our World,* August 17, 1992, The American Presidency Project, http://www.presidency.ucsb.edu/ws/index.php?pid=25847.

40. William J. Clinton, "Clinton Campaign Speech," April 22, 1992, C-SPAN, https://www.c-span.org/video/?25724-1/clinton-campaign-speech.

41. Clinton, "Clinton Campaign Speech."

42. *Energy Tax Options, before the Committee on Energy and Natural Resources,* U.S. Senate, 103rd Cong. (February 24, 1993) (statement of Senator Malcolm Wallop).

43. Terence L. Barnich, "Clinton Energy Tax—Worse than It Seems," *Wall Street Journal,* March 3, 1993.

44. Jane Mayer, "The Koch Brothers' Covert Ops," *New Yorker,* August 30, 2010.

45. *Administration's Energy Tax Proposals: Hearings before the Committee on Finance,* U.S. Senate, 103rd Cong, (1993) (testimony of Victor G. Beghini, Marathon Oil; testimony of John J. Collins, American Trucking Associations; statement of American Farm Bureau Federation).

46. William J. Clinton, "Remarks on Earth Day," April 21, 1993, The American Presidency Project, http://www.presidency.ucsb.edu/ws/index.php?pid=46460.

47. "H.R. 2264 (103rd Congress): Omnibus Budget Reconciliation Act of 1993—House Vote #199—May 27, 1993," GovTrack.us, https://www.govtrack.us/congress/votes/103-1993/h199.

48. As quoted in Bob Woodward, *The Agenda: Inside the Clinton White House* (New York: Simon & Schuster, 2005), 204.

49. Ezra Klein, "Did the House GOP Get BTU'd?" *Washington Post,* May 5, 2011.
50. Mayer, "The Koch Brothers' Covert Ops."
51. Chris Casteel, "Both Senate Candidates Near $1 Million in Fund Raising," NewsOK.com, October 23, 1994, http://newsok.com/both-senate-candidates -near-1-million-in-fund-raising/article/2481504.
52. Karen Fisher-Vanden et al. "The Second Generation Model of Energy Use, the Economy, and Greenhouse Gas Emissions" (prepared for the U.S. Department of Energy, September 1993).
53. Daniel Spiegel, U.S. Mission Geneva to Secretary of State, "Memo re: Conference of Parties," July 31, 1996, National Security Archive, George Washington University, Electronic Briefing Book, No. 537, Document 2.
54. Howe, *Behind the Curve,* 191–193.
55. "Senate Debate over Byrd-Hagel Resolution," Congressional Record 143, no. 107 (July 25, 1997), Electronic Briefing Book, No. 537, S8117.
56. Jeffrey R. Shafer, "Memo to Deputy Secretary Lawrence Summers re: NEC Meeting on Climate Change," February 21, 1997, National Security Archive, George Washington University, Electronic Briefing Book No. 303, Document 1.
57. "Denver Summit: Developing Countries and Climate Change," April 1997, National Security Archive, George Washington University, Electronic Briefing Book, No. 537, Document 10.
58. Madeleine K. Albright, "Memo to President re: Denver Summit of the Eight," June 1997, National Security Archive, George Washington University, Electronic Briefing Book, No. 537, Document 13.
59. "US Embassy Beijing 5483 to Secretary of State re: Cool Chinese Response to US Proposal for a Climate Change Protocol," February 19, 1997, National Security Archive, George Washington University, Electronic Briefing Book, No. 537, Document 7.
60. Senator Chuck Hagel as quoted in "Senate Debate over Byrd-Hagel Resolution," S8115.
61. Senator John Kerry as quoted in "Senate Debate over Byrd-Hagel Resolution," S8118–S8120.
62. Senator Robert Byrd as quoted in "Senate Debate over Byrd-Hagel Resolution," S8117.
63. Timothy E. Wirth and Stuart Eizenstat, "Memo to Secretary of State Madeline Albright," September 5, 1997, National Security Archive, George Washington University, Electronic Briefing Book No. 303, Document 6.
64. Senator Chuck Hagel as quoted in "Senate Debate over Byrd-Hagel Resolution," S8116.
65. This campaign is well documented in studies including Eric Pooley, *The Climate War: True Believers, Power Brokers, and the Fight to Save the Earth* (New York: Hachette, 2010); Oreskes and Conway, *Merchants of Doubt*; Howe, *Behind the Curve.*

66. Senator James Inhofe as quoted in "Senate Debate over Byrd-Hagel Resolution," S8113.

67. Senator Chuck Hagel as quoted in "Senate Debate over Byrd-Hagel Resolution," S8115.

68. Institute of Medicine, National Academy of Sciences, and National Academy of Engineering, *Policy Implications of Greenhouse Warming: Mitigation, Adaptation, and the Science Base* (Washington, DC: National Academies Press, 1992), 68.

69. Wirth and Eizenstat, "Memo to Secretary of State Madeline Albright."

70. Howe, *Behind the Curve,* 191–194.

71. Greg Wetstone, in "Global Warming: Dateline Kyoto," December 11, 1997, Natural Resources Defense Council, https://web.archive.org/web /19980207100917/http://www.nrdc.org/field/kyoto.html.

72. Rafe Pomerance, "Developing Country Paper," July 15, 1997, National Security Archive, George Washington University, Electronic Briefing Book, No. 537, Document 15.

73. Christine J. Gardner, "U.S. Churches Join Global Warming Debate," *Christianity Today,* October 5, 1998.

74. Chuck Hagel, "Global Warming Conference: Closing Remarks," Competitive Enterprise Institute, July 15, 1997, https://cei.org/outreach-regulatory -comments-and-testimony/global-warming-conference-closing-remarks; "Don't Sign the Kyoto Protocol: Climate Treaty Is Dangerous to U.S., World," Competitive Enterprise Institute, March 15, 1998, https://cei.org/content/don't -sign-kyoto-protocol-climate-treaty-dangerous-us-world.

75. Brett D. Schaefer and Jay Kingham, *How the Global Warming Treaty Will Harm the Economic Health of the States* (Heritage Foundation, November 21, 1997), https://www.heritage.org/global-politics/report/how-the-global -warming-treaty-will-harm-the-economic-health-the-states.

76. Natural Resources Defense Council, "Earth out of Balance," advertisement, *New York Times,* October 29, 1997.

77. Senator Trent Lott as quoted in "Senate Debate over Byrd-Hagel Resolution," S8124.

78. C. Boyden Gray and David B. Rivkin, "A 'No Regrets' Environmental Policy," *Foreign Policy,* no. 83 (1991): 53.

79. "Bush Mandatory Emissions Caps," September 29, 2000, C-SPAN, https://www.c-span.org/video/?c4488136/bush-mandatory-emissions-caps.

80. "Environment," accessed March 30, 2017, Gallup, http://www.gallup.com/poll /1615/Environment.aspx.

81. "Debate Transcript: The Second Gore-Bush Presidential Debate," October 11, 2000, Commission on Presidential Debates, http://www.debates.org/?page =october-11-2000-debate-transcript.

82. George W. Bush, "Governor George W. Bush Remarks on Energy," October 13, 2000, Georgewbush.com, http://webarchive.loc.gov/all /20001018063225/http://georgewbush.com/news.asp?formmode=sp.

83. Darren Dochuck, "Moving Mountains: The Business of Evangelicalism and Extraction in a Liberal Age," in *What's Good for Business: Business and American Politics since World War II,* ed. Kim Phillips-Fein and Julian E. Zelizer (New York: Oxford University Press, 2012), 72–90.

84. Douglas Jehl, "Moves on Environment Disappoint Industry: Bush's Early Acts Anger Oil and Mining," *New York Times,* March 11, 2001, A24.

85. Christine Todd Whitman, "Crossfire: Christine Todd Whitman Discusses the Bush Administration's Environmental Policy," transcript, CNN online, February 26, 2001, http://transcripts.cnn.com/TRANSCRIPTS/0102/26/cf.00 .html.

86. Christine Todd Whitman, "Speech: G8 Environmental Ministerial Meeting," March 2, 2001, EPA.gov, https://archive.epa.gov/epapages/newsroom_archive /speeches/1e4ce7633567acd38525701a0052e36c.html.

87. As quoted in "Shell Withdraws from Global Climate Coalition," *Oil & Gas Journal,* May 4, 1998.

88. George W. Bush, "Letter to Members of the Senate on the Kyoto Protocol on Climate Change," March 13, 2001, The American Presidency Project, http://www.presidency.ucsb.edu/ws/?pid=45811.

89. Myron Ebell, "Congratulations and More Work to Do on CO2 and Kyoto," e-mail, March 14, 2001.

90. On Competitive Enterprise Institute funding, see Union of Concerned Scientists, *Smoke, Mirrors and Hot Air: How ExxonMobil Uses Big Tobacco's Tactics to Manufacture Uncertainty on Climate Science* (Cambridge, MA: Union of Concerned Scientists, 2007), 32–33.

91. Bill Dawson, "The Politics of Energy: Coal," Center for Public Integrity, December 3, 2003, https://www.publicintegrity.org/2003/12/03/3150/politics -energy-coal.

92. Spencer Abraham, "The Bush Administration's Approach to Climate Change," *Science* 305, no. 5684 (2004): 616–617.

93. Data drawn from CAIT Climate Data Explorer, accessed April 6, 2017, http://cait.wri.org.

94. Andrew D. Lundquist, ed., *Reliable, Affordable, and Environmentally Sound Energy for America's Future: Report of the National Energy Policy Development Group* (Washington, DC: Government Printing Office, 2001); George W. Bush, "Remarks Announcing the Energy Plan in St. Paul, Minnesota," May 17, 2001, The American Presidency Project, http://www.presidency.ucsb .edu/ws/index.php?pid=45617.

95. Natural Resources Defense Council, "Slower, Costlier and Dirtier: A Critique of the Bush Energy Plan" (NRDC, May 2001), https://www.nrdc.org/resources /slower-costlier-and-dirtier.

96. See note 4 in John D. Leshy, "Natural Resources Policy in the Bush (II) Administration: An Outsider's Somewhat Jaundiced Assessment," *Duke Environmental Law & Policy Forum* 14 (2004): 347–362.

97. Chris Mooney, *The Republican War on Science* (New York: Basic Books, 2005).

98. Climate Change Science Program and the Subcommittee on Global Change Research, *Strategic Plan for the U.S. Climate Change Science Program* (The U.S. Global Change Research Program, July 2003), https://www.globalchange.gov/browse/reports/strategic-plan-us-climate-change-science-program.

99. "Bush Administration Launches Historical Federal Climate Change Initiatives" (press release from the U.S. Climate Change Science Program, July 24, 2003), http://web.archive.org/web/20030803121755/http://www.publicaffairs.noaa.gov/releases2003/jul03/noaa03089.html.

100. Global Climate Science Communications Action Plan, April 3, 1998, is available from Union of Concerned Scientists, Climate Deception Dossiers, http://www.ucsusa.org/global-warming/fight-misinformation/climate-deception-dossiers-fossil-fuel-industry-memos#.WSMdZbGZPMU.

101. Pooley, *The Climate War*, 46–48.

102. Andrew C. Revkin, "Bush Aide Softened Greenhouse Gas Links to Global Warming," *New York Times*, June 8, 2005; Andrew C. Revkin, "Former Bush Aide Who Edited Reports Is Hired by Exxon," *New York Times*, June 15, 2005.

103. Tim Dickinson, "Six Years of Deceit," *Rolling Stone*, June 28, 2007.

104. Committee on Oversight and Government Reform, *Political Interference with Climate Change Science under the Bush Administration* (Washington, DC: U.S. House of Representatives, December 2007).

105. As quoted in Oliver Burkeman, "'What Would Jesus Drive?' Gas-Guzzling Americans Are Asked," *The Guardian*, November 14, 2002.

106. As quoted in Katharine K. Wilkinson, *Between God and Green: How Evangelicals Are Cultivating a Middle Ground on Climate Change* (New York: Oxford University Press, 2012), 25.

107. "Environment," Gallup.

108. "To Establish a Renewable Portfolio Standard," Senate Amendment 791, 109th Cong. (2005).

109. Mike Soraghan, "The Fracking 'Loophole' That Just Keeps Growing," E&ENews, August 18, 2015, https://www.eenews.net/stories/1060023558.

110. Carl Hulse and Michael Janofsky, "Congress, after Years of Effort, Is Set to Pass Broad Energy Bill," *New York Times*, July 27, 2005.

111. Energy statistics drawn from the Energy Information Administration, https://www.eia.gov.

112. Mark Holt and Carol Glover, *Energy Policy Act of 2005: Summary and Analysis of Enacted Provisions* (Washington, DC: Congressional Research Service, 2006).

113. Benjamin Hanna, "FERC Net Metering Decisions Keep States in the Dark," *Boston College Environmental Affairs Law Review* 42 (2015): 142–143.

114. Data from the Energy Information Administration, https://www.eia.gov.

115. Steven Mufson, "CEOs Urge Bush to Limit Greenhouse Gas Emissions," *Washington Post,* January 23, 2007.

116. Intergovernmental Panel on Climate Change, *Climate Change 2007: Synthesis Report* (Geneva: IPCC, 2007), 30, 39.

117. Barry G. Rabe, *Statehouse and Greenhouse: The Emerging Politics of American Climate Change Policy* (Washington, DC: Brookings Institution Press, 2004).

118. Ryan Wiser and Galen Barbose, "Renewable Portfolio Standards in the United States: A Status Report with Data through 2007" (Lawrence Berkeley National Laboratory, 2008).

119. Massachusetts v. EPA, Oral Argument, S. Ct. 05-1120 (November, 29, 2006).

120. Massachusetts v. EPA, S. Ct. 05-1120 (2007).

121. Jennifer Parker, "Supreme Court Rejects Bush in Global Warming Debate," *ABC News,* April 2, 2007, http://abcnews.go.com/Politics/story?id =3000959&page=1.

122. "Climate Stewardship Acts," accessed May 29, 2017, Wikipedia, https://en .wikipedia.org/wiki/Climate_Stewardship_Acts.

123. Alliance for Climate Protection, "Nancy Pelosi and Newt Gingrich Commercial on Climate Change," accessed May 22, 2017, https://www.youtube.com /watch?v=qi6n_-wB154.

124. Mayer, "The Koch Brothers' Covert Ops."

125. Barack Obama, "Address before a Joint Session of the Congress," February 24, 2009, The American Presidency Project, http://www.presidency.ucsb.edu/ws /index.php?pid=85753.

126. "Fact Sheet: The Recovery Act Made the Largest Single Investment in Clean Energy in History, Driving the Deployment of Clean Energy, Promoting Energy Efficiency, and Supporting Manufacturing," press release, February 25, 2016, The White House, https://obamawhitehouse.archives.gov/the -press-office/2016/02/25/fact-sheet-recovery-act-made-largest-single -investment-clean-energy.

127. *At a Glance: American Clean Energy and Security Act* (Pew Center for Global Climate Change, June 26, 2009), https://www.c2es.org/site/assets/uploads /2009/06/Waxman-Markey-short-summary-revised-June26.pdf

128. Myron Ebell, "Statement on Waxman-Markey Energy-Rationing Bill," Competitive Enterprise Institute, June 23, 2009, https://cei.org/content /statement-waxman-markey-energy-rationing-bill.

129. "The Cap and Tax Fiction," editorial, *Wall Street Journal,* June 25, 2009.

130. Sir Muir Russell (Chair), "The Independent Climate Change E-Mails Review" (University of East Anglia, July 2010), http://www.cce-review.org/pdf /final%20report.pdf.

131. Chris Horner, "Climate-Gate E-Mails Released by Whistleblower, Not Hacker," Competitive Enterprise Institute, November 30, 2009, https://cei.org /content/chris-horner-climate-gate-e-mails-released-whistleblower-not -hacker.

132. Senator Jim Inhofe, "FoxNews—Climategate Provides Vindication for Inhofe on Global Warming," December 1, 2009, https://www.youtube.com/watch?v=b2JLqXS7-Ig.

133. "Sensenbrenner to Tell Copenhagen: No Climate Laws Until 'Scientific Fascism' Ends," *Fox News,* December 9, 2009.

134. "Environment," Gallup.

135. "Hot Air Tour in Rapid City—AFP President Tim Phillips," DakotaVoice, September 4, 2009, https://www.youtube.com/watch?v=gFoJXiLvhR8.

136. Joe Manchin, "Dead Aim—Joe Manchin for West Virginia TV Ad," October 9, 2010, https://www.youtube.com/watch?v=xIJORBRpOPM.

137. "Hot Air Tour in Rapid City."

138. Theda Skocpol and Vanessa Williamson, *The Tea Party and the Remaking of Republican Conservatism* (New York: Oxford University Press, 2012).

139. James Wanliss, *Resisting the Green Dragon; Dominion, Not Death* (Burke, VA: Cornwall Alliance, 2011); Right Wing Watch, *The 'Green Dragon' Slayers: How the Religious Right and the Corporate Right Are Joining Forces to Fight Environmental Protection* (People for the American Way, 2011), http://www.rightwingwatch.org/report/the-green-dragon-slayers-how-the-religious-right-and-the-corporate-right-are-joining-forces-to-fight-environmental-protection/; Wilkinson, *Between God and Green,* 70.

140. "Protect the Poor: Ten Reasons to Oppose Harmful Climate Change Policies," Cornwall Alliance: For the Stewardship of Creation, 2014, http://cornwallalliance.org/landmark-documents/protect-the-poor-ten-reasons-to-oppose-harmful-climate-change-policies/.

141. Harry R. Jackson and Tony Perkins, *Personal Faith, Public Policy* (Lake Mary, FL: FrontLine, 2008), 212–213.

142. David C. Barker and David H. Bearce, "End-Times Theology, the Shadow of the Future, and Public Resistance to Addressing Global Climate Change," *Political Research Quarterly* 66, no. 2 (2013): 267–279, at 272.

143. Matthew B. Arbuckle and David M. Konisky, "The Role of Religion in Environmental Attitudes," *Social Science Quarterly* 96, no. 5 (November 2015): 1244–1263.

144. Scott Clement, "The Tea Party and Religion," Pew Research Center's Religion and Public Life Project, February 23, 2011, http://www.pewforum.org/2011/02/23/tea-party-and-religion/; Daniel Cox and Robert P. Jones, "Religion and the Tea Party in the 2010 Elections," Public Religion Research Institute, October 5, 2010, https://www.prri.org/research/religion-tea-party-2010/.

145. Environmental Protection Agency, "Endangerment and Cause or Contribute Findings for Greenhouse Gases under Section 202(a) of the Clean Air Act; Final Rule," *Federal Register* 74, no. 239 (December 15, 2009): 66496–66546.

146. Colin P. Kelley et al., "Climate Change in the Fertile Crescent and Implications of the Recent Syrian Drought," *Proceedings of the National Academy of Sciences* 112, no. 11 (March 17, 2015): 3241–3246.

147. As quoted in *Climate of Doubt*, October 23, 2012, Frontline, http://www.pbs .org/wgbh/frontline/film/climate-of-doubt/.

148. James Hohmann, "The Daily 202 Live: Q&A with Gingrich on How Trump Will Change Washington," *Washington Post,* December 20, 2016.

149. Kate Sheppard, "Meet Romney's—and Obama's—Climate Change Adviser," *Mother Jones,* May 29, 2012.

150. Barack Obama, "Remarks by the President in the State of the Union Address," The White House, February 12, 2013, https://obamawhitehouse.archives.gov /the-press-office/2013/02/12/remarks-president-state-union-address.

151. Environmental Protection Agency, "Fact Sheet: Clean Power Plan" (EPA, 2014).

152. Environmental Protection Agency, "Fact Sheet: Clean Power Plan Benefits" (EPA, 2014).

153. "UMW Rally in Pittsburgh July 31, 2014," https://www.youtube.com/watch?v =N84FIWkwxbM.

154. Stan Diel, "Pray God Blocks EPA Plan, Chief Regulator of Alabama Utilities Tells Consumers," AL.com, July 28, 2014, http://www.al.com/news/index.ssf /2014/07/post_14.html.

155. Cliff Sims, "Coal Miner Walter Parker Gives Emotional Testimony at EPA Hearings," *Yellowhammer,* July 30, 2014, https://content.jwplatform.com /previews/HfXva8W6-1x1j34K9.

156. Department of Energy, *2017 U.S. Energy and Employment Report* (Washington, DC: Department of Energy, January 2017), 29.

157. "U.S.-China Joint Announcement on Climate Change," The White House, November 11, 2014, https://obamawhitehouse.archives.gov/the-press-office /2014/11/11/us-china-joint-announcement-climate-change.

158. Barack Obama, "Remarks by the President on the Paris Agreement," The White House, October 5, 2016, https://obamawhitehouse.archives.gov/the -press-office/2016/10/05/remarks-president-paris-agreement.

159. Michael Bess, *The Light-Green Society: Ecology and Technological Modernity in France, 1960–2000* (Chicago: University of Chicago Press, 2003).

160. DeSombre, *Domestic Sources of International Environmental Policy.*

161. Alex Epstein, *The Moral Case for Fossil Fuels* (New York: Portfolio, 2014), 1.

162. Donald J. Trump, "An America First Energy Plan," May 26, 2016, archived at https://perma.cc/2MMZ-4K45.

Conclusion

1. In 2001, Congress passed legislation to reduce the the federal inheritance tax. Deborah Solomon, "The Wordsmith," *New York Times Magazine,* May 21, 2009; Molly Ball, "The Agony of Frank Luntz," *The Atlantic,* January 6, 2014.

2. Frank Luntz, memorandum to Bush White House, *The Environment: A Cleaner, Safer, Healthier America* (Luntz Research Companies, 2002).

3. Karlyn Bowman and Eleanor O'Neil, "AEI Public Opinion Study: Polls on the Environment, Energy, Global Warming, and Nuclear Power—2017," American Enterprise Institute, April 20, 2017, https://www.aei.org/publication/aei -public-opinion-study-polls-on-the-environment-energy-global-warming -and-nuclear-power-2017/.

4. Luntz, "The Environment."

5. Monica Anderson, "For Earth Day, Here's How Americans View Environ- mental Issues," Pew Research Center, April 20, 2017, http://www.pewresearch .org/fact-tank/2017/04/20/for-earth-day-heres-how-americans-view -environmental-issues/.

6. Luntz, "The Environment."

7. "Statement by President Trump on the Paris Climate Accord," The White House, June 1, 2017, https://www.whitehouse.gov/the-press-office/2017/06/01 /statement-president-trump-paris-climate-accord.

8. Murray Energy Corporation, "Murray Energy Corporation Applauds President Trump's Announcement that the United States will Withdrawal [sic] from the Paris Climate Accord," press release, June 1, 2017, http://www .murrayenergycorp.com/wp-content/uploads/2017/06/2017.06.01-MEC -PRESS-RELEASE-Murray-Energy-Corporation-Applauds-President -Trump's-Announcement-that-the-United-States-will-Withdrawal-from-the -Paris-Climate-Accord.pdf.

9. "New Report Examines Costs to U.S. Industrial Sector of Obama's Paris Pledge," U.S. Chamber of Commerce, March 16, 2017, https://www.uschamber .com/press-release/new-report-examines-costs-us-industrial-sector-obama-s -paris-pledge.

10. "CEI Commends President Trump's Decision to Cancel Paris Climate Agreement," Competitive Enterprise Institute, June 1, 2017, https://cei.org /content/cei-commends-president-trumps-decision-cancel-paris-climate -agreement.

11. H. Sterling Burnett, "Trump Bids Paris Adieu!," Climate Change Weekly, June 2, 2017, https://www.heartland.org/news-opinion/news/trump-bids -paris-adieu.

12. E. Calvin Beisner, "Paris Climate Agreement No Help to People or Climate, Harmful to Both," CNSnews.com, June 5, 2017, https://www.cnsnews.com /commentary/e-calvin-beisner/paris-climate-agreement-no-help-people-or -climate-harmful-both.

13. "MIT Issues Statement Regarding Research on Paris Agreement," MIT News, June 2, 2017, http://news.mit.edu/2017/mit-issues-statement-research-paris -agreement-0602.

14. Scott Pruitt, "Speech on Paris Accord, as Prepared," June 1, 2017, http://web .archive.org/web/20170602213656/https://www.epa.gov/speeches /administrator-scott-pruitt-speech-paris-accord-prepared.

15. Roger A. Pielke Jr., "Forests, Tornadoes, and Abortion: Thinking about Science, Politics, and Policy," in *Forest Futures: Science, Politics, and Policy for the Next Century,* ed. Karen A. Arabas and Joe Bowersox (Lanham, MD: Rowman & Littlefield, 2004), 145. See also Roger A. Pielke, *The Honest Broker: Making Sense of Science in Policy and Politics* (Cambridge: Cambridge University Press, 2007) 40–41.

16. Pielke, "Forests, Tornadoes, and Abortion," 144.

17. On the challenges for environmentalists in advancing a "science-first approach" to climate change, see Joshua P. Howe, *Behind the Curve: Science and the Politics of Global Warming* (Seattle: University of Washington Press, 2014), 6–10.

18. "Daily Press Briefing by Press Secretary Sean Spicer and EPA Administrator Scott Pruitt," The White House, June 2, 2017, http://web.archive.org/web /20171219182256/https://www.whitehouse.gov/briefings-statements/daily -press-briefing-press-secretary-sean-spicer-epa-administrator-scott-pruitt -060217/.

19. Pruitt and Zinke articulated their priorities in media interviews. "Interview with Environmental Protection Agency Administrator Scott Pruitt," The Situation Room, CNN, February 28, 2017, http://transcripts.cnn.com /TRANSCRIPTS/1702/28/sitroom.02.html; "Scott Pruitt on Balancing Environmental, Economic Priorities," *Fox News,* April 2, 2017, http://www .foxnews.com/transcript/2017/04/02/scott-pruitt-on-balancing -environmental-economic-priorities-mitch-mcconnell-on-gorsuch -nomination-health-care-reform.html. "Secretary of the Interior Ryan Zinke," *The Hugh Hewitt Show,* May 5, 2017, http://www.hughhewitt.com /secretary-interior-ryan-zinke/.

20. Pruitt, "Speech on Paris Accord, as Prepared."

21. James M. Inhofe et al., "Letter to Secretary of State John Kerry," November 3, 2016, https://www.epw.senate.gov/public/_cache/files/244c9583-e2ec-47cf -a329-28c7c9f64fe3/letter-to-unfccc-re-paris-agreement-final.pdf.

22. For examples of such critiques, see Nicolas Loris, "The Many Problems of the EPA's Clean Power Plan and Climate Regulations: A Primer," Heritage Foundation, July 7, 2015, https://www.heritage.org/environment/report/the -many-problems-the-epas-clean-power-plan-and-climate-regulations-primer; H. Sterling Burnett et al., "Heartland Institute Experts React to President Obama's Signing of the Paris Climate Agreement on Earth Day," Heartland Institute, April 22, 2016, https://www.heartland.org/news-opinion/news /heartland-institute-experts-react-to-president-obamas-signing-of-the-paris -climate-agreement-on-earth-day.

23. Christopher M. Klyza and David J. Sousa, *American Environmental Policy: Beyond Gridlock,* updated and expanded ed. (Cambridge, MA: MIT Press, 2013); Judith Layzer, *Open for Business* (Cambridge, MA: MIT Press, 2012); David J. Sousa and Christopher M. Klyza, "'Whither We Are Tending':

Interrogating the Retrenchment Narrative in U.S. Environmental Policy," *Political Science Quarterly* 132, no. 3 (September 2017): 467–494.

24. Claudia Copeland, *EPA and the Army Corps' Rule to Define 'Waters of the United States'* (Congressional Research Service, January 5, 2017), 9.

25. Gary Baise, "Inside EPA's WOTUS Ruling: Does This Impact Private Property Rights?," Farm Futures, June 15, 2015, http://www.farmfutures.com/blogs -inside-epas-wotus-ruling-does-impact-private-property-rights-9907.

26. Eric Lipton and Michael D. Shear, "E.P.A. Broke Law with Social Media Push for Water Rule, Auditor Finds," *New York Times,* December 14, 2015.

27. "EPA Administrator Scott Pruitt," speech to American Farm Bureau Federation Advocacy Conference, FarmBureauTV, February 28, 2017, https://www .youtube.com/watch?v=yVzz3IYrpac.

28. Chriss W. Street, "Trump EPA to Dump 'WOTUS'; Frees 247 Million Acres of Farmland," Breitbart, June 28, 2017, http://www.breitbart.com/california/2017/06 /28/trump-epa-to-dump-wotus-control-over-247-million-acres-of-farmland/.

29. "Elected Leaders Praise the Trump Administration's Move to Rescind WOTUS," news release, Environmental Protection Agency, June 27, 2017, https://www.epa.gov/newsreleases/elected-leaders-praise-trump -administrations-move-rescind-wotus.

30. Ariel Wittenberg, "Big Legal Question: Is Trump's WOTUS Repeal 'Reasoned'?" E&E News, June 28, 2017, https://www.eenews.net/stories /1060056742. On the legal complexities regarding the actual finalization of Trump's proposed rollback, see Ariel Wittenberg, "Worried about High Court, Trump Admin Wants to Delay WOTUS," E&E News, November 6, 2017, https://www.eenews.net/stories/1060065765.

31. *Sage-Grouse Conservation: Background and Issues* (Congressional Research Service, 2016), https://www.everycrsreport.com/reports/R44592.html.

32. "Secretary Zinke Signs Order to Improve Sage-Grouse Conservation, Strengthen Communication and Collaboration between States and Feds," Department of the Interior, June 8, 2017, https://www.doi.gov/pressreleases /secretary-zinke-signs-order-improve-sage-grouse-conservation-strengthen -communication.

33. Ryan Zinke, *American Commander: Serving a Country Worth Fighting For and Training the Brave Soldiers Who Lead the Way* (Nashville, TN: Thomas Nelson, 2016), 172.

34. National Mining Association, "DOI Cancellation of Sage Grouse Land Withdrawal Highlights Unreasonable Nature of Proposal It Recognizes Was a 'Complete Overreach,'" National Mining Association, October 5, 2017, https://nma.org/2017/10/05/doi-cancellation-sage-grouse-land-withdrawal -highlights-unreasonable-nature-proposal-recognizes-complete-overreach/.

35. Eric Lipton, "Why Has the E.P.A. Shifted on Toxic Chemicals? An Industry Insider Helps Call the Shots," *New York Times,* October 21, 2017.

36. Environmental Defense Fund, "EDF Files Lawsuits to Defend Reforms to Chemical Safety Law," Environmental Defense Fund, August 14, 2017, https://www.edf.org/media/edf-files-lawsuits-defend-reforms-chemical -safety-law.

37. Independent Lubricant Manufacturers Association, "Regulatory Updates," accessed November 7, 2017, https://www.ilma.org/ILMA/Issues/Regulatory _Updates/ILMA/Regulatory/Regulatory-Updates.aspx?hkey=fd4f3376-5cc7 -42f0-98c5-6f1b8518a6f4.

38. Christopher Sellers, "Trump and Pruitt Are the Biggest Threat to the EPA in Its 47 Years of Existence," Vox, July 1, 2017, https://www.vox.com/2017/7/1 /15886420/pruitt-threat-epa.

39. Ryan Zinke, "Memorandum to the President re: Final Report Summarizing Findings of the Review of Designations under the Antiquities Act [draft deliberative]," 2017, accessed December 8, 2017, https://www.documentcloud .org/documents/4052225-Interior-Secretary-Ryan-Zinke-s-Report-to-the.html.

40. National Congress of American Indians, "NCAI Opposes Executive Action on the Reduction of National Monuments," December 4, 2017, http://www .ncai.org/news/articles/2017/12/04/ncai-opposes-executive-action-on-the -reduction-of-national-monuments.

41. Eric Lipton and Lisa Friedman, "Oil Was Central to Decision to Shrink Bears Ears Monument, Emails Show," *New York Times*, March 2, 2018.

42. As quoted in Christopher Sellers et al., *The EPA under Siege: An In-Depth Analysis of the EPA under Trump and Administrator Scott Pruitt* (Environmental Data and Governance Initiative, May 2017), 55, https://envirodatagov .org/publication/the-epa-under-siege.

43. Darryl Fears and Juliet Eilperin, "Zinke Says a Third of Interior's Staff Is Disloyal to Trump and Promises 'Huge' Changes," *Washington Post,* September 26, 2017.

44. Dino Grandoni, "EPA's Budget Finds Unexpected Defenders in Congress," *Washington Post,* June 16, 2017.

45. "FY 2018 Budget," Data and Tools, Environmental Protection Agency, May 17, 2017, https://www.epa.gov/planandbudget/fy2018.

46. "Interior, Environment, and Related Agencies Appropriations Bill, 2018: Omnibus Agreement Summary," United States Committee on Appropriations, March 2018, https://www.appropriations.senate.gov/imo/media/doc /FY18-OMNI-INTERIOR-SUM.pdf.

47. Nick Stockton, "The Grizzled, Stubborn Lawyers Protecting the Environment from Trump," *WIRED,* June 16, 2017.

48. Eric Lipton, "Courts Thwart Administration's Effort to Rescind Obama-Era Environmental Regulations," *New York Times,* October 6, 2017.

49. John McQuaid, "One Big Legal Obstacle Keeps Trump from Undoing Greenhouse Gas Regulation," *Scientific American,* April 26, 2017.

50. Pew Research Center, *March 2016 Political Survey*, http://www.people-press
.org/files/2016/03/03-31-2016-Political-topline-for-release.pdf.

51. NBC News / Wall Street Journal Poll, September 2017 [survey question],
https://www.wsj.com/public/resources/documents/17363NBCWSJSeptemberP
oll09212017Release.pdf.

52. Faiz Shakir, "Video: Luntz Converts on Global Warming, Distances Himself
from Bush," Think Progress, June 27, 2006, https://thinkprogress.org/video
-luntz-converts-on-global-warming-distances-himself-from-bush
-6035c9521c50/.

53. "Pollster Frank Luntz Releases New Polling Results: Bipartisan Public
Support for National Climate Legislation," Environmental Defense Fund,
January 21, 2010, https://www.edf.org/news/pollster-frank-luntz-releases-new
-polling-results-bipartisan-public-support-national-climate-le.

Acknowledgments

We began this book in December 2016 as we observed the ascendancy of a Republican administration determined to remake environmental policies in the United States. As we contemplated the potential changes to the nation's environmental laws and commitments, we asked the simplest of historical questions (deceptively simple, as it turns out): how did we get here? This book, written for the most part over the course of 2017 as some of the changes to federal environmental laws and policies unfolded, is our answer to that question.

A related how-did-that-happen question is, how did we manage to finish this project? In large part, the answer is, with a lot of help. It is a pleasure to thank the institutions that supported us and the people who offered us their time and their insights. We are fortunate that Wellesley College and Temple University are institutions that have created communities of scholars that support and encourage research and writing. At those institutions and beyond, we benefited from the insights of a number of scholars in history, political science, and environmental studies. For their comments on the manuscript, we are deeply grateful to Pete Alagona, Lila Berman, Ann Bone, Beth DeSombre, David Farber, Levi Fox, Sherry Gerstein, Steve Hausmann, Josh Howe, Chris Klyza, Jim Kopaczewski, Kevin Kruse, Peter Lavelle, Ryan Quintana, Adam Rome, Travis Roy, Gary Scales, Chris Sellers, Bryant Simon, Adam Sowards, Howard Spodek, and Alexandra Straub. In ways both large and small, their comments immeasurably improved this book. Lindy Crowley, Sarah Koenig, and Eva Paradiso were enormously helpful in assisting us in fact checking the manuscript, although any errors that remain are our responsibility. The anonymous readers for Harvard University Press provided generous and critical feedback that played an important role in our revisions. From the start, Thomas LeBien's enthusiasm for this book and his editorial insights helped us sharpen both our argument and our narrative. We appreciate his support and advocacy, as he shepherded this book from proposal to publication. Lastly, we are especially grateful to our families and friends who put up with many early mornings and late nights, as this book occupied more of our time than we expected over the past year.

Index

Abbey, Edward, 76–77
"Abortion politics," 203–204
Acid rain, 52, 108, 112–121, 153
Acid Rain Program, 67, 117–120, 163, 180
Adler, Jonathan, 214
Agricultural interests, 4, 61, 90, 130–131, 132–134, 140–141, 208–209
Alagona, Peter, 83, 93
Alaska National Interest Lands Conservation Act (1980) (Alaska Lands Act), 48, 53, 75–76
Algae, "dead zones" caused by, 132
American Clean Energy and Security Act (2009), 182, 183
American Electric Power, 118
American Enterprise Association, 24
American Liberty League, 24
American Petroleum Institute (API), 64, 172–173
American Recovery and Reinvestment Act (2009), 182
Americans for Prosperity, 181
Anti-intellectualism, 29, 42, 51

Antiquities Act (1906), 3, 79. *See also* National monuments
Appropriations bills, 16, 72, 137–138
Arctic National Wildlife Refuge (Arctic Refuge), 72, 154, 168–169
Arrhenius, Svante, 150
Aspinall, Wayne, 21, 30

Babbitt, Bruce, 78, 99
Badger, Evelyn, 85
Baker, Howard, 38
Ball, Jim, 175
Barker, David, 188
Bearce, David, 188
Bears Ears National Monument, 103, 211
Beck, Nancy, 210–211
Benedick, Richard, 146, 147
Berlin mandate, 163, 164, 166. *See also* Kyoto Protocol
Bess, Michael, 192
Biden, Joe, 119
Billings, Robert, 49–50
Bishop, Rob, 93

Black, James, 150
Bozell, L. Brett, 26
Bradsher, Keith, 155
Brower, David, 34
Brown, Lewis H., 24
Brown, Pat, 40
Brownback, Sam, 209
Browner, Carol, 133
Bryan, Richard, fuel economy
    proposal, 154, 155, 167, 194
Bush, George H. W.: environmental
    protection acts signed by, 5;
    reclassifies Powder River Basin, 68;
    oil production under, 72; public
    lands reform under, 77; and threats
    to Endangered Species Act, 86; and
    Clean Air Act, 116–119; climate
    policy under, 149–157; and 1992
    presidential election, 158
Bush, George W.: energy development
    under, 72, 168–178; forest protection
    under, 80–81; public lands manage-
    ment under, 80–81; and threats to
    Endangered Species Act, 89–93;
    regulations on nitrogen oxides
    emissions under, 121–122; and
    Clear Skies Act, 122–126; Clean Air
    Act overhauled under, 122–128; and
    New Source Review program, 126;
    and Clean Air Interstate Rule,
    127–128; climate policy under,
    168–178, 179
Business Roundtable, 102–103
Byrd, Robert, 115, 119, 160, 163, 164
Byrd-Hagel resolution, 164–166

California Environmental Quality
    Study Council, 40–41
Callendar, Guy, 150
Campaign donations, 95, 148, 162
Cap and trade, 117–118, 122, 124,
    126–127, 180, 181–192
Capitalism, 23, 26, 41–44

Carbon dioxide emissions. See
    Greenhouse gas emissions
Carson, Rachel, 33, 34
Carter, Jimmy, 48–49, 62–63
Cato Institute, 44
Chafee, John, 84, 106, 131, 137, 165
Chafee, Lincoln, 91
Chemical Safety for the Twenty-First
    Century Act (2016), 211
Cheney, Dick, 72, 92, 122, 172
Chesapeake Bay, 132
Chevron doctrine, 110, 125, 126
Chevron USA, Inc. v. Natural Resources
    Defense Council (1984), 110, 125
China, 191
Citizens for a Sound Economy, 160,
    161
Civil Rights Act (1964), 27–28, 30, 33
Cizik, Richard, 187
Clean Air Act: and evolution of
    environmental problems and
    governance, 12, 13; co-sponsored by
    Goldwater, 31; and bipartisan
    support for environmental reforms,
    32, 33; coal industry and, 69;
    overhauled under Reagan, 104–105,
    106, 108–110; and acid rain,
    112–113, 114, 117–120; and smog,
    121; overhauled under Bush,
    122–128; impact of, 128, 129,
    142–143; threats to, 141–142;
    regulation of ozone-depleting
    substances under, 146, 188; and
    climate policy under George W.
    Bush, 170, 179–180; and climate
    policy under Barack Obama,
    190–192
Clean Air Interstate Rule (2005),
    127–128
Clean Power Plan (Obama), 4, 180,
    190–191, 192, 194, 207
Clean Water Act: Trump on, 4; and
    evolution of environmental

problems and governance, 13; and bipartisan support for environmental reforms, 32, *33*, 37–39; overhauled under Reagan, 104, 106–108; and problem of nonpoint source pollution, 129–134; Job Creation and Wage Enhancement Act and overhaul of, 136–137; deferred reform to, 139–141; threats to, 141–142; impact of, 142–143; Pruitt's attack on, 208–209

Clean Water Initiative (Clinton), 133–134

Clear Skies Act (George W. Bush), 122–126

Climate Action Plan (Obama), 189–190

Climate change: Republican denial of, 1–2; addressing, 148, 192–195; and understanding history of U.S. climate policy, 148–149; warnings regarding, 149–150; policies under George H. W. Bush, 149–157; policies under Clinton, 157–168; policies under George W. Bush, 168–178, 179; incremental progress regarding, 178–181; policies under Obama, 181–192, 206–207; Luntz on discussing, 198–199; policies under Trump, 199–201, 202–208; opposing action on, 206; American belief in, 216

Climate Change Action Plan (Clinton), 162

Climate Change Science Program (George W. Bush), 172

Climategate, 183–184

Clinton, Bill: oil production under, 72; public lands reform under, 77–80; and roadless rule, 80; and threats to Endangered Species Act, 86–87, 88–89; regulations on nitrogen oxides emissions under, 121; and New Source Review program,

125–126; and Clean Water Initiative, 133–134; on Job Creation and Wage Enhancement Act, 136; climate policy under, 157–168

Coal, war on, 176–178, 190–191

Coalition for Vehicle Choice, 155

Coal production, 65–69, *70*, 143, 210

Cold War, 156

Command-and-control regulations, 37, 80, 104–108, 115, 123–124, 131–132

Commoner, Barry, 118

Competitive Enterprise Institute, 167, 170–171, 183

Comprehensive Environmental Response, Compensation, and Liability Act (Superfund Act), 48, 111

Congressional gridlock, 15–16, *17*

Conscience of a Conservative, The (Goldwater), 26

Conservatism: studies on environmental politics and, 7–8; as factor influencing Republican reversal, 8–10; environmentalism and rise of, 19–20; origins of, 23–29; emergence of partisan environmental politics and rise of, 41–52; anti-environmentalism harnessed to, 196–197, 199–200, 203–206

Conservative interest groups, 10–12, 78–79, 113, 137, 157

Conservation movement. *See* Gifford Pinchot; Theodore Roosevelt

Contract with America, 16, 78, *88*, 134–139, 141, 186, 207

Conway, Erik, 9, 152–153

Cooney, Phil, 173–174

Coors, Joseph, 44, 45, 61

Corporate political action committees, 44

Cost-benefit analysis, 105–106, 120, 135–136

Courts as venue for regulatory reform: 15–16, 80–81, 83, 208; and Endangered Species Act, 83, 87–89; and Clean Air Act, 109–110, 126–128, and Clean Water Act, 109, 140–141, 209; and climate change, 179–181, 188, 190

Cramer, Katherine, 96

Crane, Jasper, 25

Creation care, 11, 175

D'Amato, Alfonse, 119

DDT, 9, 51–52

"Dead zones," 132, 133

Deepwater Horizon, 73–74

Deep Water Royalty Relief Act (1995), 71

Department of the Interior, 3, 64–67, 70–72, 75, 92, 94, 209–212

DeSombre, Elizabeth, 147

DeWitt, Calvin, 50

DiBona, Charles, 70

Dochuk, Darren, 11, 64

Dole, Bob, 128

Dominion Power, 118

Dominion theology, 11, 187. *See also* Evangelical Christians

Dukakis, Michael, 116

Ebell, Myron, 170, 189, 201

Edison Electric Institute (EEI), 105, 151

Ehrlich, Anne, 34

Ehrlich, Paul, 33, 34

Endangered Species Act (1973), 32, 56, 59, 81–93

Energy crises, 46–47, 49, 62–63

Energy plan, under George W. Bush, 172

Energy Policy Act (1992), 154–155

Energy Policy Act (2005), 175–178

Energy tax debates, under Clinton, 159–161, 162

Environmental Action, 34, 39

Environmental Defense Fund, 115–116, 166, 178, 182

Environmentalism: and defense of environmental laws, 15–16, 62, 76, 87–88, 126–128, 213–214; and contributions to public health, 17, 101, 141–142; and rise of conservatism, 19–20; origins of, 21–23; emergence of partisan environmental politics and, 43; American support for, 215

Environmental justice, 17, 124, 143–144, 212, 215

Environmental Protection Agency (EPA): Trump plans to eliminate, 1; Pruitt appointed administrator of, 2–3; creation of, 5, 35, 98–99; Ford on, 46; purpose of, 99; Reagan's attack on, 101–112; and Clear Skies Act, 125, 126; and Clean Air Act, 128, 188; and Clean Water Act, 132, 133; and *Massachusetts v. EPA*, 179–180, 188, 190; Pruitt's agenda for, 205; lowered morale in, 212; rules reinstated by, 213–214

Epstein, Alex, 193

Evangelical Christians, 11, 49–50, 64, 68, 87–88, 167, 186–188

Evangelical Climate Initiative, 175

Evangelical Environmental Network, 87–88, 175

Exceptionalism, 9, 45, 149, 194, 197

Executive action as reform strategy, 16, 91–92, 103, 107, 189–190, 207–208. *See also* Clean Air Interstate Rule; Clean Power Plan; New Source Review program; Roadless rule; Waters of the United States rule

Exxon Valdez, 154

Fallon, George, 34

Falwell, Jerry, 49

Farber, David, 27

Federal Coal Leasing Amendments Act (1976), 65

Federal Land Policy and Management Act (1976), 76

Federal public lands, 56–62; energy development and, 63–65; and public lands reform, 75–81; management of, 76; reshaping debate over, 76

Fifield, James, 26, 49

Fish and Wildlife Service (FWS), 82–83

Ford, Gerald, 45–48

Forestry policy. *See* National forests, management of; Roadless rule; Salvage rider

Fracking, 176, 190, 193, 203

Friedman, Milton, 24, 25–26

Fuel economy standards for vehicles, 154, 155, 158, 162, 167, 175, 190, 194

Gaetz, Matt, 2

Galbraith, John Kenneth, 28

Gas tax, 161. *See also* Energy tax debates

George C. Marshall Institute, 152–153, 165

Gingrich, Newt, 73, 88, 134–135, 181, 189

Global Climate Coalition, 165, 170

Global warming. *See* Climate change

Global Warming: What Does the Science Tell Us?, 153

Goldwater, Barry, 19–20, 22–23, 26–27, 28, 31

Gore, Al, 150, 158, 161, 166, 168–169, 178

Gorsuch, Anne, 102, 103–104, 110–111

Gorsuch, Neil, 110

Government subsidies, reduced under Reagan, 75–77

Grand Staircase-Escalante National Monument, 79, 80, 211

Grant, Ulysses S., 22

Gray, C. Boyden, 117

Grazing policy, 76–79

"Green drift," 142, 208, 214

Greenhouse gas emissions, 150–152, 167–168, 170, 171–172, 179–181, 188, 190

Gridlock on environmental issues. *See* Party divergence

Grudem, Wayne, 73

Gulf of Mexico, 71–72, 132, 133

Habitat Conservation Plans, 84

Hagel, Chuck, 164, 165

Halliburton loophole, 176

Hansen, James, 149, 152, 153

Harrison, Benjamin, 22

Hayek, Friedrich, 25, 29–30

Heartland Institute, 184, 201

Heinz, John III, 115–116, 117

Heritage Foundation, 44, 183, 187

Hickel, Walter, 35

Horner, Chris, 184

Hot Air Tour, 181, 184–185

Howe, Joshua, 156

Huber, Peter, 13

Humphrey, Hubert, 21, 27, 34

Hurricane Katrina, 178

Hurricane Sandy, 188–189

Inconvenient Truth, An, 178

Inhofe, James, 2, 161, 165, 184, 187

Intergovernmental Panel on Climate Change (IPCC), 150–152, 162–163, 178

Iranian Revolution, 49

Jastrow, Robert, 153

Jeffords, James, 124–125

Job Creation and Wage Enhancement Act, 135–137

Job loss, 142–143

Johnson, Bill, 3–4

Johnson, Lyndon, 21, 23

Katrina, Hurricane, 178

Keeling, Charles, 150

Kelly, Mike, 92

Kerry, John, 164, 165
Klamath River Basin, 89–92
Klyza, Christopher, 16, 142, 208
Knowland, William, 39
Koch, Charles, 44, 161–162
Koch, David, 161–162
Koether, George, 25
Krupp, Fred, 115–116, 216
Kuchel, Thomas, 40
Kyoto Protocol, 163, 166–167, 169, 179

Lake Erie, 132
Lavelle, Rita, 111
Layzer, Judith, 214
League of Conservation Voters, 34, 39, 176
Lieberman, Joe, 180
"Light-green society," 194
Lincoln, Abraham, 22
Livermore, Norman, 40, 101–102
Logging, 75–80, 84–87, 94. See also Roadless rule
Lott, Trent, 167
Luntz, Frank, 196–199, 201, 216

MacDonald, Julie, 92
Manchin, Joe, 184
Market-based regulations, 115–121, 122–125, 128, 180, 182. See also Cap and trade; Energy tax debates
Marshall Institute, 152–153, 165
Massachusetts Institute of Technology, 202
Massachusetts v. EPA (2007), 179–180, 188, 190
Mayer, Jane, 161
McCain, John, 139, 180, 181
McCarran, Pat, 58
McCarthy, Gina, 189
McCloskey, Pete, 34
McCurdy, Dave, 161
McEvoy, Arthur, 32
Mercury pollution, 123–124, 126–128

Mining, 65–66, 118. See also Coal production
Mobil Oil, 151
Moderate Republicans, 27–28, 39–40, 87–88, 174–175, 212–213
Montreal Protocol on Substances that Deplete the Ozone Layer, 145–147
Moral Majority, 49–50
Moses, Robert, 43
Mountain States Legal Foundation (MSLF), 45, 61
Mountaintop removal coal mining. See Strip mining
Mount St. Helens, 52
Murray, Robert, 200
Murray Energy Corporation, 3, 200
Muskie, Edmund, 35, 39

Nader, Ralph, 42
National Academy of Sciences, 165
National Association of Manufacturers, 160
National Environmental Policy Act (NEPA, 1970), 32, 59
National Forest Management Act (1976), 76, 80
National forests, management of, 22, 80–81
National Marine Fisheries Service, 89, 92
National monuments, 94–95, 96, 211–212. See also Bears Ears National Monument; Grand Staircase-Escalante National Monument
National Oceanic and Atmospheric Administration (NOAA), 82–83
Natural gas production, 176–177, 190, 203
Natural Resources Defense Council (NRDC), 135–137, 166, 178, 182
"Navigable waters," 140–141, 208–209
Needham, Andrew, 59

New Deal, 23–24, 26–27, 28, 32, 59
New Source Review program,
    125–126
Nierenberg, William, 150, 153
Nitrogen oxides emissions, 121–123, 127
Nixon, Richard, 5, 34–39, 82, 98
Nonpoint source pollution, 129–134,
    136, 139–140
Northern spotted owl, 84–87, 209
Northwest Forest Plan, 86–87
Norton, Gale, 89, 90

Obama, Barack: Pruitt's opposition to
    regulatory agenda of, 2–3; energy
    policy of, 73–74; and threats to
    Endangered Species Act, 92;
    national monuments created by,
    94–95; implementation of Clean Air
    Act under, 128; supports action on
    climate change, 181; climate policy
    under, 181–192, 206–207; on Paris
    climate accord, 191–192
Offshore drilling, 35, 69–74, 94, 158
Oil crisis, 46–47, 49, 62–63
Oil production, 65, 69–74, 176
Oppenheimer, Michael, 113, 149–150
Oregon Lands Coalition, 85
Oreskes, Naomi, 9, 152–153
Ozone hole, discovery of and interna-
    tional negotiations concerning,
    145–147. See also Montreal Protocol

Palin, Sarah, 73
Paris Climate Accord, 4, 191–192, 193,
    200–201, 202–204, 207
Parker, Walter, 191
Party divergence: and passing laws,
    15–16; widening of, 17; bipartisan
    consensus preceding, 29–41;
    emergence of environmental, 41–52
Pelosi, Nancy, 181, 189
People for the West!, 78–79
Percy, Charles, 38

Persian Gulf War, 154
Pew, J. Howard, 25, 26
Phillips, Tim, 184–185
Phillips-Fein, Kim, 10, 24, 44
Pielke, Roger, Jr., 7, 203–204
Pinchot, Gifford, 58
Point source pollution, 129, 136
Pombo, Richard, 81, 87, 91
Population Bomb, The (Ehrlich), 34
Population growth, 32–34, 44–45
Portney, Paul, 119
Powder River Basin, 67–69, 70
Powell, Lewis F., 41–43. See also Powell
    memo
Powell memo, 41–43, 95, 103
Power Shift, 166–167
Project 88, 115–117
Project Documerica, 98
Proposition 9 (California), 51
Pruitt, Scott, 2–3, 192, 203, 204,
    205–206, 208–209, 211, 212
Public interest right, 11, 81, 92, 95, 141,
    172, 174, 184, 221n25

Rabe, Barry, 179
Randolph, Jennings, 106
Read, Leonard, 24
Reagan, Ronald: environmental
    protection acts signed by, 5, 40–41;
    and beginning of Republican
    reversal, 8–9, 19–20, 52–53, 55, 101,
    201; and origins of conservatism,
    28–29; and bipartisan support for
    environmental reforms, 39–41; and
    rise of conservatism and emergence
    of partisan environmental politics,
    50–52; and "War on the West," 54–55,
    60; and gospel of more, 63–64; public
    lands reform under, 75–77; attack on
    EPA, 101–112; and acid rain,
    112–115; and Clean Water Act,
    130–131; and Montreal Protocol,
    145–147

Redwood National Park, 50
Regional interests, 30–31, 114–115
Regulation Reality Tour, 181, 184–185
Reich, Charles, 42
Reilly, William, 117
Renewable energy, 155, 158, 160, 169, 177, 179, 182
Renewable energy portfolios, 179
Republican reversal: beginnings of, 5–6, 19–20, 52–53, 55, 101, 201; characteristics of, 6–7; studies on, 7–8; causes of, 8–15; consequences of, 15–18, 214–215; evolution of, 201–211
Republicans and science, 2, 9–10, 13, 52, 90–92, 151–154, 165, 172–173, 197–201, 203–205
Republicans for Environmental Protection, 174–175
Resource Conservation and Recovery Act (1976), 47–48
Rey, Mark, 80
Road to Serfdom, The (Hayek), 25
Roadless rule, 80–81
Rohrabacher, Dana, 2
Romney, Mitt, 189, 190
Roosevelt, Franklin D., 23–24, 26–27
Roosevelt, Theodore, 3, 5, 22, 58, 205, 211
Rove, Karl, 92
Ruckelshaus, William, 39, 112, 113–114, 130–131
Rural communities, 8, 78–79, 89–90, 94–97, 181–182, 184–185
Rush, Erik, 73

Safe Drinking Water Act (1974), 33
Safe Drinking Water Act (1996), 138
Safe harbor rule, 89
Sagebrush Rebellion, 60
Sage grouse, 209–210
"Salvage rider," 79

Sandy, Hurricane, 188–189
Santa Barbara oil spill, 34–35
Santini, James, 60
Saylor, John, 21, 22, 30–31
Schlafly, Phyllis, 24
Science and Republicans, 2, 9–10, 13, 52, 90–92, 151–154, 165, 172–173, 197–201, 203–205
Scott, Doug, 62
Sears, Earl, 128
Seitz, Frederick, 153
Sellers, Christopher, 211
Shultz, George, 145
Shuster, Brad, 136, 137
Sierra Club, 109
Silent Spring (Carson), 34, 178
Simon, Julian, 44–45
Simpson, Alan, 77, 84, 128
Smith, Robert, 81
Smog, 121–128
Snowe, Olympia, 180
Solar power, 48, 73, 177, 191. See also Renewable energy
Sousa, David, 16, 142, 208
Speth, Gus, 148
Spiritual Mobilization, 26
Stafford, Robert, 106
Stavins, Robert, 116
Steele, Michael, 73
Stevens, Ted, 55
Stockman, David, 26, 104, 114
Strip mining, 3, 65–66, 69, 143, 190
Subsidies, reduced under Reagan, 75–77
Sulfur dioxide emissions, 52, 112–114, 117–120, 127
Sununu, John, 119, 152
Superfund Act, 48, 111
Surface Mining Control and Reclamation Act (1977), 33, 65, 66
Sydnor, Eugene, 41

Taft, Robert, 23–24
Tall stacks, 108, 112. *See also* Acid rain; Clean Air Act
Tea Party, 181–182, 185–186, 188
Televangelism, 49–50
Tellico Dam, 83
Tennessee Valley Authority v. Hill (1976), 83
Thomas, Lee, 145
Threatened and Endangered Species Recovery Act (2005), 91
Tornado politics, 7, 203
"Total maximum daily load" (TMDL) plans, 139
Toxic Substances Control Act (1976), *33*, 47–48
Train, Russell, 39, 84
Trans-Alaska Pipeline, 47
Trump, Donald J.: anti-environmental agenda of, 1–6, 194, 197, 199–201, 202–208, 211–216; appointees of, 3–4, 210–211; on climate change, 3–4, 199–201; reduces size of national monuments, 3–4, 96, 211–212; energy policy of, 74, 192; on Clean Water Act, 141, 208–209; compared to Reagan, 201–211; weakening chemical regulations, 210–211; budget cuts proposed, 212–213; challenged by moderate Republicans, 213; challenged in court, 213–214
Two Energy Futures: A National Choice for the 80s, 64

United Nations Conference on Environment and Development (Rio de Janeiro, 1992), 156–157
United Nations Framework Convention on Climate Change (UN-FCCC), 157, 162, 164, 182–183, 192. *See also* Kyoto Protocol; Paris Climate Accord

United States Climate Action Partnership, 178
Unsafe at Any Speed (Nader), 42

Values, politics of, 198, 203–205
Voter concern, environment as, 34, 39, 41, 138–139, 168, 197, 215
Voting Rights Act (1965), *33*

Wallop, Malcolm, 159
War on coal, 176–178, 190–191
"War on the West," 54–55, 78
War Powers Resolution (1973), *33*
Waterhouse, Benjamin, 103
Waters of the United States rule, 140–141, 208–209. *See also* Clean Water Act
Watt, James: Hickel and, 35; as head of MSLF, 45; as evangelical, 50; as secretary of Interior, 55–56, 60–62; energy development and, 63–67, 69–71; viewed as threat by environmentalists, *63*; and threats to Endangered Species Act, 83–84; resignation of, 94
Western states: conservative Republican versus environmentalist views on, 56–62; reorientation of coal industry to, 66–69; public lands reform in, 76–81; and threats to Endangered Species Act, 81–93; national monuments created in, 94–95; support for environmental protection in, 95–96. *See also* Rural communities
Wetlands, protected under Clean Water Act, 140–141
Weyrich, Paul, 49–50
Whitman, Christine Todd, 121, 123, 126, 169, 174
Wilderness Act (1964), 21–23, 30–31, *33, 59. See also* Roadless rule
Wilderness Society, 62, 76

Wind power, 177, 191. *See also* Renewable energy
Wirth, Timothy, 115–116, 162–163, 165–166
Wise Use movement, 78, 86
Woodwell, George, 150

Xi Jinping, 191

Young, Don, 87, 88

Zelizer, Julian, 10
Zinke, Ryan, 3, 74, 205–206, 210, 211, 212